The Pyramid Builder

Also by Christine El Mahdy

Mummies, Myth and Magic
Exploring the World of the Pharaohs
Tutankhamen: The Life and Death of a Boy-King

The Pyramid Builder

CHEOPS, THE MAN BEHIND THE
GREAT PYRAMID

Christine El Mahdy

headline

First published in 2003
by HEADLINE BOOK PUBLISHING

Christine El Mahdy would be happy to hear from readers with
their comments on the book at the following e-mail address:
christine@bcegypt.com

10 9 8 7 6 5 4 3 2 1

Cataloguing in Publication Data is
available from the British Library

ISBN 0 7553 1008 X

Typeset in Palatino by
Letterpart Limited, Reigate, Surrey

Printed and bound in Great Britain by
Mackays of Chatham plc, Chatham, Kent

HEADLINE BOOK PUBLISHING
A division of Hodder Headline
338 Euston Road
LONDON NW1 3BH

www.headline.co.uk
www.hodderheadline.com

This book is dedicated to the awesome foursome
with all my love
Mark and Traci, Tony and Sam

Contents

Acknowledgements

M any people have been involved in the conception and birth of this book. However, for posterity I would like to record first and foremost my grateful thanks to the Somerset advanced hieroglyph reading group, who have discussed, cogitated and finally formed conclusions over complex Egyptian texts, most importantly the Dream Stela text. In alphabetical order, these are Paul and Carol Bradbury, Marion Carter, Gavin Elseworthy, Mark Fletcher, Kareena Gillard, Jill Lackford, Chas and Loma Linsell, Richard Lunn, Donna Nunn, Steve Oxbrow, James Ridgewell, and Paul and Maggie Wade-Williams. I would like to thank Paul Wade-Williams for his help and his T-shirts; David Elkington for his good humour and delightful eccentricity; Ian Jameison for his advice; and especially David Couling for his forbearance, patience and constant support. I would like to thank my children, Mark and Tony Hobson and Nadine and Yasmine El Mahdy for their love and support of an eccentric Mum. Thanks go to all staff at Dillington House, especially Wayne Bennett and Geoff Hewitt, who welcomed the British Centre for Egyptian Studies (BCES) into their domain. I would like to extend my hand of thanks to all my students, past and present, through Yeovil College, Somerset College of Arts and Technology; Wadham School, Crewkerne; and, worldwide, the students of the BCES, all of whom keep me on my toes, and

David Paterson of Ferndown School, Dorset, for help with maths. Finally, to all my friends and colleagues in the field of Egyptology all over the world: we may not always agree in everything, but our love and enthusiasm for our field bring us together no matter what our language and background. Through our joint cooperation, may the torch of Egyptian studies never be extinguished.

Preface

Egyptology is a science. On a certain day, the first stone of a pyramid was laid. On another, the final stone was put into place. So by using the best methods science can devise, and giving careful attention to the archaeological evidence, it should be possible to ascertain these dates with something approaching accuracy. The very least one could expect would be to know the name of the man for whom it was all done.

If only it were that easy! Here is a challenge for you. Take any two books on ancient Egypt, of any date and by any authors – the choice is yours. Now check the names of the kings who built the pyramids during the Fourth Dynasty of Egypt's ancient history. Look at the lengths of their reigns and the suggested dates. Do you see the problem?

The truth is that even given all the methods available to us today, all our knowledge of Egyptian writings, and two centuries of excavation, we still cannot agree even about the basic principles. This leaves the argument over names and dates seeming somewhat futile, as no matter what decision is taken, many will disagree.

However, a stance must be taken. This book concerns arguably the greatest of the kings of the Fourth Dynasty, the builder of the Great Pyramid. Historical inscriptions record his name in hieroglyphs as Khnum-Khufu, although few people would recognize him by that name. Many unaccountably abbreviate it to Khufu. He is better known popularly as Cheops which is the Greek spelling of his name as recorded in Book 2 of the *Histories* of Herodotus. Under these confusing circumstances, I have decided, for the purposes of this book, to use the Greek version, Cheops. Readers may decide for themselves whether or not they agree!

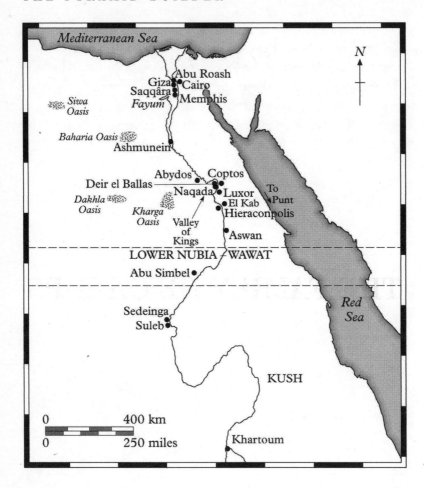

Egypt and Nubia

PART ONE

THE FAMILY OF CHEOPS

INTRODUCTION

Monumental Mystery

——

Have you ever been lucky enough to visit Egypt, and stand at the foot of the pyramids of Giza? If you have not, how can I even start to create an image of them for you? No picture can ever do them justice. If you stand at the base of the Great Pyramid and look upwards, the entire sky seems filled with stone and the height of the apex makes you dizzy.

Only one thought fills your mind: why?

What on earth could persuade anyone to build something so vast and apparently useless? And why and how did they ever complete the task? Surely it would have been so much easier at some point to call it a day – to accept a flat-topped edifice instead of a pointed one? Think of the time and stone you could save! The sheer scale of the building is an effrontery to common sense. Little wonder that visitors from the ancient Greeks to Hollywood producers see it as the physical proof of cruel slavery, of the indignities carried out on some men by a dictator.

So what was he like, the man who ordered it built? Was he a dictator, the builder of this monstrous work? Was he, perhaps, the world's first true fascist leader, forcing men to live and die in agony just to build his massive desert monument? What exactly was he like? What did he look like and sound like?

Once you start to think in this way, can you also start to hear the distant echo of the voices of the long-dead men who built the pyramids? Did the men who cut and moved the stone, those who screamed out the orders, ever ask themselves, even then, that eternal 'Why?' What motivated them to get out of bed each morning, knowing what they would face that day? Was it, as some think, fear of the whip in the hand of a Hitleresque sadist?

Or could it have been religious fervour? Was the builder, then, some sort of charismatic preacher, addressing his men across vast meeting grounds? Did he use words of power to persuade them, urging them on so that they could share in his life after death? Was he the first one to start, 4500 years ago, sales meetings, urging the delegates to higher figures on the productivity charts?

Would you have been urged on by such a plea? And if your answer, like mine, would be 'No thank you, I would prefer to stay in bed where it is safe and warm,' then what else could it have been? Perhaps, like Napoleon the pig in George Orwell's *Animal Farm*, the pyramid builder used unarguable communist principles for the collective good. Were collections of agreed rules carved up in hieroglyphs on some lost board – 'All builders are equal, only some are more equal than others'? Was the pyramid like the windmill in *Animal Farm*, the very symbol of their unachievable freedom to be bought with their lives? And did some human hulks, urged on by such ideals, toil and die here from their exertions, believing that they died for the good of all?

Or was it instead some great capitalist enterprise? Did architects wave their scrolls around on a site where concrete was being poured, knowing of the financial rewards that awaited them? Was Tim Rice right – could you 'make a fortune buying shares in pyramids' like Potiphar in *Joseph and the Amazing Technicolor Dreamcoat*?

I suspect that even as they were being built, the pyramids of Giza probably perplexed everyone just as much as they do today. While the officials – the 0.1 per cent (or less) of the population who had received an education – probably knew what they were doing, the rest, the 99.99 per cent who actually did the job, presumably just did as they were told, as was the norm in ancient Egyptian culture. Perhaps the truth is simply that there seemed nothing better to do at the time, and if they did what they were told, they would at least be fed, while if they refused they might starve. Perhaps that is the secret of the pyramids. If there had been computers around at the time, they may have found something more interesting to do with their time!

It is hard to understand any of it. What we see today on the plateau of Giza may be enormous, but it is, in truth, just another ancient crumbling ruin, something akin to the Colosseum in Rome, which today also looks very different from the way it appeared in its Imperial Roman heyday. The Great Pyramid today has lost its peak, several layers of stone and all of its once-gleaming external coating, and stands several metres short of its original height. The sides are crumbling, and many a tourist comes away clutching a stone from the base. It may be a small stone, but after over 4500 years and uncountable numbers of visitors, exactly how much of the pyramid has disappeared into the pockets of the casual visitor? Yet what are those few missing metres compared with the vastness of what is left?

The Greeks listed the pyramids at Giza as one of the wonders of the ancient world, although they were probably only writing down what had been said for many centuries. There can be no doubt that these were buildings designed from the start to impress and to last forever. If by chance their sheer scale fails to impress you, then try to think instead about their age. They were over 1000 years old when Moses led the children of Israel out of Egypt into the promised land. They were already more than 2000 years old when the Greeks and the Romans came, the world's first package tourists, shown around the site by tour guides then, as today. They left their graffiti around the sites in ancient Greek. Great world leaders have stood at their foot and been as overawed as we are, from Alexander and Julius Caesar to Napoleon. If they could speak, these stones could relate the very history of humankind.

For almost the same length of time, people have been trying to break their way inside the pyramids. The reasons are various. In the 12th century, Caliph Miamun, son of the great Haroun el Raschid to whom Scheherezade reputedly told bedtime stories to save her skin, spent a lifetime trying to find the entrance to the Great Pyramid. Once he was finally inside, Arabic wisdom informed him that if he burned the right substances, said the right words and performed the right actions and gestures in the right order, then from the stones themselves there would materialize a great emerald carved in the shape of a life-sized Sultan, seated cross-legged upon his *diwan*. Miamun and his men burrowed in like steel-clawed rabbits through millions of tons of stone. They eventually found an entrance, but it was blocked so tightly that it was easier by far to mine their own hole through the rocks. But undoubtedly, they all remained disappointed when they became the first in the current era to enter these great buildings – and found little there of much interest to them. There was no emerald; and if, instead, they did happen to find a bundle of pitiful human remains, the last physical evidence of the mysterious pyramid builder, then they would have thought so little of it. Certainly no record of it remains. Probably they simply threw the rags and bones away.

Archaeology is a destructive science. In trying to find answers to eternal questions, archaeologists systematically destroy the things they are examining. Miamun was no archaeologist, but the result was the same, or worse. Once the tiny things he found were gone, there was no second chance. Things which did not interest him went unnoticed. The depradation of the site, though, was already almost as ancient as the pyramids. It would be unsurprising if it was completely empty.

Since the Middle Ages, the Great Pyramid has stood open to all visitors. Little wonder that so little remains there today to give us clues about the man for whom it was built.

In today's times of universal scepticism and general atheism, visitors and students still ask 'why', but without the easy comfort of the answer that satisfied many generations before them – 'Only God knows.' Today, in our scientific age, this is clearly not enough. We want to know exactly who did it and for whom, how the stones were moved, and what urged on the men who did it. A century ago, either slavery or religious fervour were answers that satisfied almost everyone. Using the *Book of Exodus*, it was simple to say 'Slaves built them under duress.' Today we have moved beyond the earth and out into space, but we are still in search of answers. Now there is a newer and more positive theory. Quite clearly, 'Aliens did it.' The answers which eluded the Victorians are now immensely obvious to everyone. Of course! The ancient Egyptians were descended from a race from Mars – or, as some say, Orion. They stumbled across hidden wisdom that allowed them to build aircraft and helicopters, which in turn made the building of the pyramids so much easier. So it was quite natural that the Victorians failed to recognize this, because helicopters had not been invented in their day.

Today's popular representations of ancient Egypt, in cartoons, films laden with special effects, and books, have made everything seem not only possible but probable. As a professional Egyptologist, I have a hundred images to fight against and children to argue with who believe absolutely what they see. I am asked questions such as, 'Do stones roll down the corridors and knives come out when you go into a pyramid?' (the Indiana Jones series); 'Do you have to be very fit to jump from one stone to another inside the pyramids?' (Tomb Raider, with Lara Croft); 'Are you scared of flesh-eating scarabs?' (*The Mummy*); and of course, 'What was the Scorpion King really like?'

It seems that Egyptology is always trying to bridge the gap between contemporary knowledge and the excesses of imagination. On the whole I, like most archaeologists, tend to be more pragmatic. Several basic facts are clear. The pyramids exist – so someone built them. We have objects from them and around them which show us exactly when they were built. As I shall show you, there is also evidence, despite notions to the contrary, to indicate how they were built. I believe utterly in the power of mankind to achieve it all. I am also completely convinced that often today we are unable to 'see the wood for the trees'. Brought up in a technological era, we have become convinced that 'bigger is better'. To move a big stone, you need either a big machine or alien help, or, like Obelix and Asterix, a magic potion of some kind, or, as some are suggesting today, a big trumpet to cause the stones to resonate and thus rise up into place more easily! We fail to understand what the ancients understood. We no longer understand the simple principles, the basic properties of the materials which surround us. On a desert island, we would think of houses with rooms, heating and fitted kitchens, not of using the materials at hand to advantage. The answers are often far simpler than anyone supposes.

Many books have been written already on the subject. But none of them has yet given a satisfactory explanation of the mysteries of the Great Pyramid – until now. Within the following pages, you will hopefully start to discover the man behind the stone – Cheops, who ordered the pyramid built in the first place. And, for the first time, you will find a reasoned and logical explanation of how and why they were built.

By the end of this book, instead of asking 'Why?' and 'How?', you'll be asking yourself, 'Why has no one ever thought of that before?'

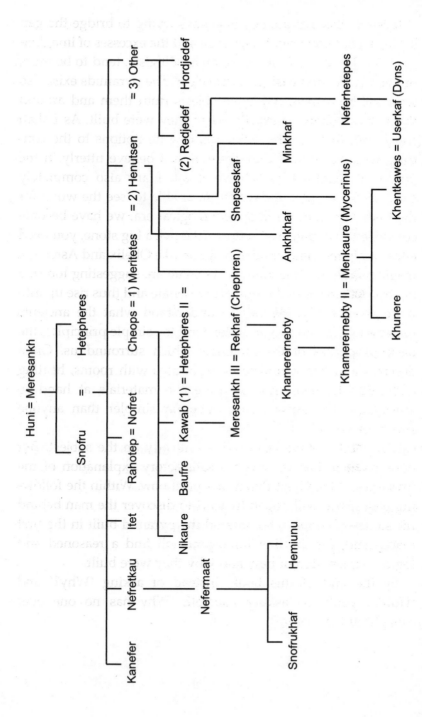

CHAPTER ONE

The Rise of the Fourth Dynasty

—

C ome with me in your imagination, if you are able, and step into the land into which the pyramid builder was born.

If has often been said that time has changed little along the banks of the Nile, and that, south of Cairo, things have not altered since the beginnings of the ancient civilization. But if you had travelled up the Nile around 2600 BCE, things would have looked very different indeed. For a start, Cairo did not exist. This is hard to imagine, for this great, sprawling metropolis, growing today at the rate of a respectable triffid, is now home to around 20 million people: the greatest, and the most polluted, city in Africa. This massive conurbation sweeps along overpopulated streets from Heliopolis in the north, once a serene and isolated small town, down to Helwan and Maadi in the south. But in 2600 BCE, there was little to be seen here but vast stretches of river and desert, with a sprinkling of farming communities that were little more than small villages sleeping under the hot sun of Upper Egypt.

The population of the entire country was then around 1.5 million, of which only around 400,000 at the most, and probably fewer, were able-bodied young men fit and able to work, who were required to support the rest. Their dependants, old women and men well into their forties, together with younger women and their children, stayed home out of the sun and waited for the food to return with their menfolk.

Settlements were scattered thinly along the river banks. On each side of the Nile, the flat banks were verdant and lush with ripening crops. The Nile was Father to Egypt, and he gave generously to his children with yearly floods so that few men were needed to work the fertile ground. Beyond the green fields stretched, on both sides of the river, the land of the dead. Here were the cemeteries where ancestors were buried and to where, every few days as laid down by custom, the living would come to leave pots of water and bread on the stone-piled graves. In between the banks, the fast-flowing river was dotted with small fishing boats.

Down by the riverside, thickets of finely branching acacia, persea and willow gave cover to great basking crocodiles, waiting, jaws open in the hot sun, to catch the girls who came down to the river to fill water jars for their mothers. In mid-river, shining areas like sandbanks were actually the backs of hippos. The Nile gave life, but it also took it away.

The largest town of all lay some 20 miles south of modern Cairo, and was called White Wall. Later generations would call it Memphis – but in 2600 BCE, that was the future. Then the Nile ran further to the west, at the foot of a great stony escarpment which today we call Saqqara. On the skyline of the escarpment stood several huge, flat-topped mud-brick buildings. These were the tombs of important courtiers who had served long-dead Kings. The buildings raised their panelled facades high above the small town, all brightly painted in bold primary colours of red, blue, white and yellow, which made the overall blue of sky and river and gold of sand even more intense. Further to the west, lying in a hollow and surrounded by a great wall, stood a pyramid, the only one of its kind and invisible to most. Only those permitted by the King ever went through the gates in the wall and beyond. But from White Wall, it was invisible.

There were no pyramids. The hills were empty and stretched into the mists north and south. There was nothing there but the wild dogs who scavenged around the cities of the dead.

In the centre of the town of White Wall there was a high, thick, rectangular wall, in all probability made of stone brought from across the river from the quarries of Tura. This was the King's palace. Little could be seen within the wall, for huge wooden gates closed the only entrance gate. Scattered around the outside of the walls were houses, some large, mostly small, and all made of sun-baked mud-brick. Between these houses, a narrow, flattened mud pathway served for those who ventured out into the strong sun – the workers, burned black with the heat, and donkeys, swishing away flies with dirty tails. Some things change little in the Middle East.

Down by the riverside there was a jetty with ships moored up side by side. Made of wood and with sails furled, these boats, scarcely bigger than a modern felucca, plied their trade up and down the Nile. There were few foreigners about, and women and children, as always, were at home, many sitting on doorsteps. Sailors lounged around, waiting for the order to move. Merchants moved vast loads off the decks and into warehouses. Scribes in clean white kilts wrote assiduously on rolled scripts laid out along their left arms, their black wigs falling over their faces.

Inside White Wall, away from the eyes of ordinary folk and within the enclosure wall, stood the palace, created of wood and mud-brick but much larger than the houses. In front of it stood two flagpoles, embedded in mace-shaped stones. From the tops of the poles, long, brightly coloured pennants flew in the breeze blowing from the north. This was the home of the King and his family. Guards were posted around the walls at intervals. Everyone moved quietly. Within these walls there lived a god, a living bridge between the physical and spiritual worlds. This one man, so all men believed, met and conversed daily with the spirits. Mortal men lived in terror of him, afraid even to look up at his face if they ever met him, but all kept their eyes fixed firmly on the ground in front of them. Few people, other than his wives, had ever seen his face and none of them really knew what he was like.

At the rear of the palace, protected by a quiet avenue filled with seated guards, stood a second building, taller and more brightly decorated than the first. From inside there came the sound of music and singing, of clapping and stamping feet. The voices were women's. Mingling in the sound was the wail of infants, the cries of babies, the calls of children. Somewhere within the building came the chanting of boys, accompanied by their teacher. This was home to the royal wives.

And it was here, one day in an unknown month, that a child was born. His father was King of all Egypt, Snofru. His mother was the King's wife, Hetepheres. The child himself would one day, in the distant future, become King in his father's wake. But not for many years yet. Cheops would have a long wait for his turn. King Snofru was new to the throne and could only guess at what lay ahead for him and his family. He had plans for stability, wealth and peace. The birth of a son represented part of that stability, for now his line was secure. All of Egypt listened for his word, which was law.

. . . But it had not always been like that.

How Egyptian history was recorded

Fifty years ago, even less, our understanding of ancient Egypt's history seemed complete. Scholars for the previous 150 years had created a comfortable framework in which Kings and dates sat happily. Today the pattern is altogether less certain.

In 332 BCE, Alexander arrived in Egypt at the head of a joint

Greek and Macedonian army. He was welcomed as a saviour and he swore, when he died, that he would be buried there. After his death, a half-brother called Ptolemy came to the throne. Knowing nothing of the country which he now ruled, and unable to speak the language, he had to look for help. It came from a priest who had been born in a delta town in the north of Egypt. His name was Manetho, and he created for Ptolemy the very first written historical framework into which the names of the Kings of Egypt and their succession could be set.

In drawing up the account, Manetho was able to call upon centuries of knowledge, writings and folklore. This was the first definitive guide to ancient Egypt, revealing traditions and customs of a country new to Ptolemy. Manetho presumably wrote his account in Egyptian, since that was his native tongue.

The book was so useful that others copied sections of it, but the original is lost to us. An anonymous scribe translated it into Greek for the King. We cannot know how accurate that translation was, nor, for that matter, how reliable Manetho's original sources were.

Using texts, dated documents, King lists and a very generous supply of gossip to guide him, Manetho divided the past history of his country into family groups or dynasties. Starting with the founding of Egypt in the First Dynasty, he moved steadily forwards in time until the Ptolemies formed the 32nd. He listed the Kings in the sequence that he found in his researches. Their names would have been the name given to them at the time of their coronation, unique to them in the whole web of time. These are generally unfamiliar to us – take Nebhepetre, Sehetepibre and Usermaatre Setepenre – yet they are the names by which the Kings were known. These, written into an oval loop called a cartouche, later had to be translated into Greek for Ptolemy. Having gone through all of these processes, many of the names are barely recognizable. Manetho also listed the length of time each had ruled, together with what he considered to be useful and pertinent facts, such as 'He was carried off by a hippopotamus'!

The result, as may be imagined, is far from satisfactory. Yet at the time it would have served its purpose. Since few people at the time understood the concept of history at all, the account probably seemed more than adequate. The Egyptians were never interested in exactitude, as we are. They had little interest in their own background, but were comfortable knowing the basic 'facts': that there had been a First Occasion when time and life had started, and that since that time, Kings had come, stayed for a while and then gone. The lives and responsibilities of the Kings were generally alien to ordinary people, farmers and craftsmen. They were more interested in whether the floods would come at the expected time, or whether they would be able to grow food to feed their families. The cosmos, the order of the universe – those were things about which they knew nothing and they left them confidently in the hands of the godlike Kings. In all likelihood, it would never have occurred to them as being important to know in what year a certain King had lived and died. Since he *had* died, he was no longer of any real interest to anyone!

As for the state machine – the administrative officials who organized the everyday machinery of taxation and benefit – they were more interested in recording the events of the day. This meant noting the year, month and day of the present King's reign. They kept immaculate records, stored in state archives of such efficiency that, in the reign of Ramesses II, an unknown, poor widow seeking justice in the King's presence was able to request the presentation of 500 years' worth of papers logging the change of ownership of her mean patch of land – and it could be done, in an instant. So, for the Egyptians, the system worked.

But for us, it is all too imprecise. We have lost the state

archive. The officials recorded events in the year of the King they served. There might be more than one King alive at a time, with contenders in other towns – but no official, of course, would record the existence of co-rulers for political correctness in the presence of their own royal master. The King's son may well have been crowned before his time, while his father was still alive, in order to secure the succession – but the state records would not need to mention this. The records, naturally, could not record the ultimate length of the King's reign. How could they? So for us, they would have been interesting but basically unsatisfactory from an historical viewpoint. The only way today we can be certain how long an Egyptian King reigned is by the highest date on a document or object which has survived so far. Manetho's record can then be used to confirm or deny this evidence.

In theory, Manetho had all of this information available to him, and for all we know he may perhaps have recorded it faithfully. Other scholars admired his work, which was unique for its time, and copied it and used extracts of it for their own work. To our misfortune, however, these copies were frequently poor and inaccurate. The original text by Manetho does not exist, either in Egyptian or in Greek, so we are left with only the copies, most of which vary greatly from each other.

To use Manetho's record to work out what happened and when, we must therefore understand that we are using information recorded for purposes of propaganda, using unknown and possibly inaccurate sources and, frequently, unidentifiable names, and that was translated at least once and then miscopied by others. Hardly a sound historical record.

Scholars in the last 200 years, using the evidence gained from monuments and archaeological discoveries, collected Manetho's dynasties into groups. They discovered that the great pyramids were built during a high peak of Egyptian culture which they termed the Old Kingdom. Into this division were placed the Third, Fourth, Fifth and Sixth Dynasties. Another peak of civilization was encountered in the 11th and 12th Dynasties, called by scholars the Middle Kingdom. The period of military conquest and domination of the Eastern Mediterranean in the 18th, 19th and 20th Dynasties were thus termed the New Kingdom. To separate these high points, troughs of chaos, lack of information and disunity were termed intermediate periods. Between the Old and Middle Kingdoms, the First Intermediate period encompassed the Seventh, Eighth, Ninth and 10th Dynasties, the Second Intermediate period, between the Middle and the New Kingdom, the 13th, 14th, 15th, 16th and 17th Dynasties; and the Third Intermediate period, a relatively newly identified period, the 21st, 22nd, 23rd and 24th Dynasties. Before the Old Kingdom, the emergence of the unified state was termed the Archaic period. All in all, it seems a neat method of dating.

However, time and more information have shown that these boundaries must be recognized as artificial and thus may not be as clear-cut as once they seemed. The dynasties and kingdoms, with their intermediate periods – these are our tools, not the ancient Egyptians'. The Egyptians would have been totally unaware during their lives of the decline and slide from one period or one dynasty to another. The time boundaries we place, moreover, have no reference whatever to what was happening outside Egypt. There is, for instance, no correlation whatever between the Middle Bronze, a period recognized by almost all other areas of archaeology, and the Egyptian method of dating. In this, as in many other areas, Egyptology has stood proudly alone!

It is now becoming apparent that the dynasties were not as neatly organized as Manetho originally suggested. The implication from Manetho's list is that each dynasty represents a complete line of a family. While most of the dynasties are certainly family groups, and a change of dynasty generally does indicate a new line of Kings on the throne, some of the

17

dynasty breaks appear to be in completely the wrong place. For example, it is now clear that the line of succession between the Third and the Fourth and the Fourth and the Fifth Dynasties was continuous. The reasons for the dynasty breaks are unclear. It is possible that this was caused by mistakes in Manetho's original sources, or the breaks may be there for other reasons we have not yet fully understood.

It is also equally clear that the old distinctions of the kingdoms can also no longer be trusted. The Kings of the 11th Dynasty, for example, did not reunite the country after the chaos of the First Intermediate period as fully as we once believed, while the 13th Dynasty seems now to have been as important, powerful and wealthy as the 12th and per-haps should be incorporated into the Middle Kingdom. The line of Kings runs continuously from the 17th to the 18th Dynasty, yet the Kings of the 18th are considered New Kingdom, while their grandparents and great-grandparents were part of the turbulent Second Intermediate period. These artificial boundaries are thus less helpful that might have been imagined.

Using Manetho's guidelines together with the archaeological record, we can state with certainty that Cheops ruled Egypt during the Fourth Dynasty. Manetho's reign length of around 23 years for Cheops accords well also with the dated evidence we have found. The Fourth Dynasty sits neatly into the height of the Old Kingdom period. But when these 23 years actually happened is a far more complex matter!

When was the Fourth Dynasty?

In Egypt, we have a method of dating admired and envied by colleagues in other fields. The ancient Egyptians noted that the rise of the Nile floods on which they so depended followed within hours of the reappearance in the night sky of Sirius, or Sothis, the Dog Star. This star, one of the brightest in the heavens, had previously vanished from sight for many days, eclipsed from view. Its reappearance was eagerly awaited. In late July, the temperature soared almost beyond human endurance. The Nile, polluted and running at a bare trickle, was infected. The fields lay empty, the soil cracked in the scorching heat of the sun. Famine and thirst were everywhere. Only the rising waters of the Nile, red and rich with silt from the Ethiopian highlands, would save them from imminent disease and death. The reappearance of Sothis, then, heralded celebrations throughout the land. Farmers would stir from their turpitude to prepare tools and seed, women would be more contented to use stored grain, knowing more would soon follow. With the water came birds and fish – life itself.

The Egyptians believed that the King was personally responsible for the arrival of the flood. Both Snofru and, later, his son Cheops daily undertook rituals to ensure the return of the inundation. So the calendar itself depended on the King.

Yet the state had already established its own method of recording events, a fixed calendar whose roots go back to the founding of the land itself. They had divided their days into groups of 10, which we would call weeks. Three of these weeks, or 30 days, amounted to a month. Twelve months, or 360 days, made a year. On to this was added five extra days, over and above the normal months (epagomonal). According to legend, these days were sacred, days on which Nut, the sky, had given birth to four children, Osiris, Isis, Seth and Nephthys, resting from her pains on the fifth day. These days did not count for working, but were the first state holidays. So the year amounted to 365 days. Yet we know today that the year is actually 365¼ days. We account for this extra time by the addition of one extra day in the calendar every fourth year.

The Egyptians did not account for this quarter-day. In the first year, Sothis would appear, the farmers would rejoice and the state would announce the start of the New Year. Four years later, the state celebrated one day too early. Another four years on, and the calendars were two days out of line. So as the years passed, the differences grew greater, and then started to shrink as the two dates moved closer together again. We call this the Sothic cycle. Because the agricultural year focused around a fixed event, the flooding of the Nile, this discrepancy was more obvious to them that it might have been to most cultures.

The two calendars – one of land, one of state – coincided only once every 1460 years, or four times 365! So, for 1460 years, the state would be announcing their New Year's Day, the official date of the inundation, at a time when the farmers were planting, harvesting or were otherwise too occupied to celebrate what was clearly the wrong event! We know that the two calendars coincided in 139 CE, and counting back in cycles of 1460 years, the calendars would also have coincided in 1322 and 2782 BCE.

The arrival of the inundation was vital for the state, since it was also the start of the new tax year. Because of this, two documents which record the actual day when the inundation arrived have come down to us. In the 12th Dynasty, during the reign of Sesostris III, we know that the flood arrived on day 16 of the fourth month of Peret, the winter season, in the seventh year of the King's reign. Going back in cycles of 1460 years, it can be easily established that year seven of Sesostris III of the 12th Dynasty, in the Middle Kingdom, fell somewhere around 1872 BCE. Counting backwards, the start of the 11th Dynasty and thus the start of the Middle Kingdom must have been around 2050 BCE. Unfortunately, we have no earlier dates to help us to go back further in time.

We can boost our store of information by considering the Turin Canon, a list of Kings' names and reign-lengths scrawled on the reverse of a Ramesside taxation papyrus, now in fragmentary condition. The papyrus lists all the Kings of Egypt from the founder, Menes, at the start of the First Dynasty, to those of the Second Intermediate period, with each King's name appearing alongside a number, presumably their reign-length. Unaccountably, there is a divide at the end of the Fifth Dynasty rather than at the end of the Sixth Dynasty, where the Old Kingdom traditionally ends. A rubric, or red figure, of 995 years is taken generally to be the period of time from the beginning of the First Dynasty to the end of the Old Kingdom. Adding this to the date of 2050 for the start of the Middle Kingdom gives us 3045; and adding extra then for the First Intermediate period, a date of around 3100 to 3200 BCE for the unification of Egypt seems reasonable.

We must, of course, always be cautious with our evidence. On the one hand, we need to be certain not to rely too heavily on material without other evidence to back it up. On the other, we should also be careful about discarding evidence if it is all that we have! This dilemma is a real one. We have no idea who wrote the Turin Canon or why. The papyrus was found in excavations in the workmen's village of Deir El Medina on the west bank of Luxor. Here were housed the highly skilled artisans employed in cutting and decorating the royal tombs. They were all literate – but why should they have wanted to create a list of Kings? The numbers are believed to be reign-lengths; but while Sesostris III is listed as ruling for 39 years, the highest evidence from documents and objects remains 19 – a huge discrepancy. We have similar problems with many other Kings. Without this vital information, can we rely on the numbers or dates at all?

If we take the two numbers we have so far – that is, 2050 for the start of the Middle Kingdom, plus the 995 of the Turin Canon, then 3200 BCE marked the start of the Unification, or the First Dynasty, and 2050 marks the start of the 11th Dynasty and the Middle Kingdom. The years in between must be apportioned between the Kings according to the reign-lengths that we can establish. After overcoming uncertainties over the length of the First and Second Dynasties in the Archaic Period at the beginning, the length of the First Intermediate period at the end, the start of the Old Kingdom can be fixed around 2700 BCE. If the years cannot be absorbed by the First Intermediate period, nor by the reign-lengths of the Kings of the Old Kingdom, then we have no choice but automatically to lengthen the Archaic period, the time between the unification and the start of the Old Kingdom.

What is the evidence for this? Recent work has revealed beyond any doubt that there were strong Kings who ruled the Nile Valley, if not the delta, before the Kings of what was previously called the First Dynasty. As a result, a 'Dynasty 0' has come into being. Kathryn Bard suggests the First Dynasty started around 3000 BCE, thus allowing one to two centuries for the ephemeral one or two Kings now placed into Dynasty 0. This also allows 314 years for the First and Second Dynasties, or 514 if you include Dynasty 0. But this seems far too long.

Unpicking the evidence

It was suggested many years ago that the apparent divergence of the two calendars in Egypt was very curious. How could a civilization that could plan and build enormous pyramids not have realized this apparently simple problem and tried to correct it? When Egypt was under Roman occupation, the clash of the calendars was a thorn in the conquerors' side, as scholars tried to add and remove days to correct it. Is it not likely, then, that the Egyptians also tried to correct it? If, at any time, any Vizier or King had changed the date to bring the state calendar into line with the calendar of the land, then our dates, based on observations of the two dates of the reappearance of Sothis, would also be incorrect. In other words, if any one King had announced at any time a change in the calendar (which would not have had to be recorded), then our system would collapse like a house of cards. This would then make invalid the dating of those archaeologies which rely on us for dates. In other words, the whole of the dating system for all the countries of the Eastern

Mediterranean would also collapse! Other archaeologies, e.g. Palestinian, Hittite, Cretan, etc. use artefacts of Egyptian origin to date their own levels and finds rather than carbon-14. There is, of course, no one worldwide 'archaeology' in terms of dating or methodology.

On the whole, radiocarbon dates gained from testing organic materials from ancient Egypt do fit the general framework. Carbon-14, a radioactive element, is present in every organic life form. When the life form dies, carbon-14 starts to decay at a known rate over a long period of time. Counting the carbon-14 left in an organic material, whether plant or animal, enables the date of death to be estimated. Carbon-14 dating, though, is not precise, compared with Egyptian methods of dating.

However, there is one aspect of Egyptian dating which does not fit at all with conventional dating methods and which so far scholars have passed with little comment. If the state calendar had depended on the arrival of the flood, the announcement of the first day of the year would have been simple, as officials would announce it on the first day of its arrival in the Nile Valley as New Year's Day. In the same manner, if the calendar had depended on the sighting of Sothis alone, then the calendar would be easily adjusted annually. Neither of these things happened. Instead officials insisted on a rigid 365-day cycle which then took 1460 years to coincide with the inundation.

But at some point in antiquity, the state calendar must have started off at the same time as the flood. As we have seen, counting back in cycles of 1460 years from 139 CE, this would have been in 1322, 2782 or 4242 BCE. It can't have been 1322 BCE, as the two calendars had long been in existence by then. It can't have been in 4242 BCE, as that's far too early. There is no chance of any unified civilization in Egypt as far back as that, although the early Egyptologists W.M.F. Petrie and J.H. Breasted suggested this as the starting point of Egyptian history. The start of the state calendar could have been in any year at all – with the loss of a day every four years, the cycle would have been the same no matter when they started. What is equally certain is that they could not easily have predicted the year in which the two would coincide, and thus start the state calendar late in the cycle. There would have been no point! So this suggests beyond doubt that the state calendar must have been set up in 2782 BCE. The state calendar marked New Year's Day. The agricultural calendar celebrated New Year's Day on the first day of the inundation. For the state calendar to be set up, it had to be at a time when the inundation occurred and in time with the rising of Sirius. This could be in any year at all; but once started, the two drifted apart inexorably. The coincidence of the two in 139 BCE shows previous coincidences, i.e.

1460

-138 (there was no year 0)

1322 BCE (too late)

1460

2782 (only feasible date)

1460

4242 (far too early)

If the start of the state calendar was set up *differently* (and why should it be?), this could have been to anticipate a future year – and this makes no sense. So it must have been 2782 BCE.

This causes problems, however. According to legend, classical writers and archaeology, civil war in Egypt in the pre-dynastic period ultimately resulted in the unification of the towns and villages under one King, who then built the capital city, later called Memphis but at that time called White Wall. By this act of unification, the new King became, at a stroke, the owner of everything along the Nile Valley. This same King then set up accounting and taxation systems, and, in order to record the information, someone at his court set up the hieroglyphic writing system. We find hieroglyphs, used as writing rather than as simple pictures, in evidence from the First Dynasty.

In other words, if the King set up the state record system, the tax and accounting systems and the writing system at the founding of White Wall at the start of the First Dynasty, this would have to place that event in 2782 BCE, and not at 3100 BCE as usually calculated.

There is no doubt whatever, as stated above, that 514 years is far too long for the time from the unification to the start of the Old Kingdom, this being approximately the same length as the Old Kingdom itself! There is also little doubt that the First Intermediate period also needs to be shortened. This can be done while still retaining the dates gained from the observations of the reappearance of Sothis in the 11th Dynasty. If, on the other hand, some smaller leeway was to be gained after this date – in other words, that the calendar had been altered, but not by so great a margin as previously suggested – then instead of losing the Third Intermediate period altogether, something which would cause a crisis for some areas of our archaeology, it could perhaps also be shortened.

This causes us a problem. It is generally considered in most books that the unification, the start of the First Dynasty, was around 3100 BCE. After the unification, the archaic period, a time of civil disorder, was marked by a string of ineffectual Kings who may not have been able to control the entire country.

The dawn of the Old Kingdom, the direct ancestors of Cheops, is therefore generally dated to around 2780 BCE. However if, as seems reasonable, the state system started only in 2782 BCE, then the dates for the Old Kingdom and for Cheops must have been later. So Cheops may have ruled as much as 300 years later than many books currently suggest.

Taking the conventional methods of dating, then, the Nile Valley was unified between 3200 and 3100 BCE; and then, after a period of disorder, emerged 531 years later, around 2686 BCE, into the Old Kingdom. This would place the start of the Fourth Dynasty around 2570 BCE.

If we adjust our dating to incorporate the inauguration of the state calendar in 2782 BCE, this would place the start of the Old

Kingdom at no later than 2550 BCE, and the start of the Fourth Dynasty at around 2450 BCE. Both of these dates would be perfectly reasonable when matched with carbon-14 dates from organic matter from the Old Kingdom period.

The march of Egyptian history

The beginnings

The picture that emerges from all of this evidence is not the one that might have been drawn a few decades ago. Early books on ancient Egypt make it all appear so simple! Around 3100 years BCE, they will relate, a King, known to legend as Menes, first united the Nile Valley, built a new capital of Egypt at Memphis, and then attacked and subdued the north, the delta, to form a single, unified country. Yet according to archaeological evidence, no man called Menes existed at all. The word, *mn.s* in Egyptian, means 'it is consolidated'. Undoubtedly this is a title, 'The Unifier', rather than the name of an individual. Many books state categorically that this man can be identified as Narmer. But is there any evidence for this?

The little evidence that we have for this period came from excavations at Hieraconpolis, ancient Nekhen, about halfway between modern Luxor and Aswan. Two great Egyptologists, James Quibell and Frederick Green, found there what they interpreted as being the foundations of the first temple in Egypt. Somewhere in this region, from a pit or trench, came a rich mass of objects known collectively today as the Main Deposit. These pieces comprised, among the usual mix of pottery, finely carved mudstone palettes, so-called maceheads and a remarkable gold head of the falcon god Horus.

The palettes, mistakenly identified as cosmetic palettes, are carved in raised relief, often on both sides, with a variety of scenes. Each palette has an indentation on one face, in which were found traces of ground malachite. This has been described as being intended for use as eye-paint. However, as yet, not a single instance of green eye-paint has been identified on statues or paintings. It was more probably used in the preparation of faience, or glazed composition ware.

The palettes show a variety of scenes, largely identifiable with the struggle to unite Egypt. The most famous, the Narmer Palette, which is now in Cairo Museum, shows the King, on one side, wearing the crown of Upper Egypt while clubbing a foreigner. Behind him, a servant carries the King's sandals. On the top of the palette, between cows' heads with women's features, is the King's name *nr*, a catfish, and *mr*, a chisel, giving the name Narmer. On the other side, above the indentation, the King, now wearing the crown of Lower Egypt, inspects two ranks of dead prisoners, their decapitated heads lying between their legs. In front of the King, the King's water-bearer, half the size of the King, is identified by hieroglyphs as the Vizier. In front of him, half his size, are four standard-bearers, each carrying totems with the figures of birds and animals on them representing areas of Upper Egypt.

Other palettes found in the same cache do not display the same neat order of figures as the Narmer Palette. The scenes they record are often more disorderly. The Battlefield Palette, broken in the middle, shows a lion, assuredly the King, prowling around dead men after a battle. Birds are shown in the act of devouring parts of the dead. Above, the legs and feet of two figures show one man, not Egyptian in character, being taken prisoner by a personified standard, which has now grown two arms. The Libyan Palette, also broken and with only the bottom section surviving, shows on one side a rural scene, with pack asses among trees and the hieroglyphic symbol for Libya, a throwstick, while the other side shows the fall of several battlemented walled cities, their walls being undermined by attacking standards once again.

At the time of the discovery it was suggested that the material represented a foundation deposit. Although it is believed the objects were found in the one place, their exact site of discovery still remains a mystery. The falcon's head, made of solid gold with a bar of polished obsidian pierced through the head to form two black eyes, presents a great problem. Fixed into its headdress are two plumes. These plumes are clearly not of the same date as the head itself. The gold of which they are made is a different colour, lacking the patina of age of the head itself. The plumes are crudely cut with jagged edges, certainly not matching the skilled finish of the head. Even the hole into which the plumes are fitted is merely punched through the gold of the head. Interestingly, the plumes are the headdress associated with Amun, the god of Karnak. The plumes are sometimes shown in Luxor on the god often identified as Min. On these occasions, the hieroglyphs alongside refer to the figure as Amun, and in his earliest and usual forms, Min does not wear plumes. Amun is seldom represented any earlier than the 11th Dynasty, when he emerged as the local god, Tod, south of Luxor. Thus the very earliest date that might be ascribed to the plumes on the Hieraconpolis head is Middle Kingdom, although their workmanship suggests a more realistic New Kingdom date.

According to Quibell and Green, the head with the plumes was found in the same Main Deposit as the palettes. If we could establish that the Main Deposit was a pit, with objects found in layers and the head at the top, it could be argued that the Main Deposit was no more than a rubbish tip used over a long period of time. This seems unsatisfactory, given the fine state of the Narmer Palette, and the lack of other material in the pit which might give credibility to this idea. If the Main Deposit, on the other hand, was a long trench, then it could be argued that it lay alongside a wall, and that different pieces, discarded from the temple, were dug into different parts of the trench at different times. However, if, as is usually claimed, the Main Deposit were one single cache of goods, then it cannot have been a foundation deposit.

The fact that several of the palettes were found broken and

that the other sections were not recovered, together with the head, suggests that, like the Karnak Cache and the Luxor Cachette, this deposit was the result of a 'spring-cleaning' exercise within the temple, or even placed there when the temple fell into disuse. If either of these were the case, then the Main Deposit, though much of it very old indeed, may cover a wider span of time that previously suggested. The Narmer Palette, given its superior carving to other pieces, could easily be commemorative rather than contemporary. In other words, it may have been made not at the time of the original victory, but at a much later date as a souvenir, perhaps to commemorate an anniversary of the event.

The Narmer Palette, then, needs to be used cautiously in the effort to unravel the story of the unification of Egypt.

Excavations on the site of Memphis have clearly shown, however, that White Wall was not, as many suppose, at the same site as Memphis itself. The earliest objects found at the site are to the south of the remains of Memphis, and lie directly adjacent to the desert plateau now called Saqqara. White Wall was built as a defensive city at the frontier with northern Lower Egypt, probably as a border fortress. Served almost exclusively by the river, it offered a good port for loading and unloading goods from the south. As time went on, the meander of the river became filled with mud – in effect, the river began to move inexorably eastwards. For some time, either the port had to be dredged or, as it became more silted up, docks began to be built on the new ground to keep pace with the river's shiftings. Ultimately, around the end of the Old Kingdom, the old city was abandoned altogether and a new palace-city was built further to the north.

There is more to this story, as the archaeology attests. Battle for control over the Nile Valley began with the sudden increase of wealth, and therefore power, of two chieftains, one based in Hieraconpolis and the other in Naqada, north of Luxor. The names for both sites are written with the hieroglyph for gold, so it is reasonable to understand that the metal figured large in local history.

The town of Naqada is close to an entrance through to a wadi – a dry riverbed – running through the Eastern desert. We know that many quarries out in the Eastern desert provided stone early on in Egypt's history. We also know that gold deposits were found here, although these were small compared to the much richer lodes in Nubia. It would seem that the war between the two places was a battle over the control of the gold supply, with Naqada fighting for the supply from the Eastern desert, and Hieraconpolis controlling the import of gold from the south.

In the battle between the places, the two leaders begged, bribed and assaulted local towns and villages until slowly they came to control people and places to each side of them. It was inevitable that the two main forces would clash. Hieraconpolis, represented in battle by a standard bearing Horus the falcon atop, and Naqada, represented by Seth, its local deity, and apparently some form of dog, fought bitterly and for some time. Legend later recalled the 'battles of Horus and Seth' and suggested they lasted for many years. The victory of Hieraconpolis over Naqada placed one man, for the first time, at the head of all Egypt, from Aswan to the foot of the delta.

This man, the unifier of Egypt and first King of the First Dynasty, then built White Wall in the north as a fortified site, able to act as spearhead for new campaigns aimed at the land to the north. The founding of White Wall is shown on the so-called Scorpion Macehead, where the King is depicted diverting the course of the Nile to build the walled palace compound. North of White Wall, the land was occupied, according to the palettes, by city-dwelling, curly-haired men. This was probably part of Libya, the name applying to the whole of the North African coast banding the Mediterranean. Having established a frontier post, the new King then appointed officials from among his family and friends, as later became the tradition in Egypt. These men, for the first time, achieved fame and fortune, not by brave deeds, but by their physical closeness to the King. In this way, his sandal-bearer would have been a very high-ranking noble-man, perhaps even his son and heir.

This founding of the capital, later subsumed into Memphis, established the government departments of the palace and also, it would seem, saw the birth of hieroglyphs, the writing that enabled the ancient Egyptian language to be written down for the first time. This seems to have occurred around 2782 BCE, as we saw on page 24. Shortly after, other First Dynasty Kings from White Wall attacked the north. Again, according to the palettes, they achieved this by undermining the walls of cities and fighting for control. As each King died, they were buried not near White Wall, in the necropolis now known as Saqqara, nor in their own hometown of Hieraconpolis, but in Abydos, the holy and sacred city north of modern Luxor already associ-ated with the god Osiris.

Who these people are is still a problem. Egypt is and has always been a part of Africa, although we identify it today as being part of the Middle East. For all of that, when pictures of its people are shown, the men are shown darker-skinned than the women, suggesting their complexion was light enough to change colour under the strong sun. It has to be emphasized at this point that establishing race by skin-colour is a very poor method! We know certainly from aspects of style and idiom that some settlers arrived here from the land between the Tigris and Euphrates – Mesopotamia, now known as Iraq. Perhaps these were the ancestors of the lighter-skinned folk. Yet many of the customs and much of Egypt's culture owe their birth to black Africa. In images of Snofru and his son, Cheops, their faces are African.

The years of consolidation

As we have seen, evidence now clearly suggests that Kings attempted to unify Egypt over two short dynasties, Dynasty 0 and the First Dynasty, in three distinct stages: controlling the Nile Valley; founding the capital; and conquering the north. Yet the hold of these Kings over the people they had already conquered seems to have been less than secure: by the Second Dynasty, the old divisions were reappearing, perhaps accompanied by civil unrest.

William Stevenson Smith observed that the reign-lengths of Egyptian Kings can be reasonably surmised by the material evidence and monuments left behind, because the longer a King ruled, the more he would have achieved during the reign and the more objects we shall find bearing his name. While the sequence of the First Dynasty Kings is established from the discovery of their tombs in Abydos, together with more evidence from King lists, labels and so on, the names and reign-lengths of the Second Dynasty Kings are much less certain. Indeed, despite the wealth of recent archaeological work on the oldest sites such as Abydos, Naqada and Hieraconpolis, only the reigns of two Second Dynasty Kings, Peribsen and Khasekhem(wy), can be established with any certainty. Peribsen's name is capped with the figures of two deities, Horus and Seth, suggesting that the brief unity of the First Dynasty was breaking apart again in the Second Dynasty. Some of the material retrieved from the First Dynasty tombs at Abydos shows that these tombs had clearly been burned. The picture overall is one of confusion, perhaps even war between rivals. After all, one King had formed a template for monarchy, and others would undoubtedly have felt better entitled to fill the new office, especially old rivals in the south.

Since the first pyramid was built at the start of the Third Dynasty, there appears to have been a sudden, dramatic stabilization of power. Almost overnight, it seems, the conflicts of the Second Dynasty simply stopped, and the country started to pull together for the first time. This blossoming of the Third Dynasty suggests a single, popular and powerful leader who could give his country the assurance of stability. These were the Kings who laid down guidelines and gathered the wealth that made it possible for the Kings of the Fourth Dynasty to contemplate the building of the pyramids of Giza. One King of the Third Dynasty, Netcherikhe – better, though perhaps not entirely correctly, known in popular books as Djoser – was able to summon up the workforce of the land to create an infrastructure capable of designing, planning and creating the Step Pyramid at Saqqara.

But the giant leap from the apparent disorder of the Second Dynasty would have been out of the question, were it not for the existence of one man in the right place at the right time.

His name was Imhotep.

Imhotep

Across the chasm of time back to the start of the Third Dynasty, faces and personalities are lost to us. Yet although we know little about him, Imhotep was counted as one of the greatest thinkers of all time. He was the Vizier, or second-in-charge of the land, under King Netcherikhe, and thus may have been related to the King. It has been suggested he may have been a brother, although there is no evidence for this. The remains of several statues bearing his name have been found around the site of the Step Pyramid. A rare letter found at Saqqara, written in hieratic script – a kind of cursive hieroglyphs – was addressed to him by an overseer of works on the pyramid site. The letter complained that to take the men from the site and sail them to the palace for the issue of their clothing would take valuable building time. Could the boat not come to the site from the palace bring them with them, to save time?

Imhotep was remembered for thousands of years as architect, mathematician, author, and healer – both a physician and an anatomist. From the face of the Step Pyramid, it can be seen very clearly that originally the site had been conceived originally as a simple *mastaba* tomb – a low, flat rectangular building with a burial shaft cut below into the bedrock. (*Mastaba* is an Arabic word for a bench which these tombs resemble in shape, hence the name.) The design of a *mastaba* was essentially flawed, since its contents were invariably stored in cell-like rooms in the superstructure of the tomb, thus making it extremely easy to break into and rob through the roof. The Step Pyramid was a bold innovation, adding a smaller *mastaba* atop the first, and then another – until a small pyramid was built up.

The architect of this was undoubtedly Imhotep himself. As Vizier, Imhotep was responsible for conscription and oversee-ing all the workshops – in short, for all goods required on the site and for all the manpower to work with them. He was the man at the top of the social pyramid, the man who needed to ensure that everything was exactly where it was wanted at the moment it was needed, and that the men on the site were fed, watered and housed adequately to ensure the building work did not falter.

The creation of such an administrative infrastructure is a mammoth task, beyond even the most able of top managers today, for it involved, in some way or another, the entire population of the country. Such daring vision, and such ability to bring a concept to fruition, is beyond the ability of ordinary men. Imhotep's reputation as a healer and physician suggests that the workers on the site would have had their accidents and injuries dealt with. Everyone today can accept that a happy workforce is an effective workforce; but 5000 years ago, in an age of raw domination and exertion of control using force and not the mind, the scope of what he planned and carried out is quite astonishing.

After his death, Imhotep was venerated. His tomb became a place of healing until the Roman period, about 2800 years after his death, when he was identified with Aesculapius, patron of healing and doctors. Prayers to Aesculapius-Imhotep, and votive statues, have been found widely through the Roman Empire right to its fringes. Even today, standard histories of medicine still incorporate his memory. What an achievement!

Netcherikhe's successors in the Third Dynasty began to build pyramids of their own. But lacking an Imhotep, their grandiose schemes, despite having the advantage of a prototype, came to nothing. To the west of the Step Pyramid complex, three unfinished pyramids still await full excavation. The surrounding walls of all three complexes, called the De Morgan Enclosures after the Egyptologist who first recorded them, can be clearly seen on any contour map. In 1954, Zachariah Goneim, an archaeologist born in Egypt, traced the entrance to one of these three lost pyramids and, without clearing the sand from above, entered through the sloping passages to a chamber beneath. Inscriptions informed him that the pyramid was once occupied by a King Sekhemkhet, although the alabaster sarcophagus found in the chamber sadly proved empty. It seems likely that the burial never took place at all, or, if it did, was robbed soon after the chamber was filled. Although the name of Imhotep was found at the site, he would have been very elderly. Perhaps it was his death which brought an end to the building of the pyramid itself.

The historical lesson from these events is clear. It was not the building of a pyramid that was the hardest part of the exercise, as the size of Giza has suggested to so many people, but rather the organization of manpower that was needed to achieve it. It could only have been done in the Third Dynasty by Imhotep. It would require men of equal genius in the Fourth Dynasty to attempt the same feat again.

It would seem, then, that the emergence from chaos into order, from the infighting of the Second Dynasty into the unification of the Third, was the action not of a King but of his Vizier, the great Imhotep. Today, assessing the evidence, the question that then arises is – why was Imhotep never King? Given his brilliance, and the loyalty he commanded, why did he never usurp ultimate power? The answer must equally be in the character, lost to us, of Netcherikhe. Kings after him in the Old Kingdom are portrayed not as men but as unapproachable demigods, their faces and figures the very epitome of Kingship, so it is hard to find the men behind the formal masks. Certainly the very nature of Kingship would have protected the holder of the office. After all, it would take an exceptionally brave man to dare to kill a King believed to be a living god. However, strong leadership brings respect, and Netcherikhe must have been strong to have been served so well by the great Imhotep.

CHAPTER TWO

Land of the Pharaohs

—

Titles for administrators and officials appear in inscriptions and dockets from the start of the First Dynasty, from the tombs of Saqqara. We know that by this date the King had appointed such people as the Vizier and posts within the household and the army. From the Palermo Stone, an annual record of the events of the Kings of the first five dynasties carved in stone and now in Palermo, Sicily (even though this may not be accurate for the early years), we can judge that the civil service, with all of its taxation, inspection, recording and law chambers, had also been established.

The emergence of the god-King

By the start of the Third Dynasty, the great Imhotep took matters one stage further. Egyptian culture was always organized around what was already known and established. Change was anathema, and any man who instituted change risked his very life if the changes he developed resulted in failure. It was always safer and easier to change nothing. Throughout Egyptian history, there are bright lights illuminating the cultural darkness, geniuses who were brave enough to have their ideas developed further. These men were so few and far between that we know all of their names – Ptahhotep,

Hordjedef, Amenhotep son of Hapu, Khaemwese and, greatest of them all, Imhotep.

With his truly brilliant and innovative mind, Imhotep developed a blueprint for building pyramids, and at the same time pulled the entire workforce of the country together in a massive combined effort. By the time of his death, the administration of Egypt had bonded into a fearsome unit, and demonstrated that it was possible, with a single person at the head, to pull together in a single task for the benefit of the King. Imhotep had thus elevated the King also, separating him still further from ordinary men, and had persuaded every single family in the land to come together just to build a funerary monument for his master. In one act, he had begun to define monarchy for the foreseeable future. He himself defined the role of the perfect servant, the one who at a stroke represented his master publicly, served him every minute of every hour. Yet he understood that the King was as far above and beyond him as a star above the earth. It was a master vision, and yet it had its flaws. By isolating the King, making a true god of a man, Imhotep removed any close contacts from the King. This King, according to Imhotep's concept, had to stand alone. Only his wives and children could ever know him as a man. And in this lay danger. Over several generations, the blueprints for government and technology which would be so useful to Cheops were laid down. By the time he became King, most of the techniques were understood, which enabled him to order the Egyptians to build for him the largest pyramid of them all.

Abode of the Kings

Few royal palaces remain from any period of ancient Egypt, and the ones which survive date from later times. Very few buildings survive from the Old Kingdom. So we have to take our evidence where we may. From the start of the First Dynasty onwards the Kings made their home a palace-estate, in hieroglyphs called *hwt*, pronounced 'khut'. From the hiero-glyph ⌷, this is a large compound with an entrance at the lower right corner. This was the walled compound with the royal residence, or *pr* (per) within.

The walls around the outer compound already followed a traditional design. This was copied from bundles of slender wooden branches, lashed together towards the top so that the sides slope inwards, and allowing the leafy tops to spread outwards into what it called a cavetto cornice.

Once the palace had been built at the start of the First Dynasty, only the King's close family and ambitious local chiefs could cluster around him, all eager to be of service to the new autocrat, all jostling for power, which came solely from proxim-ity to the King's person. Just as with Louis XIV, the man physically closest to the King was the noblest of men and elevated above his peers.

From the time of the First Dynasty until the time of Ramesses II, who built a new palace-city in the north-east delta, first White Wall and then Memphis would be the home of Egyptian government and site of the principal palace of the King. We do not know at what date the Egyptian Kings first established palaces in other cities. According to texts, the Middle Kingdom Kings established their capital at a site they called Itj-tawy, 'The Seizing of the Two Lands', but this site has still not been identified. It is clear, though, that the head of the administration and government remained always in Memphis.

We still know very little about the early capital city of Egypt. Although recent fieldwork has located where it once stood, the water table, which in recent years has risen after the opening of the High Dam in Aswan, means excavation down to the earliest levels is impossible. Once surface earth is cleared, water fills the trenches. Buildings made of sun-baked mud-bricks, as most domestic dwellings would have been, would have long ago become part of the earth once more, and unlike materials such as wood or matting, generally fail to survive in wet conditions.

The palace and the city into which Cheops was born have therefore long since vanished.

We do, though, have some clues as to what the palace would have looked like. The Step Pyramid in Saqqara stands in the middle of a great enclosure wall of limestone. Today, visitors to the site see the outer wall on their arrival and think little of it. A few decades ago, this wall was not there at all. The perimeter wall, and many other aspects of the Step Pyramid complex, owe their present existence to Jean-Philippe Lauer. This remarkable French architect has dedicated his life to rebuilding the complex. Using stones from the site, the lines of the remaining foundations and parts of low, broken walls, he had new stones cut to match the old in order to rebuild it. Slowly the site has regained enough of its ancient splendour to give us a clear image of how it once looked.

The perimeter wall of the Step Pyramid complex is intricately carved along its outer face with what is now termed 'palace-wall facading'. Common also on *mastaba* tombs of the period, this design was to be repeated as a popular motif on many items of ancient Egyptian life, from boxes for clothing to coffins, for the rest of ancient Egyptian history. It appears on the Step Pyramid wall in the form of a long line of complex doorways, each set into a series of niches within niches. The design also once included carvings on panelled sections between the niches which looked like knots in fabric. Other horizontal stone bars were carved to look like tree-trunks, lashed into position using criss-crossed ropes. The whole was once brightly painted in raw primary colours on a background of startling white. While today, the honey-gold of the weathered limestone seems to be part of the desert plateau from which it rises, 4500 years ago its colour and vibrancy would have shocked the eye.

Among the niches around the perimeter of the wall there appear at first sight to be 14 entrances at regular intervals. Thirteen of these, however, are false doors, carved out of stone and yet resembling in every detail wooden boards, complete with hinges and hasp-fastenings, with timbers marked even down to the knots in the wood. They are exact copies of true doors. Only one door, however, in the south-east corner, was a true entrance. This leads into a covered passage, within which, on each side, stand limestone columns, carved to resemble bunches of reeds or elongated willowy stems of pollarded trees, bound together towards the top with rings of rope. Above the ropes, the 'reeds' splay outwards to form the first capitals. The columns are conjoined to the walls behind them with panels of flat, uncarved stone, apparently intended to support the columns rather than fulfil any architectural or artistic purpose. The roof between the columns, like the false doors outside, is carved to resemble trunks of trees laid side by side across the span.

The first impression for the visitor is that it is all rather odd. Why should stone be carved so deliberately and carefully to look exactly like wood? It was suggested some years ago that since this was the first large building made of stone, the Egyptians had carved it to resemble the wood with which they were familiar, as they were uncertain whether the strength of the building came from the material itself or from its shape. This, it was argued, explained the conjoined columns – the Egyptian architects frankly distrusted the new-fangled material. Yet the layout is distinctly clear, for the entrance to the Step Pyramid complex is in exactly the same position as on the hieroglyphs for a palace-enclosure ⌊. This was designed from the outset as a stone-built eternal copy of a royal palace.

Walking through the colonnade, to the right, the visitor enters a long open courtyard, bounded by the outer wall on one side and a series of elegant, barrel-vaulted buildings to the west. The enclosure is square at the colonnade end and rounded at the northern end. In the centre of the southern end, there is a raised dais.

The barrel-vaulted rooms around the periphery of the court are all false. Although they appear to have entrances, there are none; they are solid stone, like the doors in the outer wall. This

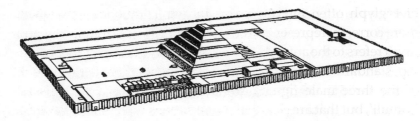

The Step Pyramid complex

style of enclosure, with the buildings around, is depicted, albeit often stylistically, in many places. One of the earliest reproductions of it is on the Narmer Macehead, today in the Ashmolean Museum in Oxford.

Raised reliefs on the Narmer Macehead

Narmer, first King of the First Dynasty, is shown, carved in raised relief, wearing the crown of Lower Egypt and seated under a baldachin or canopy on a dais. In front of him, seated in a litter, is another figure, in the characteristic shape of a woman. Behind her, three male figures carry knots in their hands, similar to the design incorporated into the outer walls of the pyramid enclosure. Below the men appear a variety of animals. Although Ian Shaw suggests that the animals and men shown represent captives, the usual Egyptian depiction of captives shows them dead or bound, and these are not. To the lower right, the man with arms raised is the hieroglyph often interpreted as meaning 'millions', though it more correctly represents an uncountable, almost limitless quantity. It refers to the animals – cattle, sheep or goats, and fowl. To the top, standard-bearers form ranks carrying their banners. In front of the three male figures are shapes that Shaw interprets as 'tumuli', but that are clearly representations of the barrel-vaulted buildings of the type found in the Step Pyramid enclosure.

It is known from inscriptions found at First Dynasty sites at both Abydos and Saqqara that Narmer was associated with a Queen called Neithhotep. This name incorporates the name of the Tutelary Protectress of Lower Egypt, Neith, meaning that the Queen was born in the delta which Narmer had conquered in battle (see the drawing of the Narmer Macehead, page 42). Above the King flies the falcon, Horus of Hieraconpolis. Above the female figure in the litter is an image of a walled city in delta-style, not Upper Egyptian. Behind the animals on the lowest register, each tadpole represents 100,000, while the fingers below each represent 10,000. Behind these numbers, a compound filled with animals, each representing a number, suggests there were 120,000 of these being presented.

The seated figure is apparently Neithhotep, and the picture records a diplomatic marriage or alliance made between Narmer of the south and Neithhotep of the north to cement the joining of the lands. Narmer sits on a dais to welcome her. Neithhotep, carried in a litter, presents her three officials to the King, who in turn brings gifts of animals in limitless quantities. The place in which this happened, with a dais for a King and barrel-vaulted buildings with open space between, can be none other than an enclosure identical in style to the court at the Step Pyramid – in other words, the royal palace.

This open court in the Step Pyramid complex is usually described as being the *sed* court. The *sed* festival is one of the first festivals ever recorded in ancient Egypt, and was vital to the continuity of the King's vitality and effectiveness. Every year, the King's life-force was physically tested. Only if the

King was fit and healthy would there be a return of vigour and vitality to the land he ruled. From many pictures, it seemed that the King was required to jog around the perimeter of the court, perhaps on several occasions. It has been suggested that each barrel-vaulted building represented a different *nome*, or county area, of Egypt, and that he ran for each *nome* in succession.

The word *sdi* in early Egyptian sometimes has the meaning 'to slay, butcher', and so it is likely, in the very earliest days, for a *sdi* festival to have ended in death for a King whose strength was found lacking. Several pictures from the Old Kingdom show Kings running the course. In later times, during the New Kingdom on, the festival was held but it is doubtful whether the King was ever required to run in public. The ceremony simply became a jubilee festival.

It would appear from the evidence of the Narmer Macehead that the palace courtyard must have been used by the King on all public and state occasions. With flags fluttering from stand-ards in front of each of the buildings, and the canopy over the throne on the dais, it would have presented a majestic and colourful spectacle.

Leaving the *sed* court, the visitor to the Step Pyramid then enters into a vast open courtyard. The northern end is domi-nated by the pyramid. Once again, a variety of buildings cluster around the perimeter of the open court; once again, all are false. Behind the pyramid and attached to its northern face, a series of small rooms lead the visitor towards what, at first, seems a blank wall. At eye-level in the wall are two holes; and by peering through, the life-size image of the King in stone may be seen peering back! In antiquity, this statue's eyes were inlaid with orbs of quartz and pupils of black obsidian. Once the false eyes had been pegged into place, the statue was lightly plastered all over and the whole painted to resemble the King in life.

Three times a day, at sunrise, sunset and late evening, offer-ings of food and drink would customarily be brought here for the soul, or *ka*, of the King. How eerie that must have been! Imagine, if you will, entering the dark, quiet complex lit only by the stars and the rushlight torch in one hand. Imagine, then, entering the silent suite of rooms – and then the light, catching the inlaid eyes of the statue through two tiny holes in a wall, suddenly brings to life the figure of the King, who appears to be emerging from the pyramid beyond! It would have taken a courageous and faithful man, indeed, to undertake such a task.

This positioning of the 'cellar' (*serdab*) behind the building is again in exactly the same place, in all later buildings, as the private apartments. It seems this is a symbolic replay in stone of the activities within the palace, where three times a day, the King would be served food in solitary private quarters behind the public buildings. This is not to say, of course, that he would not participate in banquets; but truly, it appears from evidence that yet again the King of the Old Kingdom was bound by formality and superstition to lead a solitary life.

So what, then, does the Step Pyramid enclosure represent? The notion that it was designed for the King's afterlife seems reasonable and obvious enough, but why was it designed this way? And why are so many of the buildings false? All the evidence suggests that this is an exact replica in stone of the first King's palace in White Wall. This would account for the false buildings, which, in the original, would of course have been usable rooms. It would account for the dramatic appearance of the site as one approaches the exterior today – the 'White Wall'. It would also account for the stone replicas of details of woodwork.

Of course the palace of White Wall would not have had a pyramid at its heart, but instead would contain the royal residence. Hieroglyphs show that palaces, at the time writing began, generally had two storeys, a battlemented top and a stairway which led to the roof 𓉺. Exactly the same design is shown in the rectangular shape used to contain the King's name at this early time, which we call the *serekh*. This would suggest that a multi-storey building would have been at the heart of the court of the original palace, with the King's private apartments at the rear, where servants brought his food and drink.

A serekh

The false buildings around the perimeter of the court would thus have been either workshops, offices or residences for the wealthier nobles, the King's officials.

No images have survived to show us what the inside of these buildings would have been like. In the lower chambers below the Step Pyramid, the chambers and passages are lined with brilliant blue faience tablets, inset into the wall and resembling hanging mats. So presumably, the inside walls would have been decorated and hung with bright hangings. In Upper Egypt, however, little has changed over time, in many respects. Model houses made of baked clay, 4000 years old, are exactly the same shape and design as real houses in the villages today. Since the Egyptian climate is often hot, people tend not to live in their houses as we do. Instead, they use the buildings for storage and sleeping, and cooking takes place in the open court. As a result, houses often tend to be dark, with small rooms and little furniture.

This is exactly the pattern found in one of the other few ancient royal palaces so far identified and excavated in ancient Egypt, that of Tell el Amarna. Here, adjacent to the temple in the centre of the city, lay two suites of rooms, one set each side of a great highway through the town. On one side, the west, lay the public area, courtyards flanked by columns and massive statues, with vast columned halls beyond, aimed at impressing if not over-aweing visitors. On the other side of the road, to the east, lay the privy apartments, small rooms with little decoration, most of them barely large enough to hold a bed. It seems, at first, a mean place for a King of Egypt. But although the King's private apartments were small, those of his wives, the royal ladies, would have been very different!

The royal harems

Much has been made of harems in ancient Egypt. Despite mythical stories suggesting that all men had many wives, in reality only Kings had lesser wives, and that was because a King was deemed to belong to the company of gods, not men. However, texts do suggest that Kings of the time pampered their wives. Queen Meritetes, the principal wife of Cheops, was described as 'His beloved, she who says things and it is done for her'.

Egyptian harems were not like Turkish harems. They were not places of confinement, but rather rooms where royal women chose to live together in the highest possible luxury. They were waited on by servants, both male and female (as shown by pictures from tombs at Tell el Amarna), and spent much of their day doing their hair and make-up to attract the attention of their husband; playing music, singing and dancing; and spinning and weaving (as evidence from Gurob and Amarna shows).

The houses occupied by the women were large, lavishly decorated and comfortably furnished. In the Third Dynasty, the official Metjen at Saqqara described one of these queens' houses:

> [It was] a house 200 cubits long and 200 cubits wide, built and equipped. Fine trees were planted there, a very large pool made there and figs and vines were growing round it. It was all done in accordance with the King's written command. Many trees and vines were growing and from them great quantities of wine were made.

Two hundred cubits is around 300 feet, 100 yards or 80 metres – a sizeable establishment indeed! A painting from the walls of one of these New Kingdom buildings from Tell el Amarna, now in the Ashmolean Museum in Oxford, shows the King and Queen seated on low chairs. The floor is covered with a woven covering or carpet, brilliantly coloured and with a border pattern. The children sit on floor-cushions made of material to match the carpet. Chairs would be lavish, inlaid or gilded, and, as many pictures show, would be upholstered with loose cushions and cloths over the back like antimacassars!

The building would surround a central large hall, with painted floors and walls decorated with tiles. Light would come from oil lamps, some on stands, others mounted on the wall on brackets. Drinks would be served in decorated goblets, the finest made of brilliant blue faience, or even gold and silver. Food was handed round by serving-girls from tables of food at one end, the guests being given plates with small portions. They ate with their fingers, and servants brought water to pour over their hands to cleanse them.

The royal family's daily life

Here, meals were served three times a day at the same times that the spirits of the dead were fed. The contents of those meals, although of the best available, seem to have been based on coarse bread, even for the rich. This had a dire effect on the health of all ancient Egyptians. Although complete mummies from the Old Kingdom are virtually non-existent (to date, there are only 1.5 mummies that can be confidently dated back to this time), there are many skulls. However, in the early 20th century, at a time when scholars truly believed that phrenology, the 'science' of reading the shapes of skulls, would give archaeologists all the information they would need, many skulls were collected from Old Kingdom *mastaba* tombs on the Giza plateau, and still rest today in cranaria – skull collections.

These are kept in two tombs, now sealed except, occasionally, for specialists to examine them. In the 1960s and 1970s, the skulls were systematically examined by the dentist Dr Frank Filce Leek.

Although they were the skulls of the nobility of the Fourth Dynasty, and thus mostly from close relations of Cheops, almost all of them suffered severe dental erosion, their tooth enamel worn away during their teens by sand in their bread. Leek suggested at the time, after trials, that sand could have been deliberately added to the grain by women during the grinding process in order to speed up the processing of flour in the saddle-quems, or grinding stones, used by the Egyptians. But recent microscopic examination of these grains of 'sand' suggest instead that they are minute fractures of stone, and thus more probably came from the action of the stone of the quem.

In one Old Kingdom skull from Giza, three teeth found in one lower jaw were not the original teeth. The two outer teeth were drilled through from side to side, and gold wire passed through and around the central tooth. This 'dental prosthesis', probably the world's oldest example of false teeth, was then embedded into the gums. There is little plaque on the teeth or wear on the gold wire, suggesting that the teeth may have only been inserted after death. Although from the teeth this seems likely, it is also a very strange thing to find, since the jaws of many mummies of Kings are missing some teeth, and there has been no attempt to fit false teeth for their afterlife. This body must have belonged to a man of exceedingly high rank, presumably a son, brother or both of a King. At any rate, this technological feat (dental enamel being one of the hardest substances to drill through effectively, even today) is but one example of the knowledge and skills that the Egyptians were acquiring in the use of natural materials during the Fourth Dynasty.

As I have mentioned, bread clearly formed a major and fundamental part of everyone's daily diet, even the King's closest family. The most substantial meal of the day was eaten during the cool of the evening. After workers returned home at sunset, around 5 pm, they would have a snack and a drink, but would eat properly later – today, this is around 8 or 9 pm. There is little reason to believe that Kings and nobles were any different from ordinary people in this respect, except in some of the foods that they ate. The main meal of the day would have comprised several main courses. Drinks would be beer or wine. Especially in the wealthier households, sweet puddings were always a favourite, along with fresh fruit – grapes, dates, figs, pomegranates and watermelons.

In the tomb of an unnamed noble of the Second Dynasty found at Saqqara, a full meal was found intact, although a little dry after 4500 years! There were separate dishes of: a porridge of ground barley; spit-roasted quail; two cooked lamb kidneys; a pigeon casserole; stewed fish: barbecued beef ribs; and small triangular loaves of bread made from ground emmer, a kind of early wheat favoured by Egyptians. For pudding there were small round sweet cakes; a dish of stewed fruit (probably figs); and a plate of fresh sidder berries, with cheese, and beer and wine poured from large storage vessels to finish. Truly a meal fit for a King! It is hard to imagine, seeing the meal, that it was cooked so long ago, and that, when it was made, the pyramids of Giza did not yet exist. This has to be one of archaeology's finest hours!

Outside the main harem building, in the centre of the outer courtyard, would have been a pool, fringed with plants and trees, many of them flowering shrubs heavy with the perfumes the ancient Egyptians loved so much. Flowers were gathered and used to decorate the house, while women and men carried fragrant blossoms at banquets and wore them in their hair. In the pool would dart fish taken from the river, and perhaps a turtle, as shown in some reliefs in the Saqqara *mastaba* tombs, while water-lilies, blue and white, symbols of Egypt, would float on the surface.

Every bed yet found from ancient Egypt is narrow, wide enough only for a single sleeper. The mattresses slope downwards to the foot. This makes it even more certain that the King's sexual life was carried out in the women's quarters, amid pleasant cool surroundings rather than in bed. In many houses, including the palaces, there are low daises or platforms built into the corners of rooms, and these, covered with linen, would no doubt have served the purpose well. The royal children would be thus conceived and then born in these rooms, and would spend the early years of their childhood here with the mother and siblings.

Cheops was probably taught to read and write, since in one story Snofru, his father, called for a pen and papyrus to write – the only record of an ancient Egyptian King doing so!

Snofru ruled Egypt for around 24 years, a long rule for a time when, going by evidence from the cemeteries at Abydos and Naqada, men and women would be elderly by their mid-thirties. During this time, his several wives would have borne children – we know the names of some of Cheops' brothers and sisters. These children were educated within the palace, probably at a school within the harem if the inscription of the noble Ptahshepses is accurate:

> In the time of Mycerinus, he was educated among the King's children in the palace of the King in the King's harem, being more honoured in the presence of the King than any of the other children.

We also know, both from the northern tombs at Saqqara and Giza and from tombs of the same era in Aswan, that many nobles had pets. Dogs were a favourite, and no doubt Cheops would have had their company as a child.

The evidence from texts and sites suggests that life within the palace would have been an ideal environment for a royal child, pampered and provided with everything he could wish for. Yet every child had to grow up. While others within the harem school became officials, Cheops' destiny was far greater. He was born to be King.

The establishment of Kingship

As we have seen, the completion of the Step Pyramid attests to a development of the ideas of monarchy within the new, unified state of Egypt. A King for whom the entire population would unite in the building of a monument such as this clearly had no effective opposition in the land. Yet because of our lack of direct evidence, we still cannot say with certainty what a King of the First and Second Dynasties represented to his people, although shreds of information, especially from the later time of development of the office, all point in the same direction.

Having founded the capital city and all of its governmental departments, the main task left to the Kings of the First Dynasty, apart from religious duties involving the maintenance of the cosmos, was to invade, subdue and govern the delta lands to the north. He was, therefore, primarily seen as a military leader. The military conquest of the north by Narmer may have seemed a great victory, but his marriage to Neithhotep of the north suggests that it was unwelcome or unaccepted in many places and needed the consolidation of a diplomatic union as well. The second King of the First Dynasty, Hor-Aha or 'the fighting Horus', seems, at least from his name, to have had to continue the struggle.

It has to be said here that the battles for supremacy between Hieraconpolis and Naqada were essentially the struggle of two tribal chiefs for supreme power as a local chief. There was no prior concept of what the victor would do with that power once he had achieved it, since such a situation had never existed in Egypt before. The prince from Hieraconpolis who ultimately secured victory in the fight had thus to define his post in the face of opposition and resentment from his conquered foe. In making one of his first acts the founding of a capital city, he immediately altered the status of his family and close friends. His family, by blood-ties, immediately became honoured and privileged, even though they may have been of little worth. For his close friends, promotion was a certainty. Gone were the days when only the fastest, bravest and wisest gained respect and honour, now all that depended on their relationship with one man.

Prior to the unification, the local offices had been hereditary, so this automatically continued into the new office of Kingship. However, local power was limited. Once one family had secured absolute power, then nothing short of another civil war would remove it from him and his descendants. His wife was elevated into the position of mother of future despots, while his children were born to rule by right of birth rather than right of force. This was certain to increase resentment among his enemies and may have been hard to establish in those early years.

Excavations by James Quibell and Frederick Green in the First Dynasty area of the vast cemetery of Hieraconpolis uncovered a tomb which they numbered 100. This was a simple chamber cut into the bedrock, its walls levelled, lightly plastered and then painted with scenes from the life, death and burial of one of the last local princes of the area – perhaps even the one who became the first King of a unified Egypt. The tomb is unique. The scenes lack the order of later tomb paintings, with pictures placed in no recognizable sequence. In one corner of one wall, however, the ruler is shown holding a mace and clubbing enemies who fall to their knees. This is the first iconographic record of the status of a King of Egypt, an image that would continue to be copied for the next 3000 years by every one of his successors. It can be interpreted in two ways. First, it depicts him as a man of force and violence who will subdue opposition; secondly, it shows him as bringing order out of chaos, as his disordered enemies form ordered ranks while he clubs them.

So this King of the First Dynasty was established foremost as a military leader and conqueror who smites his enemies and subdues them; as a brave warrior who personally achieves power and holds it through might, physical strength and stamina; and as a bringer of order into places otherwise filled with chaos. It is not surprising that the *sed*-race was set up to demonstrate these qualities in the earliest times of Kingship. Clearly it was the very essence of the role. A king publicly shown to be fit to rule would have needed strong, tactical advisers, initially men skilled in the arts of war. His officials should have been chosen for their physical strength and their loyalty, since a strong, trained man with a weapon would be a threat to his leader, as history shows time after time. At this stage, the appointments would not necessarily be made according to whether the person was related to the King.

Yet the moment the palace-city of White Wall stood at the head of the land, with the war ended and the vast expanse of peace and daily control stretching before him, the nobles called for different characteristics in the King. He became principal administrator, the man who now delegated mundane daily tasks to his supporters. He had first to analyse his needs and decide on the status of office-holders. The men would now be reduced to servants of his person. Was a hairdresser, for example, superior to a sandal-bearer? Was a cup-bearer more important than a fan-bearer? He could now reward even the weakest of his followers, since physical strength was no longer a basic requirement of service to him. He now needed not guards to surround him in battle, but servants who ensured his person was cared for and safe from treachery. He could easily at this stage have become a *primus inter pares*, first among equals, chief of his men in that he occupied the largest rooms and sat at the head of a table, but was still 'one of the boys'.

Instead, as the Narmer Palette shows, he appointed a

relative to undertake most of these tasks on his behalf in a post we now call Vizier. The duties of the Vizier, according to one later text, included management of the palace and its offices, control of all the other officials and supervision of almost every department within the state. He was appointed chief justice and chief ambassador, and was responsible for the counting of everything that was created or was imported. By making this appointment first, the King created an echelon of power with himself isolated at the top, totally remote, able to be contacted daily only through one man, his Vizier. Infighting now belonged to the nobility, and the King placed himself in a position to change their ranks on the merest personal whim.

Having thus relieved himself of all major administrative tasks, the King was free to define his own role. But what was that to be? The Palermo Stone records memorable events during the reigns of the Kings of the first five dynasties. During the First Dynasty, apart from recording the height of the Nile and biennial census trips up the Nile to measure the flood, few events in the lives of the Kings are listed other than the births of heirs, as in this one on the Palermo Stone: 'Year 3, Birth of two children of the King of Lower Egypt'.

This also significantly elevated the rank of his wives. From being unimportant house-managers in the time of a local hunting chief, now, overnight, they became the only living people in the land who had daily and close access to the royal person. As lover of the King's physical person, container for his seed and bearer of the 'child of his body', the royal wives had become an exclusive set. They, and only they, could look him in the face. This placed them socially above the nobles and all other officials – in other words, in front of all the important men in the land. Without them, the line of Kings could not continue. Essentially, this gave them even more power than the King himself in some respects. This was a role that was satisfactory so long as they remained loyal, but made them his deadliest enemy the moment he showed the slightest weakness.

The King's daily duties

Once the King had made himself so remote from the men he had led into battle, it seems he was rarely seen outside the palace, and this is when his physical stamina became the focus of the role. Egypt needed to see a fit and healthy man at its head, not only to lead them but to sire strong sons, heirs to the Horus throne. Hence, as we've seen, the *sed*-festival. This must have been a personally terrifying day for any man who felt himself growing weaker with age. On the Palermo Stone we find: 'Year 7, appearance of the King of Upper Egypt; year 8, praising Horus' (the King was already seen as the successor of Horus).

Along with his celebration of festivals is recorded increasingly his founding of monuments, when his duty involved pacing out the perimeter of the new building, marking the walls with ropes and, according to inscriptions within the temple of Edfu (about 60 miles south of Luxor), helping lay foundations.

> Year 17, stretching the cord for the temple called Thrones for the gods (Palermo Stone).

These buildings, like the palaces and cities, have disappeared, probably under the foundations of the later buildings we now visit and admire. According to the Palermo Stone, by the middle of the Second Dynasty, the King was already trying to extend his control further than the established boundaries of Egypt. The aim, from archaeological evidence, was to secure mineral assets – the finest stone for building, copper for tools and gold for increasing his prestige.

> Year 14, seventh time of counting gold and land (Palermo Stone).

Quarries in the Eastern desert had been opened up before the

First Dynasty to provide a steady supply of a rich variety of hard stone. But now the work concentrated purely on extracting stone for the King. Many of the best stones, complex agglomerates, were worked into the most remarkable stone vessels, finely polished, each one the work of one man over an entire lifetime. The finest granites and black diorite came only from Nubia, also the source of vast gold deposits. Copper was found in abundance in Sinai. All these materials became the personal property of the King and were placed in a treasury at his disposal. No man could have anything any more unless the King gave it to him.

The Kings were quick to exploit this. From inscriptions on the Palermo Stone and from graffiti and texts along the marching route between palace and quarry, men were conscripted by the Vizier, organized into makeshift regiments and led by the Kings purely in order to secure the mines and quarries and to ensure the safe passage of the stones and metals back into Egypt. From this time onwards, control over the quarries and movements of stone and minerals were to be in the control of the army. These campaigns were not a means of adding to Egyptian territory. There seems to have been no intent to conquer other people, but merely to secure safe routes through to the valuable sites, and then to protect the Egyptians who were trained to cut the stone or extract the ore. The expeditions left their marks on the rocks as they marched through. Yet they met with local opposition, although the Egyptians' aim for these campaigns was clearly not to fight. As a result of these attacks the King, by the last reign of the Second Dynasty, began to resort to using ships rather than marching through hostile territory. 'Year 17, building ships.'

Developments in the Fourth Dynasty

Egypt had already formed strong links with Byblos, a port on the coast of Lebanon, now Ras Shamra. Eastwards from here, an overland road which later became the Silk Route, made possible the transport of valuable traded goods from as far away as Badakhshan. This land was the source of lapis lazuli, the deep blue stone so favoured by the Egyptians that even in early predynastic times, they were already trying to find ways to make cheaper copies of it out of coloured glass! Although most of the territory north of Egypt remained essentially hostile, Byblos was so loyal that it seems to become a 'little Egypt'.

It is probable that the port had been settled by Egyptians in the first place, at the start of Egyptian history. The link was a valuable one, for on the nearby hillslopes of Lebanon grew trees – cedars, junipers and pines – that the Egyptians wanted for their own. Trees were far more numerous in Egypt than many books suggest, but it was only in Lebanon, where the climate was cooler and more conducive to steady growth, that the long, straight timbers of hard woods could be obtained.

By the start of the Fourth Dynasty Snofru, Cheops' father, was sending for cedars to build ships to sail upriver to Nubia. The Palermo Stone records: 'Year 12, building 100 cubit ships (160') of meru wood and 60 16-oar ships for the King'. Delivery of the ships allowed Snofru to sail immediately.

'Destroying the land of Kush. Bringing back 7000 prisoners, alive, together with 200,000 large and small cattle.' The movement of men and livestock on this scale was no mean feat. Even allowing for exaggeration regarding numbers of livestock, to drive so many head of cattle overland for hundreds of miles from Nubia into Egypt would have required huge organization beforehand. The animals would have to be driven across deserts, so water and fodder had to be set up along the route. In all likelihood, the Egyptians forced the Nubians to do the job for them!

In one fell swoop, Snofru had secured the stone quarries and gold mines, and their products, for himself. Not only did he personally enrich himself beyond the dreams of avarice, but by removing the men from Nubia – and 7000 men would represent communities of at least 40,000 in total, allowing for women, children and older dependants – Snofru killed several birds with one stone. First, he demoralized the Nubians, since it would take many years before the young boys he left behind became men of fighting age. Secondly, he starved the Nubians of meat by removing their cattle, thus physically weakening them. Since cattle also provided skins for shields and leather for shoes and protective garments, he also protected his army while depriving Nubia of theirs. Thirdly, he reduced the number of Egyptian military conscripts needed each year to secure the sites. This meant less expenditure on essential supplies and support for an army abroad and at the same time greater popularity for him, since serving in the army was always hated by all Egyptians. Fourthly, he ensured a fast and plentiful supply of mineral assets into his treasury with the least amount of opposition. And fifthly, he was able to feed his Egyptians at no cost to himself – the cattle and their offspring would provide fresh beef for all at no cost and little trouble to himself.

All in all, it was an extremely shrewd move. But it seems also that his action had another result he may not have planned upon. What was he to do with the Nubians once they were in Egypt? A conquered and humiliated group of men was clear trouble for the future. A stela placed by him at Dahshur gives the answer.

> The settled Nubians working on the two pyramids of Snofru are given tax exemption.

So here, it seems, we find the reason why suddenly, in the Fourth Dynasty, pyramids start to appear again on a large scale. Imhotep had shown the way at the start of the Third Dynasty with the Step Pyramid at Saqqara; but after his death, pyramid building became unsuccessful and schemes remained uncompleted. This, it seems likely, could have been caused by labour shortages. Egyptians were traditionally farmers. Conscripting them to build pyramids instead would not only have caused resentment but would have taken men from the land, and caused food shortages. Egypt needed the food; but the King needed labour.

It seems Snofru found the answer. He imported it!

The Old Kingdom monarchs

By the start of the Fourth Dynasty, then, we can see that the role of the monarch had been established, developing over a number of years and by a variety of methods. By unifying north and south, the King had set himself up as the owner of everything in the land. By appointing a Vizier, he had separated himself from the people and created an aura of remoteness around himself. By use of his intelligence, he had secured a full treasury and an enormous immigrant workforce. By utilizing the template established by Imhotep, he was now ready to build on a scale that truly represented his status in society. He had brought his people peace, food, wealth and status. He had secured trade routes to the north, through Byblos; to the east, into Sinai, and to the south into Nubia, at virtually no cost or risk to himself. The popularity he had won by all of this had changed his role from that of a violent seizer of other people's property in the Second Dynasty to a benevolent father of his people in the Fourth.

We have few texts from the whole of the Old Kingdom period. Monuments apart from pyramids are rare, and only four of the pyramids contain texts – two have full versions and two, fragmentary versions, of what are today called Pyramid texts. These tell of ceremonies undertaken to ensure the safe passage of the King's resurrected self into his afterlife but little of how he behaved during his life. We have no temples surviving from the first 1000 years of Egyptian civilization, and temples are usually the places where you find evidence of the King's exploits, albeit sanitized versions created for reasons of propaganda.

The pyramids, however, each once stood in the middle of large exterior walls, within which was an entire city of the dead, with large *mastaba* tombs built in neat rows, even streets created for various sections of society. In one area we have burials of the King's sons; in another, his wives, sisters and daughters; in another, the artisans and architects. Outside the walls, we now know from few excavations, were shanty towns built for the permanent workforces employed on building the pyramids and tombs around them, and maintaining them afterwards. All around the walls, and to the north and south, estates of land were granted solely to feed the workforce. Death had become big industry!

The *mastaba* tombs, unlike the tombs of their royal leader, have walls filled with pictures and texts. The texts list titles and major events in the careers of their occupants, starting in the early days with simple lists of titles and slowly, over time, building up into elaborate and complex autobiographies. From these we can get some insight into the relationships these people had with the King and with each other. Alongside the newly developed role of the monarch, it appears that these men, who were often the King's relatives, jostled together to outrank each other. It now became important to show posterity their success measured against that of their fellow nobles.

> He was made chief scribe for the food stores, overseer of all the stores.
> He was appointed Governor, he was appointed as judge and overseer
> of all the King's flax. He then became ruler of the southern house of
> Khed, mayor of Dep, superintendent of Myper and the house of Sepa;
> mayor of Sais; commander of the fortress of Senet.

The titles relating to any one individual are strangely mixed. Some titles are military, some relate to the King's personal household and others to administrative power. Many of these titles, we know, were purely honorary. Many men, for instance, are listed as 'King's Son' when we know the names of their father, and it was not the King! This title, like many others, could apparently be awarded to anyone for their personal service to the King. Two wills from the Middle Kingdom, carved on tomb walls, show that the wealth of individual nobles was divided. Some land and property belonged to the family in perpetuity and could be handed down freely, generally from father to elder son. Other land and property was leased to him by the King as reward for the titles he held, but these, after only a few generations, reverted to the crown. Yet again others, linked to a post, could not be bequeathed at all, but moved from one occupier of the post to the next. Since the posts were in the gift of the King, he could appoint and then sack whoever he wanted, any time he wanted.

All of this gave the Fourth Dynasty King total economic and political control. Added to all of his other powers, he was thus the supreme autocrat, dictator of the land. As a result, texts from tombs show that the King of the Old Kingdom was regarded with fear, if not abject terror, by his subjects; that while he was considered separate and essentially different from ordinary mankind, he was completely at home in the company of the gods.

What the King gave, he could also take away. Since he owned and controlled everything, it paid them always to be subservient, since, if they lost his favour, they lost everything. Images of officials in their tombs depict the normal stance which everyone had to assume when coming into the presence of a higher official – you should walk with head forward, eyes on the ground and arms lowered, palms open and forward to show no weapons were held. Sometimes, the right arm is shown clutching the left and across the chest. These stances were clearly adopted by the highest officials themselves before the King. They were not inherited from tradition, since their predecessors had been hunters and not civil servants. In the presence of the King, however, even the loftiest noble would have to drop to the ground and kiss the ground the King walked upon. In the Fourth Dynasty, Ptahshepses was singled out for an especial honour.

> His Majesty praised him, and His Majesty allowed him to kiss his foot. His Majesty did not make him kiss the ground instead!

Being allowed into the King's private rooms was an honour restricted to very few people, and an honour that could be recorded with great pride in an autobiography, as Sabu did in his tomb at Saqqara:

> When His Majesty honoured me, he allowed me to enter into the privy chambers so that I might assign the courtiers to their ranks. Never was the like done to any servant by any King, because His Majesty loved me more than any other servant of his.

Rawer, a courtier of the Fifth Dynasty, records in his tomb how, when walking through the palace, he was accidentally touched by the King's sceptre. This inspired in him such terror that he recorded the event for posterity. Another courtier, Washptah, actually died of fright in front of the King, his terror brought on by being admitted into the royal presence.

The duties of Kingship

Not for such a King the mere fulfilling of mortal roles! This King was far above and beyond ordinary men. Lord Acton famously said, 'Power tends to corrupt and absolute power corrupts absolutely.' The Egyptian philosophy of power was slightly different – that all rights bring equal responsibilities, so total rights bring total responsibility. The word for a servant in ancient Egyptian was *ḥm* (*khem*), pictured with a club ∤. This, when applied to a King, we translate as 'Majesty'. In other words, the King was the ultimate servant, not of man but of the cosmos itself!

According to Egyptian belief, out of the original chaos and non-existence came a mound of land upon which first the gods, then nature and finally humankind came into being. Existence only happened because of the performance of certain acts. Chaos, or *isfet*, was always present, waiting constantly to take over. *Maat*, often mistakenly identified as truth or justice, was the delicate and brittle equilibrium of the universe. Everything, it was believed, needed to be in balance. Pictures were always drawn or carved with another one to perpetuate and emphasize balance; hieroglyphs were carved on walls in opposite directions, flowing from a central point to ensure balance. Every good, every evil, every plant and animal, was vital to maintain the balance. This world was balanced by an equal world of the afterlife; male had female, up had down, visible had invisible. The slightest incorrect act might upset this, and Chaos would return.

The King's duty, as god among mortals, was to bridge the impossible gap between creation and the world, between mortal and immortal. He alone was content in the company of the gods, he knew their language (the *mdw ntrw* (*medoo netjeroo*), or 'speech of the gods', was the Egyptian name for hieroglyphs). To him was passed knowledge, wisdom said to be from the time of the gods. He was sent to Heliopolis, the city of the sun, while still a prince, to acquire the wisdom he needed from the men who guarded it. This knowledge would ensure that he would carry out the correct acts, say the right words, to ensure the safety and continuity of existence.

In order to attain this, the King needed to enact daily ceremonies in which he would ritually restore creation by repeating the same acts that had once brought the world into existence. To us, in a frequently irreligious and sceptical age, this may seem like an easy option – the Vizier does the work, while the King's only duty is to carry out simple ceremonies. Yet to Egypt and the Kings, it was not this way. To them, the role of the King was the most onerous of all. If he got it wrong, the sun might not rise, the Nile may not come and men would certainly die. So below the King on the social pyramid there was a certain contentment. Every man had a role to fulfil, and that role was equal to, though different from any other role. To gain a promotion meant acquiring more responsibilities, so many men were happy to let others rise through the ranks. Yet everyone knew that they played an essential part in the jigsaw of life, while the King's role, which did not concern the working man in the least, was to ensure that by ritual the world continued to exist.

Whatever the King of the Old Kingdom ordained had to be done. If it were not done, the men may let the King down in the essential requirements of kick-starting the universe every day. Given his isolation, his wealth, his temporal power and his new workforce, the King of the Fourth Dynasty could now add religious fear. He could now be certain he would get what he wanted. And what he wanted, it would appear, was a big pyramid!

Who were the Egyptians?

We still do not know exactly where the Egyptians as a race came from. New work at Hieraconpolis has revealed archaeological support for evidence from the earliest predynastic times which the language had already suggested – that some settlers came from the south, from Africa, while others came from the north, from the Semitic lands of Mesopotamia and further east. Until the time of unification, Egypt was a mixed collection of isolated settlement sites, each with its own customs, language and beliefs, peoples who traded yet remained distinct from each other. Unification bonded them, slowly, into one nation, and this took much compromise. It is not surprising that the process was a slow one.

From the first times, cattle were vital to them. Excavations have shown time and again the presence of bones and horns of huge cattle, probably twice the height of those with which we are familiar today. References to the Apis, a divinely incarnated bull, go back to the inception of writing, while the cult itself probably went back centuries beyond this time. Yet the hunters, followers of the cattle, changed at unification to become a settled people, dependent on the Nile for the soil on which to grow their crops. According to Plutarch's, *De Iside et Osiride* (About Isis and Osiris) Osiris, the son of Nut, the personification of the sky, introduced crop-growing into Egypt. This mythological explanation of an historical fact is still at the moment beyond archaeological proof. The late, great Michael Hoffman, working on the very earliest sites, showed the almost inexplicable presence of querns, grindstones for grain, complete with the remains of the cereals, on sites he placed at around 10,000 BCE – 500 years earlier than suggested for agriculture in Mesopotamia. These people also used microliths, tiny worked flints capable only of being used on small creatures such as fish. They flourished for around 1000 years before the return of the herds and a return to big-game hunting. Hoffman called it an 'agricultural experiment'. This, in archaeological terms, may be acceptable, but in anthropological terms, 1000 years of domestication of animals and crops, linked to a sedentary style, is scarcely an experiment.

Realistically, it suggests that after the last Ice Age, as waters rose, land in the north of Africa became lush pasture. Life without hunting is easier, more reliable. With 1000 years of farming, the people who worked the land came and went as agriculturalists. In all likelihood, the very use of the land impoverished it, until it became the dustbowl we see in the Sahara today. Although the essentially rich land laid down by glacial waters began to subside was rich enough to sustain life for 1000 years, the land, well outside the Nile irrigation basin, received little rain and no floodwaters. Another possibility is that the lush lands welcomed northwards large roaming herds of animals lured by the food, previously driven back by colder conditions. The Egyptians were, and remain to this day, passionately fond of meat. The return of 'food on the hoof' could explain not only the prolific discovery of ivories at this period, but also the return to hunting. Perhaps the Egyptians were all too keen to turn away from their crops to an easy and plentiful meat source.

By the early predynastic period, excavations in 1998–99 at Hieraconpolis have revealed the burial of a baby elephant and, more recently, remains of the huge wild cattle called aurochs, onagars or wild desert asses, gazelle and ibex. All these suggest that big game was plentiful up to the time of the unification and was revered as the source of their rich life. Yet the agriculturalists persisted alongside the hunters. Images from tomb-reliefs at Saqqara show the attempted domestication of hyena as the settled Unified Egyptians attempted to redefine their lives in exactly the same way as the King was being forced to redefine his own role. Of increasing importance was the production of grain. While earliest excavations show meat was the major part of their daily diet, by the Old Kingdom, bread was the staple. Hunting, change of climate, the loss of food to support the desert herds, prolific use of wood for building and cooking – all of these elements combined to change the balance of life, very slowly.

By the time Snofru came to the throne, most of the ordinary men of the land worked in the fields, breaking the soil, sowing seed, weeding and watering, and harvesting rich yields of grain to feed the country. By the start of the Third Dynasty, meat had become more of a luxury. The use of pigeons, kidneys, etc. in the menu on page 50 showed that smaller and smaller animals, and every part of those animals, were consumed, rather than great ribs of beef and big game.

So as the game left, men settled down into their fields – and the King and his men came to tax them, to take their share. Hunting now became purely pleasurable, undertaken by the wealthy for excitement rather than for food. Manetho records the third King of Egypt as 'killed by a hippopotamus', while the Palermo Stone records in year 18 of an unnamed King's reign 'hunting hippopotami'. Ivory of the First and Second Dynasties, under a microscope, is more frequently hippo than elephant, while reliefs from *mastabas* at Giza and Saqqara show men spearing hippos, fish and turtles, and netting fish. The river by the Old Kingdom had replaced the land as the location for the hunt, while granaries collected a portion of the annual crops to feed the King, the nobles, their families and state officials.

Ordinary Egyptians left little evidence behind them to help us in our search. Illiterate, their names are lost even if their graves are still being found. Their possessions were few, and so valuable that little could be spared to accompany them to their graves, and what they took was frequently soon removed by grave robbers. Pictures from reliefs, though, show that by the Third Dynasty, workshops had been set up to train people in essential crafts – weaving, carpentry, boat-building, animal husbandry, pottery, stone-making, bead-making and metal-work. Skilful trades also emerge, especially such things as medicine, hairdressing, chiropody, dentistry, linen weaving, dyeing and sewing as well as baking and brewing. From the Third Dynasty, the titles of successful men show they all had responsibilities in some of these workshops. Peace and a settled existence under a strong leadership brought prosperity to each individual Egyptian, although, from the graves, they still led hard and very short lives that would be dominated by hard work and pain.

From the start of the Third Dynasty, also, men began to formulate philosophies for daily living. Some men started to have the leisure and the training for introspection, to try to lay down basic rules for survival. Although often these so-called 'Wisdom Texts' come down to us only in copies of copies, one of the earliest was composed by Kagamni, a Vizier of Huni and Snofru, at the end of the Third Dynasty. Another, of which only a small fragment survives on an ostracon in Munich, was apparently written by Hordjedef, a son of Cheops. In these, it was laid down in writing how they believed people should treat each other, a moral code which set guidelines for an emergent society, telling how people should look after each other and behave in polite society. Wider in scope than Greek philosophy, which was based on Egyptian prototypes in existence for 3000 years before its own heyday, they lay down clear guidelines of ethical behaviour. These were not dependent, as Judaistic and Greek ideas were, on the notion that if you transgressed you would be punished, but rather on the notion that all men, no matter what their station, fit into an entire plan for existence, and that, since we all exist together, we need to respect each other. While this could have been the means for the wealthy to impose rules on the poor, as the Romans tried through their division into patrician and plebeian, the 'haves' and the 'have nots', or to form castes as did Indian society, in Egypt it was based on the simple precept – you may be rich today, but tomorrow you could easily be poor. If, as a rich man, you despise and mistreat the poor, then how can you expect, when you become poor, to be treated with understanding? This, it seems, is the basis for the 'modern' concept of 'what goes around, comes around'.

Kagemni dictated the script, from the end of the text:

> The Vizier had his children called, having related what he understood of the ways of men, when their ways had come upon him. He said to them, 'Take notice of all that is written in this writing. Listen to it as I said it and do not exceed what has been written down.' Then they prostrated themselves on their bellies and read it (exactly) as it had been written, and it seemed better to them than anything else in the entire land.

Kagemni then laid down some ideas for living.

> A man who is respectful shall do well. A humble man shall be praised. Rooms are opened up before the man who is silent, and there is lots of

room for the quiet man, so do not gossip!

When you sit with those whom you love, decline food which you desire.

A single sip of water will satisfy the thirsty man; a single portion of herbs will bring back energy [literally, strengthen the heart]. One good thing represents goodness, a little stands in place of much. A man whose stomach still wants more after a meal is despised.

When you drink with a drunken man, drink only when his heart is content. Do not fall on meat when you sit next to a glutton but take what he gives you. Do not refuse and it will satisfy.

Let your reputation go before you but let your own mouth be silent. When you are called do not brag about your strength among those of the same age, or you will be opposed.

Hordjedef, one of Cheops' sons, advised men to behave in the same restrained manner, for life is short.

When you do well, then build a house, take a wife who is mistress of her own heart [i.e. knows how to manage a household] and a son will be born for you. You build your house for your son when you make a house for yourself. Take care of your home in the necropolis, make certain of your place in the West. Follow this, for death shall bring us low just as life lifts us up, but the house of death is forever.

The advice is humbling, seeing its extreme age. It helps us to understand that the time passed between us and them is just a brief moment in the overall pattern of existence. It also suggests the basic belief in philanthropy, of caring for others, no matter how exalted a position you may occupy. Of course this would not guarantee the good treatment of the poor, since this is in the hands of individuals, but it laid down a general precept that continued through several thousand years of continual civilization and became absorbed into Christianity and Islam.

If the wealthy nobles heeded the advice, and the poor and ordinary people had benefit of it, then Egypt must have been an extremely pleasant place to live, despite the problems of daily existence. Interestingly, even to this day, the same attitude prevails along the Nile Valley, and the visitor can be assured always of a warm welcome.

The Egypt into which Cheops was born had changed dramatically from its early times. Cheops inherited a land which was settled and well ordered, where every man knew his place and had pride in it – a land that was united in fear of him, rich and with a labour force, assembled by his father, at his disposal. For those people who, for generations, have speculated on what they believe to be the sudden appearance of pyramids on the scale of those at Giza, they have missed the essential points. First, the journey had taken over 1000 years, from the predynastic times. This was no sudden development, but the Egypt which Cheops inherited was already an ancient land. Secondly, given the resources and the philosophies of life current in Cheops' time, the building of great pyramids could almost be predicted. How else could the identity of such a great ruler be recorded for posterity but by the building of a palace-city for him in death, a palace-city dominated by a stone monument which reflected the very status of the man himself?

Looked at in this light, the building of the Great Pyramid should be no surprise at all. It was inevitable.

CHAPTER THREE

Childhood of a Pharaoh

—

C heops was born, by currently accepted dating, in around
2550 BCE. We know nothing of his birth, but this is not
strange, since the royal Egyptians never dwelt on their children
until they came of age and acquired status of their own. In 3000
years there are virtually no pictures of Princes before they
inherit the crown.

There could be several reasons for this. For a start, infant
mortality rates were always extremely high, and the chances of
any child living beyond the perils associated with weaning at
three years old were less than 50:50. Even within the royal
family there could be no guarantee that a child who had been
weaned would grow old enough to inherit the throne. The
Egyptians believed then, and still do today, in the 'evil eye'.
This is the quirk of fate which takes away from you those things
you most treasure. The more you want something, or the more
you or others praise it, the more likely you are to lose it. Such
has always been the case with sons. Every parent needed sons
both to inherit what property or skills that they had, and to act
as the 'staff of old age for their parents'. The birth of a son is
still to this day regarded in Egypt as a time of greatest joy; and
by the same token, any praise that comes for the newborn son is
likely, so they believe, to result in his death. The superstition is
an ancient one. Thirdly, and more likely, childhood in Egypt

was almost non-existent for all classes in society. Children were regarded, and usually pictured, as miniature adults. Toys were few and far between and work began usually as young as five years old. There was not, as in many countries today, any reverence or delicate emotions for children. The duties of a child were towards his parent. Simply, they may not have been considered important enough, until they acquired their own titles, to merit an image.

Birth of Cheops

We do, though, know several things about Cheops at his birth. You may recall from Chapter 1 that his father was called Snofru, and his mother Hetepheres (pronounced 'hetep – hair – ease'). His father, Snofru (or Soris, as Manetho called him), was recorded by Manetho as the first King of the Fourth Dynasty, although the Palermo Stone seems to link him with the family of the end of the Third Dynasty.

Dynasties did not actually exist in ancient Egypt. They were an invention of Manetho's, which we still maintain to this day even though we have long learned that his works contain too many mistakes to be reliable. On the whole, dynasties changed with a change of family line, whenever the line of Kings came to an end and a newcomer took the throne.

In this instance, Manetho goes further and declares the Fourth Dynasty outright as being 'eight Kings of Memphis, belonging to a different line'. Since Memphis did not actually exist at the start of the Fourth Dynasty, we must gather that Manetho is referring to the previous city, White Wall. So can we also trust his statement about the change of line? It is hard to prove, as the origin of a King of Egypt was never recorded. Once he became King, he was so elevated above the normal station of men that his mortal origins were completely forgotten.

We know nothing at all about Snofru's predecessor, Huni,

other than a colophon, or ornamental postscript, in Papyrus Prisse, in the National Library of France, Paris. This states simply, 'The Majesty of King Huni died and the Majesty of King Snofru ascended the throne as King of this entire land.' There are other references to the name Huni, so that we can be confident archaeologically of his existence, but little more. The Palermo Stone gives the name of his wife as Meresankh. Manetho adds to the problem when discussing the end of the Third Dynasty by saying, 'The six remaining Kings did nothing worthy of mention.' Manetho suggests that Snofru reigned for 29 years, although the Turin Canon of Kings, as well as workmen's graffiti around Dahshur and in stone quarries, indicate a reign of around 24 years. This latter is now accepted as more likely.

What is positive is that Hetepheres is listed on furniture from her reburial (see Chapter 7) as 'the Daughter of the King of Upper and Lower Egypt'. It is clear that she is of pure royal descent, probably the daughter of Huni. But of Snofru's birth we have no indication. He could have been a minor son or cousin. It is very unlikely that he was unrelated, as the Old Kingdom Kings were so closely protective that they never extended their line outside their own family.

The longer you study the culture of ancient Egypt, the more you become aware that something dramatic happened at the end of the Old Kingdom. All the rules for life, for Kingship and statecraft changed at this point beyond recognition. It is often almost as if you are looking at two different countries altogether. The Old Kingdom took its rules regarding the nature of Kingship from their experience at the time Kingship was established, the unification. As we saw in the last chapter, this view reckoned the King a god who belonged to the spirit world. He was expected to remain aloof from all men around him. After the watershed of the end of the Old Kingdom, the King was seen as mortal, but with knowledge or skills which made him able to communicate with the spirit world.

Before, the King patterned his life on the lives of his spiritual relatives, the gods; after, he may have adopted the *persona* of a god for state occasions, but he was nonetheless a man, who ate, drank, slept and loved as a man.

Royal marriages

The unification of Upper and Lower Egypt was achieved not only by conquest but also by marriage. The Narmer Macehead, now in the Ashmolean Museum, Oxford, shows the arrival of Neithhotep (pronounced 'nayt – hotep'), with gifts, before the unifier, Narmer. We know little of Neithhotep although her name proves she was Lower Egyptian. She brought with her notions of female power and regality if they were not there before. A monument built for her at Abydos suggests that she was a mighty ruler in her own right when she was persuaded, for diplomatic reasons, to marry her Upper Egyptian conqueror Narmer. Moreover, in the succeeding generation, two women believed to be her daughters, Merneith and Herneith, also had huge *mastabas* built for them. Titles associated with Merneith especially suggest she was a regnant Queen in her own right.

The notion that in ancient times absolute power could be held only by men is a modern concept. There seems to have been no differences in the rights of men and women at this stage. Neithhotep and Merneith seem to have set the pattern for the succeeding Old Kingdom. According to this belief, just as all gods and goddesses were equal and demanded equal respect, so the King and his women were also regarded as equals.

Since the King was a god, he lived as a god – and following the example of all Egyptian gods, from Shu and Tefnut to Osiris and Isis, this meant marriage with his sister. After the Old Kingdom watershed, although Kings associated with their sisters on the throne, their sister-wives were merely heads of state, not wives. They had been brought up within the royal family

75

and thus knew the demands that would be made upon them. Before the watershed it was different. There is no doubt whatever that during the Old Kingdom, not only Kings but also their sons married their own sisters. There was no concept whatever of improper bonds of union. These were full and fruitful marriages, just as the mythical marriages of gods and goddesses were fruitful.

The idea seems barbaric to us today – but this is our difficulty and not theirs (see page 83 for a fuller discussion of the impact of incest in the ancient world). In fact, there seem to have been many logical reasons behind these brother-sister marriages. First, it kept everyone else out. This was vitally important, to maintain the myth of divinity within the family. No royal man could risk exposure to a non-royal woman of less than divine nature. Now that one family had finally succeeded in taking the throne and absolute power, they did not want other families being given even the slightest foothold within their palace.

Secondly, it united two separate but equal strands of power. There is also no doubt whatever that, before the watershed, right to the throne passed in the line of the women rather than the men. Again, we can see that this originated with Neithhotep: through her marriage with Narmer she handed him the right to the throne of Lower Egypt. In her daughter Merneith, we see clearly that she bore the rights inherited from her mother, and she conferred these upon the man she married. In the Fourth Dynasty, the eldest daughter carried the bloodline, and though she would not inherit the throne, she would hand it to the man she married.

Thirdly, it allowed the royal family to maintain their distance from the rest of mankind and continue to keep up the illusion of divinity, since they and they alone could copy the social behaviour of the gods. In effect, it gave them total freedom to behave in any way that they wished.

Over time, this had an alarming effect. Since the Kings were socially distanced from the rest of society, they could have no close friends, and thus their women were the only ones who had full access to them. A King, if troubled, either had to be strong enough to sort matters out alone, or had to confide in his women or sons or brothers. This was fine in some respects – it resulted in close-knit extended families, and outsiders had no opportunity ever to become close to a King and dominate his thoughts. It also, at a stroke, removed any opposition to the King from other families, since the royal family could dictate the conditions under which others served them. But in other respects it meant that if problems brewed up within the family, it would result in rivalries and jealousies that could blow the clan apart. And no time was more ripe for this than in the interim between the death of one King and the accession of the next. It meant that the man who controlled and married the great heiress gained the throne for himself. It was a dangerous situation.

Since this was the general pattern, it would seem that Hetepheres, as the daughter of Huni, carried the right to the throne in her blood, and that whoever she married would thus gain the throne. By the same token, it seems improbable that Snofru was an 'outsider'. So little is known of Huni that we can only guess at how long he reigned and where he was buried. Many books state with assertion that Huni was buried in the pyramid of Meidum. As we shall see, the evidence from the site suggests this pyramid was built during the reign of Snofru. But until we know more about Huni, we can only surmise that his reign must have been short, since he left no clear major monuments behind him; and that he had very few children, since we have no nobles entitled 'sister' or 'brother' of the King of that generation. Perhaps, indeed, Snofru and Hetepheres may actually have been brother and sister, or half-brother and sister.

The family of Cheops

We can use the knowledge that we have to count backwards to find out more of the birth of Cheops. We know that Cheops would rule Egypt for 23 years. We also know that shortly before his death his son and heir, the Crown Prince Kawab, died unexpectedly, too soon to inherit the throne. Kawab is shown in images in his tomb and in statues as a portly, elderly man with thinning hair. He cannot have been less than 40 years old at his death. This means he was born to Cheops many years before his father became King, perhaps at least 20 years. In one story, Prince Baufre, one of Cheops' sons, visited his grandfather Snofru. Snofru was young enough to think frisky thoughts, while Baufre was old enough to go and find a magician and bring him back home for his royal grandfather (see page 80).

If Cheops was old enough to father children 20 years before he became King, and Snofru ruled for 24 years, then Cheops was also born to Snofru and Hetepheres long before they came to the throne. If Cheops had been born at the start of Snofru's reign he would only have been four years old or less at the time that we know he became a father. If we accept that a reasonable age to father a child would be 16, then he was born 12 years before Snofru became King.

We do not know whether Cheops was the oldest son, although we can surmise that he was since we know the names of many of his brothers and sisters, and might assume that if they were older, they would have taken the throne and not him. However, some of these siblings were buried at Meidum, at the side of the pyramid. Whether Meidum pyramid was built during the reign of Huni or Snofru, this suggests that these siblings of Cheops died before he became King. If they were older than he was, and died of old age before their father Snofru, then Cheops may have been a younger and less significant child until his time came at his father's death. If he were a younger child, then it would also be reasonable to increase the age at which Snofru sired Cheops, since he would have sired others before him.

We can be certain, then, of at least two things. We know that Snofru would have been elderly when he came to the throne.

We also know that Cheops was elderly when he inherited the royal titles.

The remarkable things about all of this is that it all suggests that Manetho's assertion that Snofru was 'of a different line' almost certainly has to be wrong. Hetepheres carried the blood-line, and whoever she married was destined to become King; and she married Snofru and bore him children at least 20 years before he became King; so Snofru's destiny was clear from the start. If it is also correct, as it seems, that Huni ruled for only a very short time, then there is also a good chance that neither Snofru nor Hetepheres were his children. They may well have been his brother and sister. Huni's predecessor is as little known as he is. His name was Khaba, and he chose to have a pyramid built for him at modern Zawiyet al Aryan. This is intriguing, for all of Khaba's predecessors appear to have chosen to be buried at Saqqara. Khaba was the first to break this rule, and Huni apparently followed him. This implies that Khaba himself was not of the main royal line.

So perhaps this is where Manetho's information came from. If Khaba indeed were of a different line – a cousin of the previous King and not a son – and Snofru were his son and a younger brother of Huni, then Hetepheres, as daughter of Huni, would carry the royal blood and her marriage to her uncle Snofru would thus seem more reasonable. We know certainly that Hetepheres lived into the reign of her son, Cheops, as she is listed as 'Mother of the King of Upper and Lower Egypt'. This agrees with the reconstruction suggested, making her much younger than Snofru.

So the image that emerges is this. Khaba rules Egypt and has two sons, the elder Huni and the younger Snofru. At his death, Huni becomes King and sires a daughter who carries the right to the throne. He marries her to his own brother, Snofru, Hetepheres' uncle, certain then that they will inherit the throne. But since we know Huni ruled only a short time, Hetepheres herself may have only been a very young girl.

History has been kind to Snofru. He is regarded as a gentle man, somewhat of a bumbler. It has often been stated that our concepts of the kindness or cruelty of these ancient Kings are laid down by the monuments they left behind them. Since Cheops left the largest pyramid, history – thanks to Herodotus – regards him as the greatest tyrant. This is clearly untrue, however, since, as we shall see, evidence points strongly to Snofru as having originated the building of not one but three pyramids.

The chances are, therefore, that legend has kept some of the truth alive, and that Snofru, the uncle of his wife, was a kind and generous man. Papyrus Westcar, now in the Egyptian gallery of the Berlin museum, records a story said to have occurred when Snofru was King. Snofru was visited by his grandson Baufre, Cheops' son. Snofru was bored, and Baufre offered to find some entertainment for him. He goes and finds a great magician, Djadjaemankh. Djadjaemankh offers a solution. 'Let your Majesty go to the lake by the palace. Fill a boat with all the beautiful young girls of the palace. Your Majesty's heart will be refreshed at seeing them row.' Snofru thought this an excellent idea, but added a little more to it. 'Let there be brought out twenty maidens with rounded bodies and breasts and long hair, who have not yet opened up to give birth [i.e. virgins]. Also bring out twenty nets and give them to the girls instead of clothes.'

As he watched, the story goes, 'His Majesty's heart was *very* much refreshed thereby'. Snofru was enjoying himself hugely when one of the girls, who had been playing with a fish-shaped clasp which hung from her braid, dropped it in the water. Distressed, she stopped rowing, and all the other girls lost their rhythm and stopped also. Snofru ordered them to row again, but the girl refused. 'I shall replace it,' he urged. 'No, I want my own back,' she persisted. It seems likely that the clasp was something special, perhaps representing her virginity or palace status. At any rate, a replacement would not do. Djadjaemankh was summoned again. After having the situation explained, he went to the lake and 'folded back the water', collected the clasp from a potsherd on which it lay, then 'returned the water to its place'.

Although the story is clearly apocryphal, it is delightful for the insight into the man, not the King, it gives us. Snofru appears as a voyeur, an elderly man who delights in watching nubile, young, semi-naked girls. The one who drops her clasp is not afraid to challenge Snofru and demand her rights. Even though everyone walked in terror of the Old Kingdom King, Snofru was seen as too kind and fair to be unreasonable, and the girls understood that a plea to him would be fairly considered.

It would seem from this story that the household of Snofru, with an elderly father and a young mother, was a delightful and happy place. We do not know how many wives Snofru had, but since it was usual for a King to maintain a number of wives, we can assume it was the same for Snofru.

One of the most significant children of Snofru was Nefretkau, their daughter. She lived into the reign of her brother Cheops and was buried near him (tomb G7130). She was married to her brother, Khufukhaf, whose tomb (tomb G7140) is in the other half of the *mastaba* in which her tomb was found. They are shown, in various places, with two sons, Nefermaat and Khufukhaf (known as Khufukhaf II), and a daughter. A Nefermaat, together with his wife, Itet, was found near Meidum pyramid, their tomb being the source of the famous panel of Meidum geese. However, this could not have been Nefermaat the son of Nefretkau, since his mother was buried at Giza, and we have the tomb of her son Nefermaat nearby. As was the Old Kingdom custom, her son was probably named after someone of an older generation. So probably, the Nefermaat of Meidum was a brother of Snofru. Cheops, or Khnum-Khufu, was probably the older son and heir to the throne.

Another brother, Rahotep, married to his sister Nofret, was also found buried at Meidum. The famous pair of statues of Rahotep and Nofret, now in Cairo Museum, give us the best chance we have of glimpsing the family into which Cheops was born and brought up. The faces of the two are set but tranquil. They are heavily built, square of jaw and shoulder. Rahotep appears a physically fit man, with a moustache. Although ancient Egyptians are well known for being close shaven, the men of Cheops' family frequently wore moustaches. Although we know little of her, another daughter, probably the older daughter or even their first child, was Meritetes. It was she, ultimately, who married Cheops and became one of his principal wives. Since we know Cheops had many wives, one of them known by name to be Henutsen, he probably had many other siblings, the sisters becoming minor wives.

If the life of Snofru is otherwise cloaked in darkness, then so too is his death. However, since he was elderly when he became King and ruled for 24 years, then he had a full and long life, and we can only wish for him that he died tranquilly and in his own bed, as all Egyptians desired.

As for Cheops himself, only one tiny image of him survives as King. This tiny ivory figurine, barely 2 inches tall, bears his name, although recently even this has been questioned. The face, like that of his brother Rahotep, is square and full in the jaw. The figurine is unpainted. If painted, most likely he, too, would have been shown with a moustache. In some ways, he appears Nubian. We know that Snofru brought back thousands of Nubians into Egypt, so perhaps this was an artistic stylism of that time.

Like his father, Cheops married at least two of his sisters long before he became King. This seems certain, since we know the names of many of the sons and daughters he had by Meritetes and Henutsen, and many of them died in his reign as elderly people.

Once again, this is against all popularly held opinion. It was acceptable, even desirable, for Kings to have bevies of wives, but no ordinary man could or should. Although polygamy is often asserted for ancient Egyptians, it is harder to prove. One scholar, trawling through ancient history, discovered that in the whole of ancient Egyptian culture, some 3000 years of written records, there are only five instances of men associated with more than one wife at the same time (where a man married more than once because previous wives died, the dead wives, although listed and pictured in their tomb, are always declared 'true of voice', which means they were dead). As he also pointed out, this does not mean that these five men did not divorce one to marry the other.

In other words, only Kings could marry more than one wife. So why, then, was Cheops allowed to marry more than one of his sisters before he came to the throne? The only reasonable suggestion is that Cheops was Crown Prince and as heir apparent was allowed some of the royal rights of a King before he assumed them. This had interesting consequences later, as we shall see.

The incestuous marriage of full brothers and sisters is obviously not a social experiment which can be observed or repeated today. Although it is frequently asserted, through genetic studies, that the child of a close incestuous relationship risks many types of mental and physical weakness, there is no evidence of any weakness having appeared in the Old Kingdom. Only at one other time in Egyptian history did full brothers and sisters marry, and that was during the Ptolemaic dynasties, from 325 BCE until 30 BCE, when the new Kings were persuaded by the native Egyptians that marriages of this kind were the norm. The history of the Ptolemaic dynasties is much more complete than that of the Old Kingdom dynasties; and we can observe here that there were certainly grave problems. In every generation of the Greek rulers, the men became weakened generation by generation until scarcely fit to rule, while their sisters retained all their mental capacities and, in contrast to their feeble brothers, became dominating and cruel to such an extent that they made Caligula and Nero seem insignificant!

There is a genetic basis for this degeneration. All coding for personal characteristics is carried on the X-chromosome. If a faulty gene was present in the ancestors of the family, this would be passed down on the X-chromosome. Males have one X and one Y chromosome, so whatever genes they inherit on their X-chromosome will be displayed in their characteristics. A female, on the other hand, has two X-chromosomes, one dominant, whose genes she will display, and one recessive, which will never appear but which she may pass down to the next generation. So if a woman inherits markers of mental incapacity, they may never show but she will stand a good chance of passing it down to her children. If the child is a male, and inherits her genetic weakness, then that weakness will be shown. In other words, the women passed the problems on, but only the men displayed them.

So we have two possibilities for the Old Kingdom. The first and unlikely notion is that their stock was genetically pure. If this were the case, then incestuous inbreeding would present no problem whatever. This would have given the Fourth Dynasty royal family the advantages of keeping out other families; of not weakening their healthy stock with impure lines from others; and of being certain that their heirs were suitable rulers. The other more feasible possibility is that genetic weakness did exist; that it was handed down and demonstrated in the men; but that it was hidden from contemporary Egyptians and similarly from us because of the nature of Kingship, which kept him a mere cipher, personally invisible to all but his family.

We certainly know that Cheops was a fecund man and that his heirs were many. The tombs around his pyramid, as we have seen, all held his family members. Although Strudwick (*The Administration of Egypt in the Old Kingdom*) suggests, after earlier scholars, that many titles given to these, either 'King's Son' or

'King's Son of His Own Body', are incorrect, and were handed out freely to nobles of other families, there is no logical reason why this should be so. The determination of the Fourth Dynasty Kings to 'keep it in the family' suggests that these were, indeed, sons, perhaps by lesser wives and thus not of prime rank, but royal nonetheless. It is all the more strange, then, that Cheops' line died out after two generations. This could indeed suggest that there were problems with inbreeding which meant, for reasons we can no longer trace, that his children and grand-children were unable to bear and maintain children.

Cheops came to the throne an elderly man, probably in his early forties. His first children by his principal sister-wife, Meritetes, were a son called Kawab and a daughter called Hetepheres, named after her grandmother. They were followed by another daughter, called Meresankh after his grandmother, the wife of Huni, and a brother called Horbaf, although he was probably the son of Cheops by a different Queen. To destinguish these girls with similar names from each other, we call them Hetepheres II and Meresankh II, although there are no numbers after their names in ancient Egyptian. In time, once the girls reached adulthood, Kawab married his principal sister Hetepheres II, while Meresankh II married Horbaf. Both unions also bore children.

Trying to draw a family tree to reflect these intermarriages and children adequately is extremely complex. As well as his children by Meritetes, Cheops was also the father to many children by another sister, Henutsen. We know the names of her sons – Akhkhaf, Minkhaf and Khufukhaf were three. The fourth, whose name was to become better known in time, is known to history as Chephren, thanks to Herodotus. His name is actually written as Khaefre. In fact, following the pattern of his brothers by Henutsen, his name should more probably be Rekhaf. At any rate, the children of Henutsen, both by name and by the ranks they eventually achieved, were lesser in status than those of Meritetes. It is apparent that Meritetes' daughters,

Hetepheres II and Meresankh II, were considered the principal ladies of the land after their mother, and Hetepheres II carried within her the line of royal blood, again suggesting that she was either the eldest child or the eldest daughter of the union.

Relatives in high places

Klaus Baer and Nigel Strudwick have both, in their time, considered the lists of titles of the nobles, both male and female, of the Old Kingdom, and found pronounced patterns which demonstrate the superiority of some titles over others. Simply stated, not all titles were of the same rank; and a lesser wife could never expect her children, no matter how able they were, to attain the highest titles. In other words, within Cheops' palace, rank came from your birth and not from any consideration of your abilities and characteristics – if you had the wrong mother, you lost before the game began!

In later times, the highest rank a civilian could attain outside the professional army was that usually translated as Vizier. In the New Kingdom, the Vizier Rekhmire describes the post as 'not sweet, but bitter as gall'. By this time Viziers were in full charge of every department of the administration, as well as being principal minister to the King for most of them. So as well as supervising the activities of, for instance, the law courts, they were also Chief Judge and reported in this manner to the King. Not only did they count and record the imports that were handed to Egypt from their foreign holdings, but they were Foreign Minister and Chief Ambassador, as well as being Head of Spies. The Vizier, at this date, was a civilian, promoted by the King because of his aptitude; and many of them, such as Hapusoneb in the reign of Hatshepsut, were commoners.

Once more, we have clear evidence of the watershed at the end of the Old Kingdom. The Kingship established as a result of experiences during the unification was unsuccessful, and had later to be renegotiated. On these terms, then, the rank and duties of Vizier before the watershed are hard to ascertain.

What is clear is that the office seems to have started under Snofru. It is true that on the Narmer Palette, the King's sandal-bearer has 'Vizier' (or *tjaty*) written over his head. Whether the full rank of Vizier in the Old Kingdom derived from this early indication is uncertain. Nor, surprisingly, do we have the great Imhotep listed anywhere as Vizier either, although a letter found on papyrus, dating to the building of the Step Pyramid and addressed to a great official who distributed food and clothing to the foremen of the site, was probably intended for him.

The first, true Vizier, then, was appointed in the middle of the reign of Snofru. His name was Nefermaat, and it seems likely that he was Snofru's brother.

Here we get a clue as to the choice of a typical Old Kingdom Vizier – he seems to be always either a younger brother or older son of a King, whose existence could be threatening to the King. After all, since no outside family could marry into the royal family and cause problems, then rivalries started within the family instead. The post of Vizier was thus given mainly to quieten opposition before it happened. Within a royal family as confined and antisocial as the family of the Fourth Dynasty, what would otherwise befall a younger brother born to the same important mother? What trick of Fate was it that allowed rank to fall according to birth and the identity of the mother, but where the younger brothers of a crowned King by the same mother had no rank to reflect their position over others in the family?

As such, the rank of Vizier was probably just a rank and little more. It is often associated with a title 𓄿𓃀 *sab*, which appears to describe a legal role – perhaps 'Judge' might be a fair translation. For an autocratic and divine King to hand over any daily administrative roles would require three qualities in the candidate: membership in his family, a real ability to do the job, and social standing that would cause problems if the person remained unchosen.

In the reign of Cheops, the first role of Vizier was apparently held by his oldest son by Henutsen, Akhkhaf. He seems to have held the post for just a few years at the start of the reign, and it is not too imaginative to suggest that when Cheops was crowned, while his eldest son by Meritetes won total acclaim as the King's heir, his eldest son by Henutsen was totally eclipsed, a nonentity. The Vizierate was a good means to give him some recognition. But once again, it emphasizes the problems that being born to the 'wrong' mother might create within a family where the rank of the mother took precedence over everything.

Within a very short time, the title was given to the eldest son of the previous Vizier, Nefermaat. This man, Hemiunu, seems to have been an excellent organizer, since his name is found on graffiti at Giza, suggesting that it was he who started the building of pyramids and supervised the buildings of the Giza plateau. It is also easy to understand that an able son of a previous Vizier might expect the title to revert to him, and he must have been bitter when it was given to Akhkhaf instead. Was Akhkhaf dead by then? Or was he removed from office and superseded? We have no means of telling, but it is very clear that the intense rivalries within the royal family would cause problems.

One further clue about these rivalries can be seen by the passing of the role of Vizier, when Hemiunu died, to Crown Prince Kawab. It could well be that the rivalries between the two halves of the family had become so impossible to judge that Cheops decided to give it to the one son who already had so much power that other brothers would not be tempted to oppose him. The premature death of Kawab, bearing all of his father's hopes and expectations, must have been a bitter blow. After Kawab's death, for a very short time, the younger brother of Akhkhaf, Minkhaf, took the post. The sons of Henutsen would not simply accept their lower ranking, it seems.

With a King as remote and isolated as Cheops, then, there

was almost no chance that he, as his descendants later frequently did, would lead the army. Perhaps he was incapable of doing so. In any case, at this period there was neither a standing army nor really the need for one. The status of the King was reflected in the country, which, during the Fourth Dynasty, became as isolationist as the royal family. It is true that the port of Byblos in the north, always in the pocket of Egypt, has revealed several inscriptions of the reign of Cheops; and it is also true that his name has been found on the route to the copper mines of Serabit el Khadim in Sinai, and in Nubia. However, all of these are places with which Egypt traded. The trade expeditions would be protected en route by conscripts, posted at intervals to ensure nothing that had been extracted could be stolen. These would be supervised by professional soldiers. At Giza, tomb 1203 belonged to one Kanefer, who was named 'Head of the Bowmen', and tomb 2110 to Nefer, 'Overseer of Scribes of the Crews and Commander of Conscripts'. Although we do not know of their relationship to Cheops, again they were undoubtedly related to him. Once again, there is clear evidence that your rank was ascertained not by your ability – and the ability to command and control an army was quite simply beyond them.

Egypt, then, traded both to the north and the south and protected their trade routes as best they could, although there was no hint of imperialism whatever. Cheops was content to remain in his palace and content to let other countries rule themselves.

Cheops' line

As well as children by his two principal wives, we also have evidence that there were other wives also bearing his children, although they cannot be identified by name. We know the names of many of the children, but since the name of their mother is unstated or missing, we can only guess at their relationship with the King.

First of these is Baufre, whom we have met already. For this Prince to be conversant with his grandfather Snofru, and to help him by bringing the services of a great magician, suggests he may well be the son of one or other of the great ladies. However, his name appears as someone keen to assist his grandfather, but with no hint of rivalries, and this may suggest he was a son of Meritetes herself.

The second is Hordjedef. This young man seems to have been remarkable, a genius of his time. He was buried at Giza, but his words of wisdom lived on for thousands of years after his death. He seems, in some way, to bear a little of the genius of Imhotep.

> When you have grown wealthy, build a house and find a healthy wife so that a son will be born to you. You build your house for your son when you make a house for yourself. Prepare your tomb within the cemetery, make honourable your place in the west. For you understand that death brings us down just as life has raised us up. Your tomb has to last forever, so appoint for yourself some fertile fields [to provide food and drink].

Many centuries after his death, Hordjedef was still being regarded as a great sage and had a cult set up in his honour until the Late Period. However, the identity of his mother is lost to us. In all likelihood, it was the same woman who also gave birth to Redjedef, since the names are so very similar. We shall hear more of this later story in Chapter 9.

Two other sons were named: Nikaure, perhaps a full brother of Baufre and thus a child of Meritetes; and Shepseskaf, who was probably a son of Henutsen.

So the ladies' quarters of the palace of White Wall, while Cheops was King, were filled at first with the cries and laughter of children and grandchildren, all directly bearing his blood. The future must have seemed golden and assured. With so many children, and the prospect of their bearing grandchildren as numerous as the sand of the desert, Cheops should have had few reasons for concern.

The Westcar Papyrus, however, tells us a different story. This papyrus, ostensibly several tales concerning magicians, has a deeper political origin. It was written at the start of the Fifth Dynasty. These Kings, who bore little relation, if any, to the Kings of the Fourth Dynasty, seem to have worried over the legitimacy of their claim. As a result, they appear to have ordered a 'false prophecy' to have been written. The first stories of this cycle demonstrate the uncanny abilities of Egyptian wise men and magicians, who had power over all aspects of nature and were filled with wisdom both to instruct and entertain their King. The later stories deal with the prediction and then the birth of triplet sons to an unknown minor, 'wife of a priest of Re of Sakhbu'. These children, we are told, are destined to rule, and were none other than the Kings of the Fifth Dynasty.

It is clear that the tales are a means of impressing everyone with the rights of the Fifth Dynasty Kings to take the throne after the demise of the great Fourth Dynasty. But how will this all happen? The scene turns to the court of Cheops, where his son, Hordjedef, tells his father of a wise man called Djedi living near Meidum. He brings the old man to the royal court. Cheops treats him with suspicion, and Djedi must carry out several spectacular magic tricks to prove his identity.

Once his abilities have been confirmed, the voice of Cheops is finally heard.

'It is said that you know the numbers of the secret chambers of the hall of Thoth.' Djedi said, 'I do not know their number, my Lord, but I know the place where it is.'

Djedi tells Cheops the place. It is stored in a protected and secret chest. Cheops orders Djedi to go and get it for him.

'O King my Lord, it is not I who shall bring it.' 'Who, then?' said his

Majesty. 'It is the eldest of the three children who are in the belly of
Ruddjedet.' His Majesty said, 'I want it.'

Djedi tells Cheops that one of these boys will 'assume this
beneficent office in the whole land' – in other words, will be
King. Cheops grows despondent. Is his line not secure? 'I say
this,' said Djedi. 'First your son, then his son and then one of
them.'

The prophecy was, of course, false, and given with hindsight.
In fact the prophecy, as archaeology tells, was not fulfilled. After
Cheops there came, in turn, two of his sons; and then a grandson, although one of the Kings of the Fifth Dynasty, and the wife
of one of the triplets, were both direct descendants of his.

So what went wrong? The troubles were clearly brewing
within the palace, born of the frustration of a large and healthy
family whose ambitions were thwarted before they were born,
purely because of the order of their birth.

The reign of Cheops might, then, have been quietly prosper-
ous and contented, even if the pall of false hope hung over
them. But it was not for this that Cheops is remembered.
Instead, at the start of his reign, under the authority of
Hemiunu, the first stone of the pyramid of Giza was laid. The
building of the pyramid would completely dominate his reign.
Herodotus suggests that the character of Cheops was cruel
and despotic.

> Up to the time of Rhampsinitus Egypt was excellently governed and
> very prosperous, but his successor, Cheops, to continue the account that
> the guide gave me, brought the country into untold misery. He closed
> all of the temples and then, not content with denying his subjects the
> practice of their religion, compelled them almost without exception to
> work as slaves for his own advantage. Some he forced to drag stones
> from the quarries in the Arabian hills to the Nile, where they were
> ferried across and taken on by others who had to haul them to the
> Libyan hills.

No crime was too great for Cheops. When he fell short of money, he sent his daughter to work in a brothel with orders to charge a certain sum (they did not tell me how much). She did this but added a further price of her own; with the intention of leaving behind something after her death she asked each client for a block of stone and of these stones was built the middle pyramid of the three which stand in front of the Great Pyramid.

Herodotus' tale still stands, despite all efforts by Egyptologists to decry it. He was no witness, as some imagine, but went to Egypt around 2000 years after the pyramids were built. He had no more notion of how and why a pyramid was built than we, today, can say how Cleopatra's voice sounded or what her favourite tipple was! These were, in fact, mere dragoman's tales. But they persist, and the vision of Cheops as the cruel despot remains a popular myth that has assumed the proportions of truth. Even Hollywood took on the same tale, and enjoyed every second of the imagined cruelty, from Cecil B. de Mille's epic of slaves driven by whips, to the pathos of Charlton Heston's screen mother getting her scarf trapped under the rollers of blocks being used for the King's pyramids in *The Ten Commandments*. And let us not, of course, forget the youthful Joan Collins being seduced to her death by treasures hidden within a pyramid, in *Land of the Pharaohs*. It makes for good, entertaining fiction. But this is all it is. As we shall see, there is virtually no truth in any of it.

PART TWO

BUILDING PYRAMIDS

The Great Pyramid

W e have seen a picture emerging of Cheops as the autocratic ruler of a united country with an almost perfect
administrative system. But you will have realized by now how
little we know about Cheops as a person. Indeed, during his life
he was swathed in so much secrecy that probably few people
other than his wives and children ever got close to him. It must
have been a lonely existence.

Cheops' life had been laid out before him from birth. Married
to several of his sisters, he became a great King whom people
feared. While we know of his presence in neighbouring countries, it is one thing only which dominated his reign – the
building of his pyramid.

In this section we are going to try to find answers to some of
the most perplexing questions a sked about the pyramids at
Giza – who built them, why and how?

The Great Pyramid is the largest of three solid stone pyramids which dominate the Giza plateau on the west bank of the
Nile. Today a suburb of Cairo has all but engulfed them, as the
desert all around has burst into life in a massive suburban
sprawl. Barely a few yards away, city traffic roars and honks
with frustration. Any attempt to make these wonders of the
world seem mysterious fades away in traffic jams.

The Great Pyramid is the northernmost of the three and

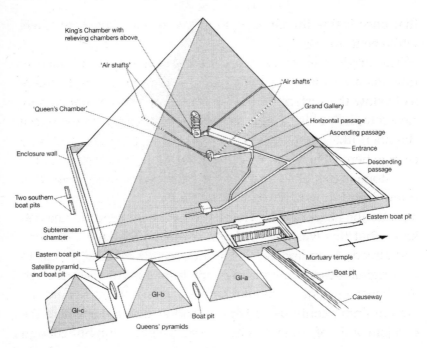

King's Chamber with
relieving chambers above

'Air shafts'

'Air shafts'

'Queen's Chamber'

Grand Gallery

Horizontal passage

Ascending passage

Entrance

Enclosure wall

Descending
passage

Two southern
boat pits

Eastern boat pit

Subterranean
chamber

Mortuary temple

Eastern boat pit

Boat pit

Satellite pyramid
and boat pit

GI-a

Causeway

GI-b

GI-c

Boat pit

Queens' pyramids

The Great Pyramid

appears smaller than the one in the centre. The central one was
apparently used by Chephren, a son of Cheops. It was built on
a higher part of the plateau and despite actually being 10 feet
shorter than Cheops', appears to dominate it. The third and
smallest pyramid is that of Mycerinus and looks insignificant
next to the other two. Place it alongside any of the other 95
Egyptian pyramids, on the other hand, and it would look
gigantic.

The modern entrance into the Great Pyramid, on its western
face, is through a robbers' hole. The real entrance, some 30 feet
above the robbers' hole, is still blocked with ancient stone, and
impassable. This pyramid is deceptive and not for the faint-
hearted or those with physical problems. It may look big on the
outside, but the passages within are frequently small. The only
real difference between this and the pyramid of Mycerinus is

that once inside the Great Pyramid, you have longer to travel while bent double.

The original entrance descended into the pyramid sharply towards a chamber cut in the rock of the plateau itself, many feet below the surface of the desert outcrop. This chamber, now closed to the public, seems to have been designed as the burial chamber, like other earlier pyramids. But there was a design change here. Where the descending passage struck through the limestone it was lined with granite slabs brought from Aswan. A few metres down, however, another passage, this one ascending into the heart of the pyramid, joins the descending one. We know that this was a later change of plan. The layers of stone had already been laid, so where the ascending passage joins to the original descending passage, the tunnel is quarried through the limestone. Only when it emerged into new layers could the granite lining continue as before. And at that point where the two join, a lip of stone was left – barely significant, but enough to make the precisely cut widths of the passage suddenly narrower.

The ascending passage continues upwards towards the heart of the pyramid. The ceiling is low and the angle steep. The only way to move through it is bent over. If you are of average height, this is just about manageable; but if you are more than 6 feet tall, then your knees must also bend, or your back will grate across the ceiling. It almost seems to last forever, and then, at last, it reaches a junction.

Here, in front, the passage levels out horizontally and eventually opens into a small chamber. This chamber is solid and square, its roof gabled in the centre. For this reason the early Arabs called it 'the Queen's chamber', since women were traditionally buried in gabled tombs in the Arab world. A small niche interrupts the eastern wall, apparently unfinished. Further back, at the junction again, today a grille on the floor covers up a dark vertical shaft, narrow, its course and bottom unfathomable.

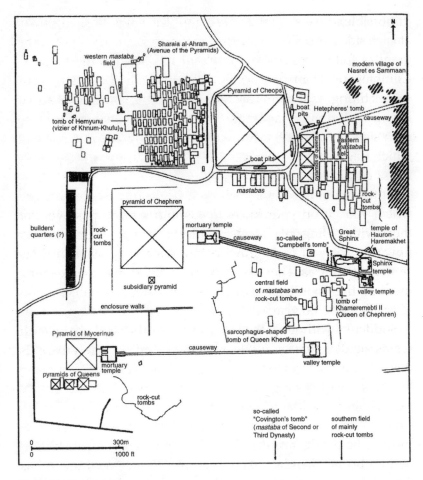

The plateau of Giza

At this point, deep in the heart of solid stone, the walls under your hands are clammy, moist with transferred sweat off the bodies of tourists clambering in and out. Above and to the right, the ascending passage continues to rise, but inexplicably and for the first time since entering the pyramid, even the tallest can straighten up. The passage suddenly soars to a breathtaking height of 26 feet. The walls here are polished granite, with joints so immaculately made that it is quite

100

impossible to see even the tiniest gap. The walls close in slowly at each side, corbelled towards a narrow ceiling. The lines of the granites follow exactly the angle of the floor of the passage. Climbing up from time to time, you become bemused, your senses tilting, as it seems as if the chamber is in fact level and it is you who simply have trouble walking. Above your head, to each side and about 8 feet up are holes in the walls, in some of which fragments of wood remain (we shall see what they were intended for in a moment).

At the top of the Grand Gallery, a small square hole, through which you go on your knees, leads into a small passage. For those with feelings of claustrophobia, this is not the time to look upwards, for you must crawl below three great slabs of limestone, portcullises. They are secured firmly, with stones keeping them off the floor. Unless of course, that stone crumbles – and after all, it is 4500 years old . . .

Suddenly, without warning, you are in the final chamber. It seems smaller than you had imagined, and strangely bare. Is this what it is all about, this cold, dark granite cube? Against the west wall, facing the western horizon, lies the empty sarcophagus, broken at one corner. Everyone peers inside, of course. A few people, if the opportunity presents itself, will take turns to lie inside, arms crossed. So this is what it feels like, to lie in a burial chamber like a mummy. Of course, no one has done it before you! Over the thousands of years since it was built, this sarcophagus has held bodies of all shapes and sizes, all ages and all colours. Only once, so far as we know, did it hold a dead body. And that was so long ago, with so much history in between, that the stone itself has long forgotten the feel of bandage against granite.

If you look up in this bare chamber, you will observe against the edge of ceiling and wall how the ceiling slabs have broken through in several places. If you have not been told, your heart may jump a little. Above you, right there, lies more than a million tons of stone – and the ceiling beams which hold it up are cracked right through! Not to worry, for the problem happened in antiquity, as the pyramid was being built. The architects saw it too and worried. So over the ceiling is a series of five 'relieving' chambers, small spaces designed to send the massive weight down through the side walls instead of on to the ceiling.

The sarcophagus seems forlorn, out of place. Was there really once gold and furniture here? Did an anthropoid image of Cheops, his broad face apparently smiling, ever young, with a pencil-thin moustache, once lie here? It seems strange to see the sarcophagus, since most today have been carried away into national museums. Then you realize that it is too large to fit down any of the passages. It must have been placed here when the pyramid was being built, when the ceiling of the chamber was still open to the sky. Somehow the sarcophagus, like the massive granite slabs which line the chamber, had had to be dragged up more than 200 feet, and then lowered into this final place.

When the tourists have gone, although the lights remain on (there is electric light installed in the burial chamber!), silence quickly resumes. This silence is more than a lack of noise. This is positive silence, a silence which seems to suck sound away, like layers of invisible cotton wool enveloping you until you can even hear your breathing and the beat of your heart. Even this seems an intrusion in this place of death.

Into this room, 4500 years ago, teams of half-naked, sweating men strained on ropes to drag the remains of the King on his last journey, up through the low passages. They would have been bent double with the weight on the ropes; perhaps they did not notice the stone ceilings of the passages.

Once inside here, the low intonations of the priests would have carried out the final acts of magic, the transformations which would allow the King to journey out to join his brethren, the gods. Once the lid slammed into place, the small entourage then passed back under the portcullis. Someone had the job of removing the supporting stones. The crash as the portcullises fell would reverberate through the empty chambers. How many men remained to the last? Perhaps only two or three, as the priests and nobles, sons and grandsons of the dead King, bent their backs to leave the pyramid to enter again the sweet air of the living. No matter how hot it is outside, the temperature within seldom varies, but the desert heat, nonetheless, is welcome.

Still inside, perhaps with a lighted torch each, the few men descend to the bottom of the Grand Gallery. Against a wall is a club or some such blunt instrument. They pick it up, test it – and then, with a mighty swing, raise it over their heads. Here, in the Grand Gallery, beams just above their heads hold granite blocks just out of reach. You would have to be swift and careful. Break the wood with just enough force so that the granite is freed. With a crash, each would fall to the floor and slide drunkenly down the ascending passage. At the end, where it meets the descending passage, it judders to a halt against the lip and stops. Backwards up the Grand Gallery the last and most faithful – the bravest – walk, cracking beams at every step, the stones following each other into the darkness beyond. With the ascending passage blocked, the air would quickly turn thick and hot, the little oxygen left to them being burned by their torches.

With the descending passage blocked totally, not even a chink of light or snatch of air coming through from the desert outside, the last few are now walled up within the pyramid, alone in the tomb, in the darkness, in the presence of a dead King whom they believed to have been transformed by magic. They would now have to come to the black shaft, today covered with a grille at the entrance to the Gallery, then open and totally unprotected. At this point they would have had to extinguish their lights, for in front of them they had a vertical climb down through a narrow shaft, down to the bottom of the pyramid, to the descending passage, where it met with the original chamber.

It is hard to envisage the darkness that must have surrounded them at this point. Although holes are cut into the walls, they are crude, and every handhold, every foothold, needed to be held as life itself depended on it. No chance, here, to hold a torch, for every handhold, every foothold separated them from life below and death above.

Once their feet touched the ground below, they were safe, and undoubtedly they ran at full tilt up the descending passage, ignoring their aching muscles. At last, the open door offered them life, to regain their freedom and breathe the air of Egypt again. Perhaps never again in their lives would they ever be asked to do anything like that, although the tale would no doubt thrill others in the telling. Until time allowed it to be forgotten.

Once outside, no doubt singing and beating drums, more blocks were pushed into the entrance from the outside. Only a few minutes, and the pyramid was solid stone. Now no one could get inside.

And no one did, for more than 3000 years.

CHAPTER FOUR

Cheops and Sons Limited

—

According to Herodotus, building a pyramid took 20 years. We know that Cheops ruled for 23. This suggests that the very first thing Cheops did, on ascending the throne, was to take aside his architect to discuss the shape, the height, and, most important of all, the site.

It must, then, have been a fraught time for the architects and builders. After all, we know, from the Turin Papyrus and other stories, that Snofru ruled for about 24 years; Cheops for 23; Chephren for 24; and Mycerinus for about 26. Now, all of this sounds extremely convenient, does it not? After all, if it took 20 years to build a pyramid, what would befall them if the King died unexpectedly and young, and suddenly needed that burial chamber? After all, life was precious. Let us compare the reigns in the mid-18th Dynasty:

- Tuthmosis IV rules for seven years (no pyramid, if he had wanted one, as he did not live long enough)
- Amenhotep III 39 years (he would have got one)
- Akhenaten for 17 years (no, not for him)
- Smenkhkare for two years (no chance)
- Tutankhamen for nine years (scarcely off the ground for this King)
- Ay for four years (no chance).

These Kings, of course, were all buried in the Valley of the Kings – which, it seems, gave them the right to relax and die early. If a pyramid took 20 years to build, then these six Kings, ruling a total of 76 years, would have had 3¾ pyramids between them – and what would have happened then? To build the two that they needed would have taken another 40 years. So would the mummies of the last two Kings, then, have to be placed into cold storage until a pyramid was complete? And what of the next Kings on the throne?

This whole thing is a great problem, for although with the benefit of hindsight we know the Kings at their crowning would live long enough to have a complete pyramid finished, the ancient Egyptians did not. If a group of fit, healthy and wealthy Kings of the 18th Dynasty could die erratically and unexpectedly too soon – then how could it be that the Fourth Dynasty Kings apparently ruled for exactly the right amount of time – and all of them, interestingly, for almost an equal amount of time?

One thing is for certain. I would not willingly have taken on such a planning enterprise, not for all the gold in Nubia, if it meant that I might be left with a half-finished pyramid and the mummy of an omnipotent semi-divine dead King to bury.

Not unless, of course, there was some other way . . .

Fallacies of the inundation and agriculture

It is well known that if it had not been for the annual inundation, Egypt could not have existed. Only the floodwaters of the Nile, annually carrying with them silt from the Ethiopian highlands, ensured the safe and continued existence of their land. This land was so lush and fertile that a stick planted in it would root, shoot, bud and fruit in almost no time. Little wonder that the Egyptians were the envy of their neighbours, whose battle to survive was more complex and less certain.

The Egyptians divided their year into three seasons, each

lasting four months. The first was Akhet, the Inundation. The second, Peret, the Emergence of the Land, was harvest season. Finally, there was Shemu, the Lack of Water or Dry Season.

Now this is relatively well known. However, it implies a falsehood: namely, that the inundation lasted for four months; that there was then one long harvest of four months; and finally that there was one long hot and arid season until the water came again.

This needs correcting. The seasons were given their names because this was the band of four months in which the event happened. So the flood would start to arrive at the start of Inundation season. However, the floodwaters reached different heights in different places at different times. The northern sites received their flood many days after the cities of the south, and at lower and lower levels the further north it spread. The force of the water, having tumbled northwards through chasms and gorges further south, was spent as it entered the flat alluvial plain of the Egyptian Nile. Its course was languid, its rise not tumultuous but almost imperceptible. If you were to observe any one town, the flood lasted no longer than two weeks at its full height before it began to recede.

As the water fell back, even a little, the farmers and administrators needed to get out at once in the land left behind. Egypt's administrative system was tightly controlled. The land was divided up into estates between the towns and villages. Although occasionally the produce of these estates was awarded by the King to certain individuals or institutions (who then had to pay full tax on it back to the King!), the land itself always belonged to the King. The state archive meticulously recorded both the boundaries of every estate and its current and past management. From the legal trial of Mes, recorded in his Saqqara tomb in the 19th Dynasty, these records could be produced in a moment, and went back hundreds of years for every patch of land. The taxation system depended on the boundaries being fair.

The floods removed all trace of previous boundaries: ditches were filled with mud until they vanished, becoming level with what had once been fields. The administrators within every district were on hand the moment the water receded even a little to demarcate the boundaries again immediately. This was vital, as following them came the farmers with their fresh seed. First they would start to redig the ditches – not for irrigation, as many might expect, but for drainage. The land was sodden, and anything planted into the wet mud would rot unless it was first drained a little. Then they would start to sow.

And so the process went on, day by day. Every day the boundaries would be appointed, the drainage ditch dug a little further, the ground broken up with hand ploughs and mattocks (it was too wet to take oxen on to drag a plough, as they would sink up to their chests!), and seed sown. To speed the process, and to aid the animals, sheep and goats would be turned loose on to the newly planted fields where they could graze as they could, drink and at the same time tread the seed into the ground, saving the back-breaking work of the farmers.

Work was remorseless, but vital. If the seed were not sown immediately, the next crop would not be ready in time. A colleague, Steve Oxbrow, has worked for many years on planting seeds, recording their time to cropping and their yields. His findings have been most surprising.

Trimestre was three-month wheat, the grain mentioned by Herodotus as grown in Egypt, and was almost certainly emmer even in Italy, where modern writers suggest spelt [both are relatives of wheat]. Even the so-called spelt in Britannia is possibly a misnomer, as I found the yield little better than emmer in the south and that emmer was hardy enough even in the Orkneys. Spring sown to take advantage of the long summer days, ninety days is long enough if the sowing date is optimized. Under irrigation a following crop of barley would, I have thought, suit the land nearest the Nile. Whether enough water could have been brought to the highest fields is doubtful but not impossible. (Barley requires less water than all wheats.)

So, if the emmer were not sown immediately, the crop would not be ready for the harvest season. Steve's finding of 90 days from sowing to harvest exactly fits the ancient Egyptian calendar. Every month was 30 days long, so every season of four months 120 days. This would allow time for the Nile to reach its full height, for the water to start to recede, for the administrators to mark the boundaries, for the farmers to start to redig their ditches, and for the seed to be hand sown into furrows broken with a hand plough. There were exactly 30 days to do this from the rise of the inundation, and then 90 days later, at the start of the harvest season, the first crop of emmer would be ready to gather. The land would then at once be ploughed with an ox-drawn cart to turn over the roots of the first crop and to sow the second. A second crop of emmer would take longer, this time, to ripen, although as Steve points out, barley would be better as it required less water to be carried up to the higher ground.

The land in Greek times was calculated by the *aroura*, a measure of land quoted by Sir Alan Henderson and other writers as being 100 cubits square, or 150 feet. A piece of land this size could yield a surprisingly heavy crop of emmer.

Steve went on:

I found net yields had not changed from Roman times until after 1957 at 2 tons/hectare (round figures). This would equate as half a ton per *aroura*, just adequate to feed three people for a year. Tax and rent would take 67 per cent of this. I assume that the pyramid builders, like the royal tomb builders, were paid in kind out of this taxation in kind.

The yield of a piece of land, less the tax, would barely be enough to maintain one worker, while the crown stores would receive the bulk of the yield. This was used, we know (see below), as daily government issue for bakers to bake bread on a massive scale to feed the workers.

Steve makes this point further:

> An *aroura* would thus equate not just to 100 cubits each way, but also a day's ploughing for a pair of decrepit oxen and enough crop to feed one person (after deductions to feed the elite and their employed artisans).

These observations, based on years of recording and growing in the southwest of England, on organically prepared ground, give us our first clear insight into the life of an Egyptian peasant. Although texts may bemoan the lot of the peasant, he figures little in our archaeology. Egyptology is almost entirely dependent on the records of the richest. How many nobles would ever tread into the fields and observe life for themselves? In their tombs, would they depict the reality – or their dreams?

It is true that Egypt is fertile, and that the land was given to them annually by the Nile. But it is now also clear that the peasant who worked the land needed to be there year round, and to work exceptionally long and hard hours, merely to scrape an existence for himself and his family. Little wonder that everyone longed for a son, who could double the amount of land worked, and thus double the income of the family and remove them from the poverty line.

Fallacies of Herodotus

> He [Cheops] closed all the temples ... And compelled them without exception to work as slaves for his own advantage ... The work went on in three monthly shifts, a hundred thousand men in one shift. It took ten years of this oppressive slave labour to build the track along which the blocks were hauled.

Before scientific archaeology began in Egypt, and before the decipherment of hieroglyphs, the picture of the ancient

110

Egyptian civilization depended entirely on two sources – classical writers and the Bible. As it happened, these sources all agreed in every respect – that the Egyptians, and especially their Kings, were as mean a bunch of individuals as you were ever likely to meet.

What was forgotten was that the sources may well be incorrect. We have already speculated about Herodotus's interpretation of Egypt. He visited Egypt about 50 years before Alexander arrived with his Macedonian army to liberate countries from the yoke of Persian domination. He spoke no Egyptian at all. We know from archaeology that there were settlements of immigrant Greeks in Egypt probably as early as the 7th century BCE. So Herodotus stayed in one such immigrant village, where at least people could talk in a language he could understand. From them, he found out what it was like to live in Egypt. Now, take any country, and any immigrant settlement who retain their own customs and language. How likely is it that they truly understand the country in which they live? We can be certain that the people Herodotus visited did their best, but they spoke to him from second- and third-hand knowledge, spiced with rumour, legend and superstition. And as I have mentioned, the pyramids were more than 2000 years old when he arrived. The truth was that they had no idea how the pyramids were built, or why.

When Herodotus describes the Giza pyramids, he even gets the measurements wrong.

> The track along which the blocks were dragged . . . it is five eighths of a mile long [about right], sixty feet wide [about 12 feet]; forty-eight feet high at its highest point [less than 20] . . . [The pyramid] is square at the base, its height 800 feet [the tallest, Cheops', was 481 feet tall] equal to the length of each side [756 feet].

There is scarcely an accurate word in this piece, yet this is something which, we are told, Herodotus observed for himself.

A pyramid whose height is equal to the length of each side is tall, thin and pointed. These proportions were followed by many early 'travellers' (most of whom had clearly never been to Egypt) to create line drawings of the Giza pyramids, to illustrate their fallacious stories. These measurements could easily have been checked, and with regard to the proportions, common sense and a little imagination would have told Herodotus they were wrong. So where did he get his 'facts' from?

Here is another passage.

> An inscription is carved upon it in Egyptian characters recording the amount spent on radishes, onions and leeks for the workers; and I remember distinctly that the man who read the inscriptions said that this was 1600 talents of silver.

In the 4th century BCE, when Herodotus visited Egypt, the tour guide had already made his appearance! And it would seem that Herodotus took advantage of such a tour to Giza, writing down or mentally noting what he was told to add to his *Histories*. We cannot blame him. In the 4th century BCE there was no such thing as history. Herodotus practically invented the field.

How should he understand the difference between fact and opinion – and would it really have mattered in any case? After all, to their understanding, the pyramid was so huge it would last forever. I doubt that the notion that future generations might regard his work as 'truth' on which to base a study ever occurred to him. His aim was to validate the story of the Greeks, in which the Egyptians were a mere passing incident. Little would he know the weight we would place on his day trip to the pyramids!

Other classical writers agreed with Herodotus. Because they regarded him as the 'father of history', they carefully used his *Histories* as the basis for their work! As for the biblical stories of Moses and his enslavement by the Egyptians, it has to be remembered that the basis of the story is the founding of Israel, the land 'flowing with milk and honey' promised to them by God in his Covenant. If the Egyptians had not enslaved them, there would be no valid reason for them to leave; if the Exodus had not happened, they would not have had to spend years in the desert; if they had not spent years in the desert, Moses would not have received the Covenant and the commandments. *Ergo* the enslavement had to happen. In fact, within the account there are clues to show that the enslavement was, perhaps, not so bad after all. Did the people not complain loudly to Moses that they had been fed well in Egypt and wanted to return? And did they not hand Aaron their gold to melt down for his idol? Gold? From slaves? Of course, this is validated by a quotation that they had borrowed the gold.

Imagine, if you will, the scene. Enslaved Hebrew knocks on the door of the palace of Egyptian. 'Hello,' he says. The Egyptian smiles and does not slam the door in his face. 'You don't know me personally. I know you are one of our Taskmasters, but I want to tell you I bear you no resentment. We are all about to leave Egypt. Now, you must not tell anyone, promise? Because we are the only ones who know about it! Now, be a good chap and lend me your gold, and I promise, Hebrew's honour, that I will bring it back to you somehow!' 'Of course,' replies the Egyptian. 'By all means take my gold and jewels. I trust you! Have a safe journey, but watch out for those tides – you can easily get trapped in them.' 'Thanks,' says the Hebrew. 'Jolly decent of you. And I'll pass the message on to our leader about the tides. Thanks again.'

Of course, it could never have happened in quite this way. The truth, as every historian knows, is that secondary sources are frequently biased and cannot be relied on verbatim, but must be used carefully for the information that they contain. You cannot, either, blame the early archaeologists, since these were the only sources of information they had. What is strange is that these unreliable sources, now proved to be based on false information, should still be used today! Unfortunately, the popular media find the stories more attractive than the truth. This is a shame, for as I have said before, truth is usually far more interesting than any fiction.

Despite what many books recently may suggest, we know quite a lot about the building of pyramids. We know, for instance, that the blocks were moved by gangs, most of which were given names. The blocks they moved would be marked in red, presumably to ensure that the block was counted as part of their daily quota. These red marks can be seen on most pyramids on several blocks where they face out, and undoubtedly, if some of the covered faces were exposed, similar marks would be seen on them. The gangs' names were generally appropriate for the King for whom they worked. 'Cheops is Content is Pleasant'; 'Chephren will Fly to His Horizon'. These are imaginative. But how do you think the foreman would have felt, when calling the daily quota, to call out 'Mycerinus is an Old Drunk'?

The truth is that slavery did not exist at all in ancient Egypt. The definition of a slave is a person who has no legal existence. His owner can thus treat him as he might a chair – kick it, break it, fling it, give it and sell it without a qualm. So it is with a slave. In Egypt, everyone was paid in food – monthly, one and a half sacks of grain, half a sack of barley for beer, together with vegetables in season and other sundries. If you were fed and maintained, you were being paid. If a man had a servant and fed him, he was paying him, while the servant had the full legal right to buy, sell, inherit and bequeath in his own right.

In one story dating from the end of the Old Kingdom, a peasant is walking his donkey when he is observed by a local landowner. The landowner covets the man's fine donkey. He lays linen across the path the next day, forcing the poor man to lead his donkey through the fields of grain. Watching carefully, he notices the donkey take a wisp of grain as he passes. He immediately demands the donkey in payment for the grain. The peasant, however, knows his right, and argues his case. His eloquence is such that he is taken into the presence of the King who, entranced, refuses to make a judgment but calls the peasant back to the palace daily so he can listen to his golden tongue! Every person, male, female, even foreigners, had the right to come into the King's presence if they so needed.

In order, then, for a pyramid to be built, the workers would have to be fed and watered or they would collapse and die, and the pyramid would not be completed. This was pay. They took outrageous names – a fine joke, and not one which a slave group might adopt!

The figure of 100,000 men to a shift – 400,000 men a year – has been taken too literally in the past. If you add on to these men their dependants – wives, elderly parents and relatives, children – then even at a mean estimate this would account for the entire male population, if the entire population was around 2 million. Can we rely on this figure?

Following Herodotus, nineteenth- and early twentieth-century Egyptologists noted from Greek and Roman texts, which they were able to read at that point, that there was often what they termed a 'corvee' – an annual conscription. Under this, an able-bodied man was required to work for several months on the King's business, be it building or fighting in the army. This, they reasoned, was so detested by the Egyptians that they created *shabtis* – little figures placed in tombs to ensure that they would not have to work the corvee eternally. Add to this Herodotus's account, and it was an easy step to surmise that the corvee lasted for three months every year (since it involved, statistically, all grown men in the country, and they would have to work every year). The obvious time for this to be done, naturally, was during the season of flooding, when the fields were under water and the farmers were idle.

Like many aspects of ancient Egyptian studies, this interpretation of events starts with an incorrect fact and then adds guesswork to become an accepted fact. Most books published today maintain this idea. It is entirely mistaken.

We know, from a study of Wisdom texts, that attitudes changed considerably in the Graeco-Roman period. Wisdom texts were purportedly written by men for their sons or future generations to teach them how to behave in society. In Pharaonic Egypt, a man was urged to treat the poor kindly. The thinking went that today, you may be rich, but if tomorrow you are poor, you would want to be treated with respect. In Graeco-Roman texts, men are urged to beat their inferiors like donkeys, for only in that way will they obey. Just because the Greeks and Romans treated workers badly (and we can understand that this was considered normal in their homeland) does not mean to say that this was an Egyptian attitude. In fact, there is no evidence whatever from ancient Egypt to suggest that any corvee ever existed.

Let us examine the problem logically. First, as we have seen, a farmer was tied to his land and there was literally no opportunity for him to sit around idle. The concept that the land was flooded for four months so he was out of work is false. Secondly, food and drink would be needed for builders, stone-movers and quarrymen just as much, if not more (given the calorific intake of manual workers) than when no building was taking place. This meant more attention to the fields, not less. Thirdly – if you want an extension built, would you get a field labourer to do it? A field labourer is a highly skilled man, who observes his crops and understands what is needed by instinct and experience to get the best yield from his land. By the same logic, a builder is also a highly skilled man. Try laying a level, equal course of bricks and you will see what I mean. They could never exchange jobs, and still be regarded as skilled.

Fourthly, throwing unskilled men into a building site or quarry does not speed up the work, but slows everything down. You can only fit a limited number of men around a block of limestone in a quarry before they start accidentally hitting each other. Unskilled men trying to move stones into an exactly calculated place only results in accidents and faulty pyramids. What you need is a small number of skilled men in the right place at the right time. This requires training and experience, which comes from years of working as an apprentice to acquire the skills, before being allowed to do work yourself. Get yourself a small piece of limestone – they are all around the place. Now strike it in order to produce one completely flat face. Unless you have the acquired skill and the eye for it, then rather like the unskilled man trying to level a table by cutting pieces of one leg at a time, all you will end up with is a very small item of no use to anyone.

Fifthly, an annual corvee of a quarter of the fit men in the land every three months could never work anyway, by definition. At the end of the three-month stint, the conscript seconded to a building site may just be starting to be useful, his hands hardened in the right place, when it was the end of his shift. Imagine the scene, for an army conscript. In the middle of a battle, he would down weapons and walk away, as his 'shift' was over! In fact, in the New Kingdom we know from texts that conscription was usual for infantrymen, who were then placed into garrisons and trained in the use of weapons before they marched off to the north. The turn of duty ended when the King returned, not before; and this did not depend on a three-month timetable!

There was no corvee in the Old Kingdom. The fields were not waterlogged for more than a few days. The field-labourers would be pressed for their tax-yield or the builders would not be fed. The stonemasons would have to be skilled men, as would the stone-movers and the builders. This is the process of logic, not of archaeology.

But as it happens, archaeology can now confirm most of this!

Mathematics of pyramid building

The logic of mathematics is inescapable. Although Mark Lehner has estimated figures for the pyramid site, I have used mathematics in my search for information about the Giza pyramids and their building for more than 30 years, and my conclusions are somewhat different.

You may recall that according to Herodotus, a pyramid took 20 years to complete. Although we have no archaeological knowledge to back up this claim, the figure sounds a reasonable one, given the length of the reigns of the Kings concerned. So let us work on this basis. The Great Pyramid comprises around 2.5 million blocks of stone, not including the granites which line the chambers and passages. This means, for the pyramid to be completed, that 125,000 stones had to be moved each year and placed into exactly the right position, or the work would not be completed on time.

30 weeks made 1 year	= 4167 stones per week.
10 days in 1 week	= 417 stones per day.

The Egyptians were the first to divide the day and night into equal segments that we today call hours. Since Aswan lies on the Tropic of Cancer, the length of daylight hours does not vary so much as in more northern or southern latitudes. There are always 12 reliable hours of light. In this calculation, we must understand that the gangs did not work at night. They needed time to eat and sleep for a full day's work the following day; and, in addition, lighting such a scheme would have been impossible.

12 hours in 1 day	= 35 stones per hour.

For the NOVA TV series *Secrets of Lost Empires* Mark Lehner and his teams tried to reconstruct a pyramid. The stones were provided at the site ready cut, and lifted into place with forklift trucks. They had to move 135 stones into place in two weeks – that's fewer than 10 per day. They did not achieve this target!

It has to be remembered that these figures do not allow for any 'weekends' or time off, except for the five extra days at the end of each year which were not part of the working calendar. It also must be understood that if, in any one hour, one stone too few were moved – then the overall target could not be reached and the completion of the pyramid would be delayed.

The base of the pyramid is 756 feet on each face.

Allowing for each stone to be
a 3-foot cube = 252 blocks per side
So the bottom layer is 252 ×
252 = 63,504 stones in total.

If the second layer of stones were placed one stone in from the previous layer (this would achieve a slope angled at 45 degrees), each layer would decrease by two stones per side.

Second layer, 250 × 250 = 62,500
If we add these together,
63,504 + 62,500 = 126,004.

This means that after one full year of concerted effort, of stones being cut and dragged to the site, then elevated into place, the 'pyramid' was still only 6 feet tall. A tall man, on tiptoe, could still see over the top of it! Scarcely, you might consider, worth the combined effort of a full workforce.

The entire pyramid, measured vertically at its centre, was 481 feet tall. If every layer was 3 feet thick,

There were 481 ÷ 3 = 160 layers of stones
from base to apex.

Every layer diminished in size, however. The second layer, of

62,504 stones, reduced by 1004 stones to form the second layer. The second layer, in turn, was then 996 stones more than the third layer. And so on.

This means that if the rate of progress remained steady (which it had to do for the pyramid to be completed on time), the bottom layers grew exceedingly slowly; and that the further up the layers you progressed, the more layers you had to complete every year to fulfil your target of 125,000 stones per year; and the faster the pyramid would rise. This was especially obvious after the pyramid reached its vertical halfway point. After this point, each layer reduced so quickly that the top half of the pyramid would have to be built in less than three years of the total 20!

Let us return to our hourly target of 35 stones per hour.

This means that 35 stones must also be cut per hour, moved per hour, and dragged into place per hour for the target to be met. This was easier at the bottom than at the top, as it would take so much longer for any one stone to go from the quarry to the top of the pyramid, where it had to be dragged into place, than to reach the bottom.

If, at any stage of the construction, a quarryman was injured, a rope or sledge broke, or a tool became too blunt to work, the stone would not be in the right place at the right time. So timing was also vital. If we allow two hours for any gang working on the pyramid to take a stone which had been brought to him, and to move it into position, and then to get 35 stones per hour into place, we need 70 gangs at a time working on the pyramid. We know from Old Kingdom quarry inscriptions and tomb inscriptions that the average group comprised 60 men, working in four gangs of 15 men each.

According to the Rhind Mathematical Papyrus in the British Museum, a ramp would be calculated to give a slope of 1 in 8, or 12.5 degrees. In the 1980s, trials at Giza, carried out by the Japanese, showed that a 2.5-ton block, the declared average weight of a pyramid block, could be dragged with relative ease up a 1 in 8 slope by eight men. Allowing for some men working hard and others slacking, and allowing for poor average health, this would seem about right.

70 gangs of 15 men working
to place the stones   = 1050 men.

These gangs would place 1 stone every 2 hours. This means 35 gangs of 15 men dragging stone up the ramp would be needed to supply them.

35 × 15   = 525 men
Total   1575 men.

These are just the men involved with the actual building. They needed a complex infrastructure to provide all of their daily needs.

The logistics of pyramid building

With any great manoeuvre requiring vast numbers of men to be present, the logistics of the operation, as we have seen from the mathematics so far, were vital. What is immediately clear is that Herodotus's 'hundred thousand men a shift' is far in excess of what was either needed or reasonable. There was limited space on an incomplete pyramid, and too many men would only create jams and thus increase accidents. As we have seen before, much of the muscle power on the site was provided by the 'settled Nubians' whom Snofru had brought into Egypt to protect his gold-mining operations there. The Palermo Stone says that 7000 Nubians were brought into Egypt; and this figure tallies well with our calculations.

Today, if such an exploit were ever to be conceived, the committees involved, the number of management stages that would be needed – all would delay the start of the building work for years. In truth, the planning would take longer than the building work!

In ancient Egypt, there was no similar previous experience on which to base the operation. The first pyramid built required predictions to be made by the man in charge, Imhotep. How many loaves would be needed per day? How many yards of rope? How many pieces of wood, turned into the various tools? Any miscalculation or estimate, and the timings would fail.

For every man on the pyramid, hundreds may be needed to support him. Every stone must be quarried, shipped to the site, dragged up the causeway, taken on to the pyramid, and then put exactly into place, or the pyramid would not end up the correct shape.

The part of the exercise which intrigues me is not the building of the pyramid. As we shall see, this can be explained from evidence. Rather, it is the human infrastructure which allowed it to be done. I ask myself questions constantly, the answers tormenting me through lack of evidence. At what time of the day did the builders eat? Were they called down to eat, or was there a mobile canteen service? Did they have a town crier, or was there a bell or gong? If they were called down to eat, was it done when they felt like it, or on a rota basis? How were they served and by whom? Who did the washing up afterwards? Did they have to go down whenever they wanted to get their drinks, or was there a water-carrier on hand to quench their thirst? Did they all wear hats against the sun? Were there medications to rub on the skin to stop melanomas, and if so, would they help us? And, most significant of all – what did they do when they had a call of nature? Were there 'portaloos' on top of the pyramids? Or was it 'Geronimo!' down the sides? And what happened if you had sunstroke? Or, for that matter, if you got the ubiquitous 'curse of the Pharaohs'? Was there an ancient Egyptian cure for diarrhoea for a builder 250 feet up on the platform of a pyramid?

As I have said, the pyramid exists, it had to be built, and

someone had to work out all the little details!

One thing is completely clear. The planning was done by one man, alone – or the system could never have worked. And, of course, we know the name of the first pyramid designer – Imhotep. Yet after his death, for many generations, pyramid building was either unsuccessful (as in the Buried Pyramid of Saqqara), or was not attempted at all.

Then, suddenly and almost out of the blue, at the start of the Fourth Dynasty, in the reign of Snofru, it started again. The progress of the years between makes it impossible that any living person could have passed the information down through the generations. Instead, someone, at the start of the reign of Snofru, must have come across the 'blueprints' for the organizational and architectural sides of pyramid construction, realized that they now had a workforce that needed employment (the Nubians) and decided to combine the two things. Or, perhaps, it could be that a committee existed which continued with the knowledge that Imhotep had assembled, but awaited the means to do it. Snofru's evacuation of Wawat (Upper Nubia) provided them with the means.

Whichever alternative was the true one, one thing is clear: the manpower for building the pyramids was immigrant Nubian labour. Once again, Herodotus's account is wrong.

Somehow, a site had to be chosen. It had to be measured and levelled. Skilled workmen had to be brought in to set up the various workshops needed – brewers to brew the beer to be consumed daily, bakers to grind the grain and bake the loaves. All this would have to be in place before a single man ever came to measure. A military text of the New Kingdom states that a man was provided with 10 loaves a day for subsistence. For our men on the pyramid, this means 15,750 loaves per day, not counting all the other workers on site who needed feeding. They needed hunters to bring in meat, butchers to kill it and cooks to prepare it. They needed fishermen to catch the fish, gut and dry it. They needed linen workers to make the linen and ropes that were needed at a moment's notice. They needed oil-makers to provide oil for cooking, for lamps and for rubbing into the skin against the fierce glare of the sun. They needed water-carriers to bring water from the Nile and provide the workers with drinks. They needed sanitary workers to carry pots for the workers to excrete into. They needed carpenters to make and repair the sledges. And this does not include the scribes to list everything; the account-ants to check everything in and distribute it; the stonemasons to carve and finish the fine stones being used; the goldsmiths and artists to decorate things.

In short, the infrastructure for our 1575 men probably amounted to many men per worker, just to ensure his needs were met at a moment's notice. If he were ill, if he were injured by some foolish miscalculation, if he were too little fed or watered to work effectively – for any reason, if the man on the pyramid was not looked after, then the job would not be finished.

And at the head of this mountain of labour, there was the man in charge. Who was this? It needed one man to co-ordinate the departments and to issue orders. It required one man who understood the figures for every single department every day of the 20 years. It needed, in other words, an exceptional administrator and leader of men. The Egyptians had this, no doubt, in Imhotep. He either taught others, or wrote down the methods.

For the building of the Great Pyramid, this man would have been the Vizier. Despite the infighting, the appointment of the Vizier was thus vital for the success of the whole operation. Cheops needed to choose the right man for the job, despite all the arguments between sections of his family.

When considered in this way, the building of a pyramid pales into insignificance beside the administration needed to ensure it happened. Logic decrees this could never have been achieved by a discontented or enslaved workforce. As it happens, archaeology confirms this also.

The pyramids were never built by slaves. They are masterpieces which demonstrate the ability of men to work together for a common goal.

But what was that goal? What persuaded them that all of this effort was worthwhile?

The Giza Plateau Mapping Project and Supreme Council of Antiquities

As we have seen from the above sections, it can be estimated, purely by logic and mathematical reason, that the numbers of men working on a pyramid were considerably smaller than previous estimates would have it, and that they were not slaves, but particularly skilled men.

The production of some of the suppliers for the pyramid crews would have been the same whether the pyramids were being built or not. Men needed feeding day in, day out, and the amount they consumed would not vary greatly. So the overall quantity of bread, meat and other foods consumed daily would not vary much from the ordinary national intake. What changed was that a greater quantity of this had to be brought to and used in one single site than was usual.

There are only two ways to achieve this. Either the things had to be brought to the site, which would involve risk, time and more labour, or it would have to be provided on site. Logic again suggests that a man arising from his bed would be best employed up the pyramid working with his skill than in travelling to and from his home village; and that, at the end of the day, he would be more contented if he could return to a local house where food and drink awaited him, and perhaps some evening entertainment around a fire. In this way, he would wake up refreshed and ready for another hard day on the site.

125

All of this could be established by logic. But since 1984, the work of the Giza Plateau Mapping Project, led by Mark Lehner of the University of Chicago's Oriental Institute, has proved beyond doubt that this is exactly what happened. East of the Great Pyramid, and south of the Sphinx, the GPMP has noted and cleared a wall. Today it is called Heit el Ghurob, or Wall of the Crow. It is stone, built with stones similar in size to those of the pyramid, and with a gateway through it some 23 feet in height. In order to clear the area, massive amounts of modern rubbish had to be cleared. Dr Lehner records this as being between about 3 and 20 feet deep, often comprising soiled sand removed from the nearby modern stables of horses and donkeys used over the plateau.

To the north of the wall, although still little excavated, lies an area called anciently the *re-esh* – 'Mouth of the Watered Land'. The valley temples of Cheops and Chephren stood here, both probably jetties into a flooded area. This was a man-made lake leading from the Nile to allow goods to be sailed as close to the plateau as possible.

To the south of the wall, discoveries made have revealed the beginnings of a huge town. In the early years, massive bakeries were uncovered, large conical baked-clay jars still embedded into areas of ash. The ash, on analysis, was from acacia wood, collected from nearby pollarded bushes. Acacia grows best at the water's edge, so the *re-esh* probably provided also a good, wet environment, while the acacias, cut down every year to ground level to encourage new, straight growth, would provide some shade and green to an otherwise arid area. The baking area was all within a building, the layers of fine ash thick and reddened, caused by immensely high temperatures. Huge vats in the floor seem to have been used to prepare the bread dough, samples showing, again, evidence for emmer having been used. The pointed bottoms of the jars were often placed facing upwards, making 'egg-box' shapes into which more jars could be stood. Hundreds of jars were found. The bakery, when in action, must have seemed like the jaws of hell, with fierce fires raging and a constant turnover of vast quantities of bread to feed all the workers on the site.

Later discoveries included a main street, paved and broad, with buildings off each side, leading southwards from the gate in the Wall of the Crow. The buildings resembled the so-called 'store-houses' which can be seen today behind the Ramesseum on the west bank of Luxor. In places, many of them have side-benches within, as well as areas of columns. The use of these is still being established, but workshop areas have been defined, including copper-working areas. Here were found copper fish-hooks and needles – precisely the implements we would surmise would be needed to provide for the site workers.

From 1992 onwards, Dr Zahi Hawass, Chief Inspector of Antiquities on the Giza Plateau, has been excavating further north of the workmen's settlement area, to the southeast of the Sphinx and below the modern village of Nasret es Sammaan. This was possible due to the renewal of sewage systems for the modern town. Here Dr Hawass has located two cemetery areas. The Lower Cemetery contained burials of workmen for the site and their foremen, while the Upper Cemetery contains tombs for the artisans, the skilled craftsmen who lived on the site. One tomb, that of a royal acquaintance called Inti-shed, contained four remarkable painted statues of undoubted Fourth Dynasty date, two of the four sporting fine Fourth Dynasty moustaches!

The skeletal bodies within the tombs so far excavated show, all of them, immense wear and tear on all of their joints. One man suffered several fractures during his life. These had all healed well and straight. Fractures must have been common, and if untreated, may have healed crooked or become infected. Since this did not happen, it demonstrates that a medical service was on hand to treat the injuries; and that the injuries were handled exceptionally well for their times. It also proves beyond doubt that these were permanent work-men, their bodies hardened by years of physical labour.

The mysteries of Meidum and Dahshur

In 1974, an engineer from Cambridge, Kurt Mendelssohn, published a book concerning Meidum Pyramid. He observed that the pyramid sits atop a mound. The pyramid is an early one. The Step Pyramid of Saqqara, the only earlier monument, developed slowly and almost accidentally when the great Imhotep decided to build one *mastaba* atop another, probably for reasons of security. This makes the Meidum pyramid the first pyramid that was built deliberately.

By the end of the Third Dynasty and the start of the Fourth, while Imhotep's plans for administration of such a mammoth enterprise could be established, and a workforce was available to build, the actual procedure for building a pyramid was by no means certain. At Meidum, the architect had chosen a novel method. Instead of starting with a flat base, and then building it up layer by layer, he started instead with a tall, narrow, pyramidally pointed tower. Around this he wrapped another layer of stone, lower than the apex of the first and with the stones angled towards the centre, giving it a safe centre of gravity.

As the layers progressed, one layer wrapped around another, the eventual result would have been a stepped pyramid. In the event, something happened. Mendelssohn postulated that after the pyramid was completed an earthquake of great magnitude flattened it.

The next pyramid to be built was at Dahshur. It had been deliberately constructed, and from the bottom layer upwards, its corners forming exactly the same angle as the collapsed pyramid of Meidum. It was thus seen to be risky, so the steep angle of the sides was altered to a gentler safer slope at the top. The result was the Bent Pyramid. This design, it was believed, displeased the King so much that he would not be buried in it. Instead he ordered another pyramid to be built. This, the Northern or Red Pyramid, so called because of the red tint of the stone used, was built from the start at the shallower, safe angle of the top of the Bent Pyramid. The Egyptians, it seems, were starting to learn lessons about pyramid building.

In fact, Mendelssohn's hypothesis, although a reasonable one, does not fit any of the evidence at all. For a start, despite its curious shape, Meidum Pyramid did not collapse at all. An earthquake strong enough to disturb the inwardly pointing levels of stone in the outer 'wrappings' would have caused immense damage. The passages and chamber within the pyramid, its weakest points, are undamaged. The pile which has accumulated around the bottom of the pyramid is not, in fact, rubble, but most of it, although covered with sand, is solid stone, the original finish of the outer pyramid. A recent field-walking exercise carried out around this base pile produced large quantities of pre-dynastic potsherds. The area around Meidum pyramid is virtually unexcavated, and no pre-dynastic cemetery is known hereabouts. Yet one exists, as the spoil demonstrates. If found, the sherds show it will have been robbed in ancient times. But for the sherds to find their way on to the bottom of the pyramid, they must have been placed there from the sand around the outside, perhaps moved there to provide 'lubrication' for the moving of stones (see Chapter 6).

Secondly, the nearby *mastaba* tomb, excavated in the 19th century, belonged to two relatives of Snofru, a brother and a son, and their respective wives. Nothing from the site indicates in any way that Huni had anything to do with it; all indications suggest it was designed for Snofru. Visitors to the site in the New Kingdom left graffiti here saying that they had visited the pyramid of Snofru. This attestation was common in ancient times and continued for more than 1000 years after his death.

129

Thirdly, the stelae at the mortuary chapel adjacent to the eastern face of the pyramid are left bare. This is most unusual if the pyramid had ever been completed and occupied. The stelae are enormous flat shafts of granite, each standing more than 15 feet high. The mortuary chapel itself is undecorated except for the graffiti left by New Kingdom visitors. The burial chamber inside has an area of the floor marked out for insertion of a sarcophagus. Although work was started on it, it was left unfinished. All the evidence suggests the pyramid was never occupied at all.

With regard to the Bent Pyramid, although there is some cracking evident in the lower courses of masonry in one corner, the work continued on the site until it was completed. This seems strange. If the site were unsafe, why not simply abandon it? The cracking seems to have been caused by the pyramid being built on top of a sand base instead of rock. Once more, a learning curve for the Egyptian architects! In my many years of teaching in the field, I have been asked thousands of questions, but only once did a five-year-old girl ask a question so logical it took my breath away: how heavy was a pyramid? While adults speak of other statistics – its measurements, its construction, its purpose – it took the mind of a child to speak the obvious. A pyramid cannot be built just anywhere; the Great Pyramid, at a mean estimate, weighs around 7 million tons. They need a solid rock base!

Another perplexing problem is that the Bent Pyramid is completely faced with smooth outer stone. This fine stone, brought from the other side of the river at Tura, is harder to work than local stone, but with work and care it can be polished to a fine brightness. It has been generally accepted that this stone was polished from the top downwards as the pyramid was completed. If the change in angle was displeasing, then why finish the polish? It would not alter the appearance of the finished monument in any way.

But who is to say that anyone found the pyramid

displeasing? The only solid facts that we have show that the angle of the Bent Pyramid was changed, and that subsequent pyramids were built at a more shallow angle. There may be another reason for this. Examine the photograph of the Bent Pyramid and observe, if the base angle were continued, how tall the finished pyramid would have been. If you are designing a pyramid, it may simply not have occurred to anyone that the finished height of a pyramid was established at the base, the moment that the angle of the slope was defined. If the pyramid had been completed at the first angle it would have taken many more layers of stone; it would have achieved at least another 50 feet in height, requiring the stone to be taken up further; and it would have needed vast amounts more cubic feet of stone. The alteration is more likely to have happened, bearing in mind its completed and polished state, because the architect realized he had inadvertently designed a giant. The lesser angles of later pyramids could thus also be taken into consideration when calculating the final height and the stone needed.

What is certain, from a stela found alongside the Dahshur pyramids, is that the 'settled Nubians working on the two pyramids of Snofru are exempt from taxation'. The stela has been much discussed. It shows clearly that two pyramids were being built for Snofru. But why? And which? If the inscriptions and monuments of Meidum are correct, then Meidum was started for Snofru, the Bent Pyramid was completed by him, and the Northern Pyramid was used for his burial.

To contemplate the organization needed for the building of one pyramid is staggering. To imagine two being built within a 20-year period seems unlikely. To believe that *three* were built is nothing short of madness! If, indeed, Meidum was never completed, and the Bent Pyramid, although completed, was never occupied, then this suggests that the building of the third pyramid as the burial place of Snofru must have taken less than

10 years. Given our logistics, this is out of the question. There has to be another explanation.

The pyramid-building industry

The work on the Giza plateau has started to prove to us what logic and reason, combined with mathematics, had already suggested. The pyramids were built by a permanent and skilled workforce, housed in a town specifically designed to be occupied by the various skilled men required to maintain the relatively few men who built the pyramids. What has remained previously unstated, yet is also logical, is that the building of this pyramid settlement itself must have taken immense work and time before the building work could commence. That this was conceived in its finest detail can be understood from the areas given over to food preparation on a gargantuan scale; and by the provision of an excellent, skilled medical team on hand to tend to wounds received on site.

The plan to build pyramids seems to have restarted under Snofru, and although he did not build at Giza but further south, it is also to be reasoned that one day soon, at Dahshur and Meidum, similar vast workmen's settlements must be found.

This involved large numbers of men, although probably not many more than the 7000 'liberated' from Wawat by Snofru.

Now let us go one stage further. Earlier we contemplated what happened if a King should die too soon, his pyramid incomplete. Another point needs to be raised. What if, on the contrary, a King were to live much longer? What if, like Ramesses II, he had ruled for 67 years instead? What then would have happened to the pyramid workers? For them, a lifetime averaged less than 40 years. If building a pyramid took 20 years, then a reign as long as Ramesses would leave them unemployed for the following 47 years! What then would happen to the settlement? How would they maintain their skills and their strength? How, indeed, would they be maintained if they were producing nothing? Would vast teams of support workers work for almost 50 years to support, in effect, three generations of pyramid builders, two generations of whom had never worked on a pyramid?

Let us add further to this point. Contemplate, if you will, the building of a pyramid. As it rises, as we found earlier, the layers would rise more rapidly; but the square footage available for the men to work on would diminish. This means that at the foot of the pyramid, where there was more space, men could work easily. Try as you will, as you reach the top 100 feet, there is no way that the 70 gangs we know would be needed could work in the space, nor that the 35 gangs needed to supply them could get the stone to them. The space simply was not there.

There are several possibilities. One is that pyramid building employed 'casual labour'. This would be needed at the bottom, and they would gradually be laid off as the pyramid rose. But, as suggested earlier, this makes no sense. Men for building projects were simply not available in ancient Egypt – all had jobs to do, mostly on the land, for which they were needed to supply the workers on the site. The skills they acquired would be lost. Another possibility is that the rate of progress was speeded up at the bottom – that each gang had, say, a doubled quota, to allow for the slower times towards the top. In this case, we must envision more men being employed, and more men laid off.

In fact, there is only one answer, and this seems to be so logical it is staring us in the face. Pyramids were not built for a specific King at all. There was a pyramid-building industry, permanently employed on several sites at once, each at a different stage of construction. Men and equipment could be moved from site to site as needed. If a new pyramid was being laid out, more men would be drafted on to the site from one nearing completion. The 'pyramid town' would be permanently manned, with skilled personnel who would move on to the work site every day. This would mean that three pyramids were built during the reign of Snofru, with one, Meidum, perhaps nearing completion. Since it was thought to be the probable place where the King would be buried, it was used to bury some of his family who died early in his reign. The Bent Pyramid was rising and half completed, as would be logical, when men were freed to start on another site because it was realized that a change in angle would reduce the height, capacity, time and workload for the men. So the Northern Pyramid was started as the Bent Pyramid reached the critical halfway point, at the lower angle. Slowly but surely, the foremen and architects were finding flaws and solving them, while the men moved around the sites. And the next dead King could be buried in the last completed pyramid.

This seems the only scenario possible. What is certain is that the pyramid settlement of Giza was indeed occupied solidly from the start of the Fourth Dynasty to the end of the Old Kingdom and the change in royal funerary practices. Inscriptions of nobles buried at later dates around the Giza pyramid necropolis give them titles such as 'Mayor of the Pyramid Town of Cheops', well into the Sixth Dynasty.

The reign of Cheops is hidden to an extent behind the vastness and grandeur of the monument he left behind. His father provided the workforce needed to build pyramids on a gigantic scale, but Cheops and his sons were the ones who devised a method to make the industry successful. During the reign of Snofru, the 'settled Nubians', trained and made fit by foremen, architects and nobles from Cheops' family, were housed in a vast and relatively luxuriously appointed city close to their building site. Here they were cosseted, fed and watered and provided with all their needs to ensure that the work was completed satisfactorily. The men in the town formed an elite, specialized in the skills needed to move and place the stones as fast as humanly possible. Their skills could not be lost or neglected, but an industry grew up, with the stone plateau to the west of the Nile, in a belt 50 miles long, used to construct a series of pyramids, rising alongside each other.

But the energy eventually ran out. The pyramid town was expensive to maintain, and the families there were supported by so many others, who also needed feeding and clothing. So by the Fifth Dynasty, the decision was taken to apply what had been learned, to reduce the base area of the pyramid in order to build small pyramids instead of huge ones. Instead, effort was channelled into the lower buildings around, which were easier to build and thus less labour intensive. As the Kings grew less effective, less able to maintain the settled Nubians who undoubtedly would have wanted to return to their own land, the corps of pyramid builders diminished.

By the end of the Sixth Dynasty, the supporters of the Kings grew tired as they watched their home areas begin to starve. Their absence from home meant that ditches were not redug, fields were saturated, crops rotted and men starved. Their energy was needed elsewhere.

Perhaps the tourist tales of Herodotus had a grain of truth in them. Not that Cheops was a megalomaniac whose obsession impoverished the country, but rather that he set into action an industry which could only exist by building one pyramid after another, and this became too expensive to maintain.

There is no evidence that he ever sent any of his beloved daughters to a brothel to pay for this work! But as time went on, the maintenance of such a town seemed to be a waste. The grandeur of the Fourth Dynasty was never to be repeated.

CHAPTER FIVE

The Gods and the Pyramids

—

I n the last chapter, we came to understand through both logic and archaeology that far fewer people were involved in building a pyramid than Herodotus was told by his guide and many people still assume. Instead of the entire male workforce of Egypt being conscripted annually into lives of misery, the picture that emerges is a very different one. The workforce was a permanent, skilled group of men, working all year round to build a succession of pyramids. As they became more skilled and began to see where faults in their designs lay, they were able to amend these in later pyramids. The men who worked on the desert sites were supported by an infrastructure of huge size and remarkable effectiveness. Field workers were not employed at all on sites, but worked even harder to produce the reliable crops needed to supply the permanent workforce with food, drink and other basic needs.

The workers on the sites were divided into gangs, each with their own name, presumably chosen by themselves, and each with a daily quota for stone moved. If we allow a working day of 12 hours, and two hours to jostle a stone into position, this means each gang had only to move six stones a day to meet their target, not an unreasonable task so long as the stones were available to them and in the correct place when they were needed.

The organization of this force is breathtaking, and amounts to a far greater achievement, in many ways, than the building of the pyramid. After all, how do you keep such a massive force of men contented for such a long period of time? The answer is – organization and planning. Each man knew his task, and, although difficult, it was not beyond him. He could be certain that no matter how small his job, in time the teamwork of the entire force would result in a monument that would stagger the imagination of the world for centuries to come.

We know that the great Imhotep had laid down certain rules for the building of a pyramid which employed a skilled work-force in an almost ideal administrative organization. At the start of the Fourth Dynasty, faced with a sudden, unexpected work-force of immigrant Nubians, Snofru was able to apply Imhotep's blueprint. The result was an industry which resulted in a series of pyramids. The organization, which involved indirectly almost everyone in the land, entirely dominated the reign of Cheops. But the question that needs answering still remains – why? Why build such a monstrous building in the first place? What was it all for?

Imagine yourself in a similar position of authority today, addressing a series of departmental heads. It would be relatively easy to motivate them, to hand out flowcharts with designated duties and quotas, and to show how each group would interlink with the other. Timetables need drawing up to show which group operates where and at what time of the day, to prevent them from falling over each other. But why should you be doing it at all? What reason could you give to persuade them that, for the next 20 years, your aim was to focus entirely on this one single project?

This still perplexes us today, almost more than trying to figure out how they built the pyramids. To find out about their methods of pyramid building, we do at least have one large piece of evidence – the pyramid itself, silent testimony to the method used. But to discover the reasons behind it, we have to try to delve into the ancient Egyptian psyche, their beliefs, the things which could be counted upon to motivate them in the first place.

The problems this raises are so great that for many decades now, people have virtually given up trying to find a reason at all. In the popular view, nothing would persuade anyone to build such things, *ergo* someone else must have built them. It is easier, on the whole, to imagine Pharaoh ordering the whipping of a bunch of recalcitrant slaves than to imagine people doing the building willingly. Or, even better, to imagine either creatures from outer space doing it, or leaving us secret methodologies in hidden chambers to tell us how to do it. Suggestions have even included emitting loud sounds and harnessing acoustic resonance to levitate the stones and thus make the job easier!

I have always said, for many years, that I am open to all viewpoints. I am willing to listen to suggestions, no matter how strange – but only if someone can provide the evidence to support it. Until that is forthcoming (and so far it is not), we are left with only one basic fact. The pyramids exist – so someone built them. And if we have no evidence of extraterrestrial assistance, we are left with the only alternative – men did it. And since we have quarry inscriptions, building clues all over the sites and the titles of men who organized it – even the bodies of those who achieved it! – then like it or not, we have to accept this.

One of our problems today is that, following Jacob Bronowski, we believe implicitly in *The Ascent of Man*. There is no doubt at all in our minds that our own generation is better than the one before. This is a fallacy. Most people marooned on a desert island would lack even the smallest basic skills which would allow him or her to survive. We have forgotten, by and large, the natural assets which surround us and how best to use them. If we cannot use large machinery, preferably remotely operated, then we are stuck. If we have a problem, we 'call someone in'. And all too often, if it is broken, we replace it since to mend it is either impossible, or would cost more than buying a new one. We live in an age of ultimate disposability.

Four and a half thousand years ago, everyone had to know how to survive. There were no shops. If you wanted to eat, drink and wear clothes, you had to have the skills and knowledge to grow or make it all yourself. If you wanted to move a stone, you did not think about blowing loud trumpets at it with the idea that it may eventually float! You grabbed a few friends and moved it, but, at the same time, you had the knowledge and the experience to understand fully the world around you. You knew the strengths of materials available to you; you knew how to take shortcuts using the few things you had. In the days before steel and electricity, you used water, wood and air, the elements around you.

In a similar way, it is too easy, when trying to find the reasons behind pyramid building, to apply modern thinking. To build something, there must be a reason. But is this necessarily true? Does the builder or welder, working high up on a skyscraper, do it because he 'believes' in the site owner? Does he respect the millionaire who is investing in the building as a 'god'? In fact, he does it because it is his job; because he has the acquired skill; and because he is paid for it. Why should this not be the motivating force also behind the pyramids? As we saw in the previous chapter, the builder would have to be well looked after – even down to 'health insurance'. His lifestyle was infinitely better and more secure than that of his colleagues out working, back bent, in stinking mud under a scorching sun.

So we may not need to find a reason why the men worked on the pyramid. We do not have evidence, as some have suggested, that the workers expected to gain an afterlife because they participated in the building of a tomb for their King. But we do need to find one reason – why did the King want it in the first place? Now, here, there has to be an answer. The multi-millionaire who is investing in a skyscraper does not do it just because he has the money, nor because he thinks it will look nice. The building will be expected to work for him in some way.

So how did a pyramid work for a King?

How the idea of a pyramid emerged

The idea of building a pyramid did not simply come out of the blue, as some have assumed. There was a long process of development from which they emerged. In the earliest, predynastic times, people were buried in simple pit-graves in the sand. However, excavations at Naqada and Abydos have shown that these pits appear to have been robbed by people who must have been present at the burial. Jewellery and other objects were removed from the pit simply by someone pushing a hand down through the sand at exactly the point within the pit where they clearly knew such treasures had been placed. Piles of stones found to have been placed over the pit-grave may well have been to mark the location, or may have been placed to make robbery in this way more difficult. In any case, these rock piles did not succeed. Other methods were tried to divert the robber. In some cases, a side chamber was cut at the foot of the pit, and the body was placed in here and sealed up, either with wood or stones, so that from above the pit would appear to be empty. However, since the evidence clearly shows that the robbers witnessed the burials and thus knew exactly what was in the grave and where, this did not work either.

By the start of the First Dynasty if not earlier, the mound of stones placed over a pit-grave grew increasingly larger. It became apparent that some superstructure might help to prevent the robberies. Discoveries at Saqqara show that this was achieved by building a large, walled mud-brick structure over the burial chamber. As we saw in Chapter 1, because of its similarity in shape to the benches on which local Egyptians would sit to rest, they became known as *mastabas*. Yet the purpose of the *mastaba* was still not achieved. The massive walls above the central burial chamber frequently contained cells, doorless rooms. This may have been to save on the massive quantities of mud-bricks needed, and the subsequent weight bearing down on a subterranean chamber, or it may have been to increase security of the body and objects placed with it. In some *mastabas*, the cells have been found to contain funerary objects, wine jars and remains of food offerings. Since the roofs of cells were relatively thin and easy to break into from above, the whole aim of the building, to increase security, was thus put into jeopardy. Not only this, but the sheer huge scale of the *mastaba* would indicate the location of the goods more easily than an inconspicuous pit-grave. It may well have been at this point that the process of tomb-robbery changed from a private crime within the family of the deceased, to a state crime carried out by professionals.

This, however, is always assuming (which one should never do in archaeology) that security was the aim of building the *mastabas* in the first instance. It could equally be the case that the size of the superstructure increased to reflect the status of the person buried within, and that robbery was not a target at all. This makes great sense. In the early, decorated *mastabas* of the Old Kingdom, the chambers contain raised reliefs on the wall showing the tomb owner carrying out offices he supervised in life. In every case, the social status of the person on the relief is reflected in the size of the carved figure. The tomb owner, whether man or woman, is shown on a grand scale. If a man, his wife is shown half his size, and their children, half that size. His followers and servants will also be shown smaller to reflect their status. So, the larger the tomb, the grander the owner's status, and the smaller the tomb, the lesser his status. By this token, the King's burial must be the largest of them all.

The first pyramids

Building a huge, flat-topped *mastaba* out of sun-baked mud-brick is a large enterprise, but nothing on the scale of pyramid building. The mud could be brought to the site in baskets hanging from the shoulders, trodden with straw, baked in the sun on the desert sand, and then used to make the walls.

But *mastaba* tombs are flat-topped; why build a pyramid?

At Saqqara, W.B. Emery found one *mastaba* which was different from the rest. Tomb 3038, dating from the First Dynasty, had a stepped structure built over the subterranean chamber, and this stepped structure was enclosed within a normal, vertical-walled *mastaba* tomb. The reason for this is clearly one of logical development. The weakest part of the *mastaba* tomb, regardless of robberies, was the area over the subterranean burial chamber. No matter how strongly wooden rafters held up the super-structure, within a short period of time these timbers would crack under the strain and break, leaving the whole *mastaba* to collapse inwards. Various methods had been tried to spread the weight of the roof, but this stepped internal structure was the ideal method – creating a series of inwardly diminishing steps which spread the upper weight evenly over the area of the lowest, largest step.

W. Stevenson Smith suggested this was probably the pyramid prototype, that the engineering needed to raise tall structures now existed. Did Imhotep later use it?

At Saqqara, the first King of the Third Dynasty was called Netcherikhe ('He of the Divine Body'). Two and a half thousand years later, and 500 miles south of Saqqara in Aswan, a forged inscription of Ptolemaic date linked the names of Netcherikhe and Djoser together. While the name Djoser does not occur at Saqqara, it is probably more accurate to record the King by his attested name, Netcherikhe. The building which we today call the Step Pyramid started life as a *mastaba*. An examination of the front face (see photo) reveals that this first building, presumably rectangular like all other *mastabas*, was built with an inner core of locally collected limestone rubble, fixed with lime mortar, and with an outer face coating of fine polished limestone. This first building was enlarged by adding a section to the southern edge, probably making it more square; and then a second, lower step extension was added, again to the south. This covered up a series of 10 parallel vertical shafts leading into the bedrock. In one of them was found the remains of a wooden coffin and a young man inside it, supposed to be a son of Netcherikhe. Presumably his heir to the throne died early and unexpectedly, thus creating a need for a semi-royal burial site.

It was at this stage that Imhotep conceived the idea of adding a smaller *mastaba* atop the first and so on, in a sequence of four. Whether this was to create a tall building, while spreading the weight, as before, or whether it was to protect the top of the first *mastaba*, who can tell? The effect, though, was to create a pyramid, albeit accidentally. Presumably the idea was a pleasing one, since it was further extended by enlarging the base and each of the first four steps to incorporate another two smaller steps at the top. As in the bottom section, however, the stones used were not deliberately cut or large in scale, but small, perhaps chipped out of a quarry or else simply scavenged locally.

The development of the true pyramids from the reign of Djoser onwards was a change in perception of pyramid building. These edifices, of solid stone with passages and chambers within, were deliberately designed on a massive scale. They were to be the focal point of entire cities for the dead. The tombs which cluster around them were created for their relatives within their huge, extended, incestuous families. They were designed specifically to allow the dead courtiers to hide their master during death, as they had during life. At the centre, the pyramid was the point of grandeur, just as the King, during life, was elevated in station above and beyond all mortal men. This was to be the tomb of a megalomaniac.

Inside the chamber of every pyramid there is either a full or partial sarcophagus, or evidence that one stood there. Whatever purpose you wish to assign to a pyramid, then, since there was a sarcophagus within it, there was presumably a body placed in it at one point.

Religion and the ancient Egyptians

What is often considered popularly to have been a complex world filled with gods and goddesses, frequently depicted with the heads of other creatures, is far from the truth. The world of ancient Egypt was in fact a far simpler place.

According to ancient Egyptian beliefs, there existed two worlds, identical in many ways, and yet startlingly different in one respect. The world of the living was a short, painful, impermanent existence centring around the weak physical body. This could not last forever. After death, everyone would become a spirit, and live eternally and painlessly in another place.

At the time of conception, forces of this world and the other combined to make a child. From the physical world, they formed a tiny body. Yet this body was nothing, could not operate, without a spirit force within it called the *ka*. The *ka* resembled you, could be freed from your body during sleep or states of unconsciousness during life, but always returned. It literally occupied your body, which, from mummification, the Egyptians knew to be nothing but a framework, bones and 'vessels'. Operating these bones, this body, was the job of the *ka*. So if you felt hunger or thirst – this was the cry of your *ka*. If you denied it, it would then find ways to punish your body – you would become ill (so much for modern diets!). A child was born of the *ka*, which provided the sperm within the male and the egg within the female. After death, this spirit was freed, but occupied a space on earth within the cemetery, above or near your grave, or within the tomb if you could afford one. Since it had provided you with its needs and longings, these needed to be satisfied after death.

At birth you inherited a *ba*. This is the very essence of life. It was formless, fluttering around, and occupied the cosmos, the skies and the stars, the towns and the plants and animals. It entered by your right ear and left via your left ear. If by any chance at birth there was no *ba* available for the child, it would be stillborn. After death, the *ba* rejoined the other spirits of the universe. It carried with it no memory, so even if it was reused, it could not recall where it had once been. This was not reincarnation as we understood it, but simply a use of elements of life within the cosmos, almost a Hindu interpretation of the world.

At death, your *ka* and *ba* left your body an empty shell. The embalmers, if you were fortunate and rich, would remove the centres of decay and wrap and perfume your body, trying to preserve it completely. On the day of burial, words said over this wrapped body, which we call a mummy, transformed it into an *akh*. This was a resurrection. The body itself, white, pure, fully equipped, could then pass into the other world.

The other world was thus occupied by the dead, those who had previously passed over. Only those who could prove that they had lived a pure life could pass across to the other side. This other world was a mirror image of Egypt in every way, complete with King, nobles, courtiers and every man to his post, just as in life. Yet this world was free of trouble and illness, a perfect place in which to live for eternity.

The location of this other world seems to have changed as time went on. In the earliest times, inscriptions show us that the Egyptians believed this was 'in heaven' – associated with the stars. They saw patterns in the stars which they associated with

145

places in which former spirits now lived, and after death, the *akh* would be raised to live there.

Later, after the watershed of the end of the Old Kingdom, these notions changed. Anubis appeared, taking upon himself the guise of Wepwawet, the local god of Assiut. Wepwawet, 'The Opener of the Ways', was pictured as a feral desert dog, and believed to live at the edge of the horizon, crouched on a mound to stop the living passing into the land of the dead. Anubis, originally associated with the ranks of embalmers, became 'He Who Sits upon His Mountain', the guardian of the western horizon. The Egyptians watched the transit of the sun. They saw it disappear over the western horizon and appear again at dawn in the east. Where had it been in between? The answer was clear – the other world did not, in fact, lie in the stars, but hidden under our own world. The sun clearly shone for us during the day, then 'dropped off' into the other world by night.

The intent, for every ancient Egyptian, was the same: they expected, as long as they lived a moral and upright life, to pass into a pure and wonderful eternity. It would be an island – the Island of Reeds, surrounded by the waters of the edge of this world. It would also be a version of Egypt, fertile, green and lush. The Greek word *paradeisos*, meaning 'garden', derived from the ancient Egyptian version of life after death and transferred neatly into modern thinking.

The two worlds lived in a precarious balance called *maat*. The King alone straddled the two worlds and could communicate with both. He was the messenger who, during his life, was able to tell the physical world of changes within the spirit world. Daily he met with the spirits in the sanctuary of a 'temple', then passed their messages on to the living. Every person who had ever lived had gone into this other world. Here they existed as benevolent spirits, often translated as 'gods'. The key to the interconnection between worlds was, the Egyptians believed, held in one place – Heliopolis, ancient Iunu. Egyptian Princes were sent here to study the keys to the connection between the universe, to be given the knowledge that they needed to be able to communicate with 'the other world'.

Yet Iunu, or Heliopolis, the city of the sun, was not always in the forefront of Egyptian beliefs. It only rose to prominence during the Old Kingdom. In fact during the reign of Cheops.

The religious revolution

According to most authorities, the only major religious revolution in ancient Egypt took place in the 18th Dynasty, the so-called Amarna period. As I showed, however, in my previous book *Tutankhamen: The Life and Death of a Boy King*, there is no evidence whatever to conclude that any real revolution took place at that time. The beliefs of the King of that period, Akhenaten, simply seem to have reverted to those of the Heliopolis system. The temples he designed exactly copied earlier solar temples. The beliefs mirrored those of Re of Heliopolis. His religion was limited to the bounds of his own city. There was, in fact, nothing revolutionary about it in any way.

It is clear, however, that a religious revolution did take place, not in the New Kingdom but over 1000 years earlier, in the middle of the Fourth Dynasty.

The Westcar Papyrus (see page 80) appears to predict the coming of new Kings once the line of Cheops has died out. These Kings, triplet boys, are developing 'in the womb of Ruddjedet, the wife of a priest of Re of Sakhbu'. Sakhbu, although unidentified, probably lay in the region of Abusir, today some 40 miles south of Cairo and on the west bank of the Nile. The Kings who were buried at Abusir were, in order, Userkaf, Sahure and Neferirkare. Their later descendants, Shepseskare, Neferefre and Niuserre, were buried in small pyramids close by. About a mile to the northwest lie the remains of two temples, one for Userkaf, the other for Niuserre. The temples, almost identical to the main temple of Re in

Heliopolis, are simple courtyards, open to the sun and dominated by a central pillar, the *benben*. This gilded tower, like a slim pyramid or squat obelisk made of small stones, was placed at the western end of the courtyard, probably to reflect the rays of the sun as it rose into the court.

It was thought until the 1950s that the title 'Son of Re' appeared before the names of Kings from the start of the Fifth Dynasty. However, the discovery of the Giza ships, found below the Great Pyramid in 1954, and excavations at Abu Roash changed all of this. The first King whose name, enclosed within a cartouche stamped into wet plaster, was entitled Son of Re was Cheops' son and direct successor, Redjedef. The names of the following two Kings, Khaefre or Chephren, and Menkaure or Mycerinus, contain the same god's name.

The change of names is startling, for it shows the allegiance of the child's parents at the time of their birth. The appearance of the name Re in sons of the royal family is also startling. The shift in religious beliefs happened during the reign of Cheops. In fact, since the Kings who bore these names were his sons, although we do not know whether the father or the mother named the children, the change must have happened in Cheops' youth, even before he became King.

The strange thing is that not all of his sons were named for Re, the new god. Yet again, as in the appointments of Viziers, we see an uncomfortable picture of a split within the family. Cheops', or Khufu's, name is similar to that of his father, Snofru; yet his sons are different. So was the change in Cheops himself? Or was it, perhaps, in one or two of his wives, those powerful ladies who were fighting for the rights of their own son to inherit the throne?

The Pyramid Texts

It is always hard to place yourself in the mind of someone else; to do so when the other person died 4500 years ago is almost an impossibility. We have virtually no information about what the Egyptians of the Old Kingdom period believed. Although a few inscriptions have survived on occasional stones, no temple designed for a cult image has yet been traced. Since the end of the Old Kingdom occurred 1000 years after the unification, this effectively means for a millennium we have almost no information about the religious beliefs which may have inspired the building of pyramids.

Four pyramids at Saqqara, dating from the end of the Fifth and start of the Sixth Dynasties, contain carved texts within their burial chambers and on the walls of some of their passages. These have become traditionally known as the 'Pyramid Texts' – a misnomer, since 96 pyramids bear no texts, and we have no means of knowing why they suddenly appeared, or, more importantly, why they then disappeared again!

The texts have been fully translated only on a handful of occasions. The first reliable copy of the texts themselves (although, since they were hand copied and by one man, they are in need of updating) was undertaken by Kurt Sethe in 1904. His translation did not appear until after his death, some 30 years later. A French translation was published in 1923 and an English in 1952; but it was not until 1969 that Piankoff published a version in the US at about the same time that Faulkner published a new, modern English version.

Faulkner states openly that 'the text upon which this translation is based is of course that of Sethe'. Recent work which I have undertaken with a group of hieroglyph-reading scholars in southwest England in the late 1990s has shown that Faulkner's reliance upon Sethe was greater than his reliance on the original texts themselves. In other words, he relied on two facts only: that Sethe's copies were accurate; and that Sethe's translation was reliable.

But we have reason for serious doubts about both of these 'facts'. The texts themselves have been taken from vertical inscriptions and transcribed as horizontal inscriptions. In some areas, the signs go from right to left, in other places, from left to right, while the transcription always goes from left to right. What is more, Sethe broke them up into 'sayings' or utterances. This is all extremely problematic. Translating Egyptian relies almost totally on reading signs together in their correct groups. If you change the position of one letter, moving it from the end of one word to the start of another, the effect on the meaning can be startling.

By transcribing them as he did, Sethe artificially formed what he considered to be logical groupings of signs, which subsequent scholars used to guide their translations. But were his groupings correct? His numerical references (which relate to the line number on the wall, as well as its position within the chamber as a whole) shows that on many occasions some words he has grouped together may be divided between the bottom of one line and the top of the next, around 15 feet or more away. In some instances, his reading and drawing of signs is dubious.

Much more disturbing is the fact that his translation is frequently completely subjective. As Sir Alan Gardiner has stated in his *Egyptian Grammar*, 'When once the exigencies of dictionary and grammar have been satisfied – and these leave a large margin for divergences – [it] is an intuitive appreciation of the trend of the ancient writer's mind.' Gardiner is being as diplomatic as he can. What he means is that frequently words, as Sethe groups them, do not exist in dictionaries at all, nor in grammars; and that once you have hazarded a guess as to what they might mean, to connect the words means the translator has to try to read the mind of the ancient writer. In other words – translations are frequently vastly different from the original texts and will differ greatly from one scholar to another. The result is not, as many imagine, a definitive translation, but one scholar's working version of what he considers it possible the translation might be!

It is entirely doubtful whether Sethe or any other scholar, no matter how great, ever intended his work to go unchecked. It is far more likely that he set the translations before the public in order to present them with a working possibility which he fully expected to be used and retranslated by others. After all, the work of an individual scholar with none to criticize him or her is unlikely to be free of errors. Unfortunately there are too few working in the field, and not enough time to check every small detail; sometimes, you have to delegate.

Faulkner, we now know from working on the Pyramid Texts, used Sethe's translation as the basis for his work, as he states openly in his preface. Thus we now have three areas where error could have occurred – the copying from wall into print; the original translation by a single scholar, working alone, into German; and the final translation from German into English. While Faulkner states that where gaps occurred in Sethe's translation, he referred to the original text, it now seems more than likely that he did not have the time to return to the original text at all.

The Pyramid Texts appear in four tombs and are different in each. Each contains certain sections. Where the sections appear in more than one pyramid, they are almost, though not quite, the same. They comprise several sections or 'spells' (a very dubious translation).

Although the language of ancient Egyptian changed little over the centuries, there are idiosyncrasies in the style of writing which at once point out the age of the text. In English, for example, we might compare the writing of Shakespeare with that of Graham Greene – the same language, but different methods of expressing it. In looking at the Pyramid Texts, we see they can be divided into three groups: very ancient pieces which speak of the King being buried in the sand and fighting off predators; old sections which speak of the King joining the stars; and sections contemporary with the pyramids and the latest texts which identify the progress of the dead King's soul with the passage of the sun across the sky.

As to their subject matter, Mark Lehner of the University of Chicago follows Piankoff's example, and states that the texts can be divided into five types: dramatic texts, hymns with names, litanies, glorifications and magical texts. I would restate this, however.

The texts are clearly mainly liturgies, designed to be read out at various points of the burial ceremonies which accompanied the King. According to the texts, words were to be spoken over all the items included within the burial. These items, surprisingly, were for the most part portions of meat, bread and cakes, and different sorts of beer and wine. This in fact agrees completely with the range of objects found in the First and Second Dynasty *mastaba* tombs of Saqqara, and the chamber-tombs of the royal burials of the First and Second Dynasties in Abydos. The items were to be offered at certain times and in special ways. At various points during the ceremonies, the words to be spoken formed longer sections of texts, also presumably accompanied by actions, which stated the intention of the acts – to ferry the King to the stars or to enable him to join with Re, the sun god, in his daily journey across the skies.

One text has been badly misrepresented, and yet this appears in one of the most publicized sections within the pyramids. Called the 'Cannibal Hymn', it is, in fact, no such thing.

The opening section includes words previously translated as 'They have seen the King appearing in power, as a god who lives on his fathers and feeds on his mothers'. The whole sense of the passage follows these words. In fact, the final verb, translated as 'feeds on', is in fact clearly 'answers, responds to, replies to'. So the passage should read: 'They have seen the King appear as a *ba*; a living god like his forefathers, who answers like his (fore)mothers'. The King is dead, and as his *ba* appears, it joins those who have gone before him. The rest of the passage, thanks to a determinative omitted in one section of Sethe's text, deals with the sacrifice of cattle, 'their large joints for the morning meal; the sweetmeats [literally, that which is inside] for his evening meal, and the delicacies are for his night-time meal'.

This simply goes to illustrate the problems that arise when using translations instead of referring to the original texts. How are we to understand the beliefs of the Egyptians who built the pyramids if the translated texts we need to use are incorrect?

All of the texts are designed to assist the King to attain his afterlife, some while physical objects are being transformed into spiritual ones so that they will be of use to him in his new form of existence; others to accompany him safely on his lonely journey to join the spirits with whom he has conversed for most of his life.

The real differences, then, lie in the different forms of language used, stages which indicate clearly that during different eras, the King was destined to travel to different places. In the earliest days, the comfort of the King in his earthly grave was sought; later, the afterlife was in the stars; and the last ones written, as we've seen, had him joining Re, and these cannot date before the start of Cheops' reign.

So one possibility, given the scale of the pyramids matching the King's persona, and its links with death in the sarcophagus within the chamber, is that the pyramid was seen as the 'machine' which would accomplish this. Within the texts, the King is said to 'ascend the staircase to the skies'. This would suggest that the soul of the King would travel up the outer slopes to join the company of the gods in their constellations. Alternatively, it could be considered to 'shoot' up the 'ventilation' shafts from the internal chambers. But if the latter were indeed the case, then why do such shafts not appear in other pyramids?

In fact, there is some evidence that they were started, at least, in the second pyramid, which today is associated with Chephren. This suggests that the religious beliefs prevalent at the time the three pyramids were designed involved the shafts, because they were completed in the first pyramid, but left unfinished in the second, when the religious ideas behind them changed.

The 'ventilation shafts'

Let's take a closer look at those 'ventilation' shafts.

Over the many centuries since the pyramids were built, men have been entranced by them, and the mystery and power that they represent. If there is nothing left inside them, it is scarcely surprising: millions of feet have trodden these passages before you. It is impossible, then, to say exactly who first observed small, rectangular 'holes' in the northern and southern walls of the so-called 'King's chamber' in the heart of the Great Pyramid. At any rate, they have always been on view in modern times, and trials showed that within the holes, narrow shafts ran horizontally for a few feet, and then turned to run steeply upwards towards the outer wall of the pyramid. However, these shafts did not emerge on to the surface of the pyramid itself. Despite this, Charles Piazzi Smythe, at the end of the 19th century, declared them to be ventilation shafts. Later writers elaborated on this, saying they were designed to maintain the temperature in the heart of the pyramid at a stable 68 degrees Fahrenheit, while allowing a passage of air through the burial chamber!

In 1947, I.E.S. Edwards, in his classic *The Pyramids of Egypt*, observed that the northern shaft appeared to be directed towards the Pole Star, Alpha Draconis, and that the southern shaft appeared to be angled towards Orion and Sirius. He postulated that these were shafts designed specifically to propel the King's spirit skywards in the right direction for it to reach the constellation of Orion.

In 1992, under the supervision of Dr Rainer Stadelmann of the German Archaeological Institute of Cairo, a robotics expert, Rudolf Gantenbrink, was given permission to send a tiny, remote-controlled wheeled robot into the ventilation shafts from the King's chamber. The robot vehicle, called Wepwawet ('the Opener of the Ways'), carried a video camera and miniature lighting system on it to allow people below the first-ever opportunity to examine the passage from the inside. Although nothing curious was observed, it was realized for the first time that the so-called ventilation shafts were extremely sophisticated indeed. Far from being tunnelled through the rising rock layers, the shafts had been lined with limestone conduits. Because of the angle of the rise from the central chamber to the faces of the pyramids, the mathematics involved in calculating the shape of each section were extraordinarily complicated. The architect had to cut hollows through the layers of limestone, as they were being built, to insert the special lining, which had to be precisely calculated to bring the shafts to the surface at an agreed point.

The following year, 1993, Gantenbrink brought Wepwawet II to the Great Pyramid, this time to explore the shafts rising from the Queen's chamber. These had only been identified at the end of the 19th century. In 1872, Waynman Dixon, a student of Piazzi Smythe, had tapped on the walls of the Queen's chamber until he heard hollow sounds. He broke holes into the walls and found the entrances to ventilation shafts behind them. The discovery had not been unexpected; after all, there were shafts in the same place within the main chamber. However, scholars had long decided that the so-called Queen's chamber had originally been planned as the main burial chamber, but that somehow, along the way, the plan had been changed. It was accepted that the Queen's chamber was abandoned unfinished in order to expand the Grand Gallery and use the space there to store the stones to seal the pyramid. The ventilation shafts in this chamber, therefore, were of little interest, since it was clear to everyone that they would only go a short distance and terminate at the level at which the Queen's chamber had been abandoned.

Wepwawet II was inserted into the shaft, which is 20 centimetres square. The lights on the forklift arrangement at the front were turned on and the video camera started to send back an image of the shaft as its predecessor had done a year earlier in the shafts in the upper chamber. To everyone's amazement, far from stopping, the little mole kept climbing, metre after metre, even further towards the outside. Something seemed wrong; if the shafts were full length, as in the King's chamber, then this smaller chamber was deliberate, and intended for a specific purpose. Suddenly there was silence, followed by a loud outburst of noise.

The TV screen showed that the mole had stopped. In front of it, closing the shaft, was a limestone block, like a door. And fixed to the front of it were two copper handles! What could lie beyond? Laser lights, shot horizontally at the tiny gap at the foot of the block, vanished and were not reflected back, proving that there was indeed a gap beyond.

Within days, theories of lost treasure in the secret passage filled papers, and pictures of the two copper handles, unseen in that shaft for 4500 years, filled the front pages of national newspapers around the world.

The mystery of this sealed 'air-shaft' continues to baffle, and yet is still far from being resolved. On 17 September 2002 Dr Hawass inserted another remote-controlled tracking vehicle into the shaft. Through drill holes in the door, cameras could now see only another short section of shaft with another blockage or 'door' beyond. It seems ever more unlikely that anything of merit can be found here. As Mark Lehner points out, the shaft is barely large enough for a rat to climb up, so anything lying on the other side of the limestone block has to be tiny! Archaeology has a habit of playing tricks on you like this: a shaft that leads nowhere but slowly peters out; a papyrus whose ending is missing and then turns up, and is seen to be actually rather boring and not at all the way scholars had imagined it. No doubt the portcullis in the shaft will turn out to be nothing exciting, probably just a barrier to stop birds or other creatures from entering the pyramid chamber!

For the moment, we are none the wiser. We know now that the so-called Queen's chamber was part of the original design of the pyramid. But for what reason? Rainer Stadelmann pointed out that as it is a closed chamber, it bore a real resemblance to the *ser-dab* chamber found at the Step Pyramid. The niche in the unfinished wall seemed to be the right size to have taken a seated statue of the dead King. He also suggested that the unfinished bottom chamber, in the bedrock of the plateau beneath the pyramid, was a ritual copy of an underworld into which the soul of the dead King might sink. This seems unlikely, however. It neither matches our information about the expected nature of the King's afterlife, nor seems particularly plausible. A nation which could organize the building of a pyramid 480 feet tall could finish clearing a small chamber if it wished! It is evident from the abandoned working of the lower chamber that the men who were cutting the room were simply called away one day, and never returned. Chippings and stone tools still lie where the last hand dropped them.

The creation myths

Could there be another explanation for why pyramids were built for Kings in the Old Kingdom?

A second and more likely explanation for the pyramids is that the King was trying to re-create a powerhouse of creation – to regenerate the circumstances at which Creation itself happened. This would then allow his soul to be re-created into the afterlife.

According to all Egyptian beliefs, at the start of time the world was a watery void of Chaos. Out of this there arose a mound. Upon the mound, all of existence came into being. The story changed somewhat at various times. Images from very early Egyptian history show the mound itself shaped like a pyramid. This would certainly make sense, especially at the time of the inundation, when the rising waters of the Nile would lap around the base of the pyramids on the Giza plateau, making them appear to be the mounds of creation rising from the fluid void.

But why three mounds? This does not tally with Egyptian theology. Or did the Egyptians not worry about this 'slight' divergence in their beliefs?

Sun rays

It has been pointed out by many scholars, including I.E.S. Edwards and R. Stadelmann, that the shape of the pyramid resembles exactly the shape of sun rays pouring down through the clouds, especially towards sunset. If you witness this, you will understand the idea behind it – that the soul of the King would rise up the slopes of the pyramid walls in order to unite with Re, the sun.

The problem with this is that when the pyramids were being designed and built, it is evident from the texts and from the architecture that the soul of Cheops and his ancestors were expected to join the constellations and not the sun. Although attractive, this idea is simply not very logical.

New notions

Over the past two decades, more and more suggestions have been made, some worthy of consideration, others a little stranger. Among the latter were ideas in circulation after tests in which razorblades placed under pyramidal shapes stayed sharp for longer, while fresh products, such as cream, stayed fresh for longer. There was no real explanation, though, about why either of these were thought to be a good idea!

In 1994, Robert Bauval, in conjunction with Adrian Gilbert, published a new work, *The Orion Mystery*, in which he proposed that the Giza pyramids had been specifically planned to mimic the placement of stars in the 'belt' of the constellation Orion. The book went much further, however, also stating that the rest of the constellation was matched by other Fourth Dynasty pyramids. He then went on to suggest that the Great Pyramid was not intended as a tomb, but as a temple, in which the King used the 'ventilation shafts' as a means of symbolically fertilizing Sirius, the star associated with the goddess Isis. Another suggestion was that the pyramid was used only to carry out the final Opening of the Mouth ceremony, a ritual designed to resurrect the dead body of the King.

Later books by Bauval, in conjunction with Graham Hancock, went even further. Discussions on the age of the Sphinx, based on weathering patterns in the trough around the statue, suggested to them that the Sphinx was far older than Egyptologists had estimated, and that this, in turn, was evidence of an earlier civilization who had left behind secret knowledge or wisdom found and used by later Egyptians to build the pyramids. They even went so far as to suggest that the model for the Sphinx was a 'simian face' they had observed on images of the surface of Mars.

The essential basis for all of these ideas, and many, many more, came from the visions of the American spiritualist and medium Edgar Cayce. While in a trance state, this extraordinarily influential man foretold that at the turn of the 20th century, remarkable discoveries would be made at Giza, centring on a lost 'Hall of Records' in which the missing wisdom would be found. As the date approached, those aware of the prediction seemed determined, come what may, to make it happen. Suggestions were made about hidden chambers under the Sphinx, passages below the plateau of Giza which would lead from the Sphinx to the Great Pyramid, and, of course, the Hall of Records. Several attempts were made to apply for permission to go and seek them out. However, the Supreme Council of Antiquities in Egypt has made it a basic requirement that all excavation, especially at the vitally important site of Giza, must be made by qualified Egyptologists. Just having an idea and a spade is not a licence to dig. This has resulted in cries of 'conspiracy' from enthusiasts who are convinced that Egyptologists know something, and that we wish to keep it to ourselves. I was attacked for this very thing recently on an American radio programme – after one contributor had asked me whether I was not aware that the Great Pyramid was no longer in its original position but had been moved!

As an Egyptologist, I can honestly say that there is no conspiracy. We know nothing that you do not know, and have access to nothing which is not publicly available. There is no attempt to cover up information at Giza.

It is quite probable that more chambers and passages remain to be discovered beneath the site. In fact, every site in Egypt is the same! Sonar tests do show that the natural limestone formation on which the pyramids stand, in a belt more than 60 miles long from Abu Roash in the north to the Fayum in the south, is filled with thousands of 'spaces'. Some of these will be natural cracks; others will certainly be man-made. It is impossible to see which is which without digging. At Saqqara, where excavations have been carried out for more than 27 years, tomb shafts have been discovered that plunge deep under the surface, sometimes five or six levels. Each contains complex chambers and passages. And of course each of these must be fully recorded and the objects found within them cared for. This is a lengthy and very expensive process. Objects found must remain in Egypt by law, and most of them go to Cairo Museum. This building, opened in 1901, is stuffed solid with material, yet there is no money or staff to conserve the objects, and nowhere to display them.

Egyptology must bear a responsibility for anything discovered. Digging haphazardly near the Great Pyramid without preparation, and without evidence of what might be found and where, would be totally irresponsible. We have too much ancient material already to cope with adequately without adding to the store. So things must take their time. Anything which may have survived 4500 years will wait a little longer in safety and secrecy until we can responsibly excavate it, although, given the high water table below the plateau, the chances of anything major surviving both the time and the damp are slim.

As I've said before, archaeology is a destructive process. Those who simply dig without reference to context – material and soil marks which may give clues as to the original layout – and with no purpose other than to 'find treasure' are not archaeologists at all but grave robbers. Egypt has suffered from enough of this. We all owe a huge debt of gratitude to the Egyptian government and Inspectorate who have done their utmost to stop the centuries of looting and depredation that have already taken place. Giza does need examination, but in a proper context and at a proper time. And until that time, we must all be patient.

The alignment of the pyramids

Could there be any truth in the notion that the pyramids of Giza were deliberately planned to mirror Orion? Two entrenched camps now dominate this discussion. On the one hand, new thinkers not formally trained in Egyptology complain that their views are misrepresented or totally ignored as fringe thinking. Yet they claim to be Egyptologists, which irritates the professionals. On the other hand, trained Egyptologists, who are traditionally shy and retiring academics unused to the glare of modern publicity, maintain a staunch silence in the hope and expectation that the others will simply 'go away'. All this has led to an impasse.

What truth could there be in the ideas? First, as we have seen, there is more than enough evidence to demonstrate the reality of the pyramid-building industry. We know now that pyramids were not built for a specific King; rather, a group of pyramids would be in various stages of construction at one time. While gangs working at the time of Cheops laboured on the Great Pyramid, as we know conclusively from graffiti, no one recorded that Cheops would actually be buried here. It would depend on a pyramid's state of readiness when he eventually died. This means there would be nothing to stop the idea of a deliberate design taking shape at Giza.

Secondly, if this were to be the case, it was unprecedented. We have seen how the builders learned their craft through trial and error. If the layout were really intended to reflect the position of stars in the belt of Orion, the chances are huge that errors would be made along the way. Those people who complain that the layout is reversed, that the Mycerinus pyramid is too small, that the ventilation shafts do not precisely align with the constellations at the right time, must try to understand that 4500 years ago, while technology had progressed by leaps and bounds, they had no computers, as we have, to work things out exactly. As we have seen in the Bent Pyramid of Dahshur, a fundamental error made at the base of a pyramid would persist as the pyramid grew. The effect of an error of a fraction of a degree in the heart of the pyramid, when aligning the remarkable shafts which led to its outside, would be multiplied as buildings progressed.

Thirdly, for those who complain that the Orion 'map' does not fit the Fourth Dynasty ground plan – this is exactly right. Images of Orion on star ceilings of New Kingdom date, and carved images on temple walls, show conclusively that the Egyptians did not see the shape of a hunter, as we see it, but only his belt.

In fact, the argument is basically of little real importance. Archaeologically, from inscriptions, artefacts and monuments nearby, we know beyond any shadow of a doubt that the Giza pyramids were built during the Fourth Dynasty. We also know, conclusively, that the design owed nothing to earlier people's lost wisdom.

We also know, beyond any doubt, that when these pyramids were planned and begun, the King believed, traditionally, that after death he would ascend to the company of other gods in a spirit world at the time associated with the stars. During the lifetime of Cheops, and for reasons now lost to us, there was a revolution in thinking. Almost overnight, Heliopolis came to the forefront and with it, the cult of Re. As we've seen, many of the sons of Cheops were named for this new god; and the texts show that as a result, the concept of the afterlife changed from the stars to a land beneath the earth, a land illuminated by the sun during the night, as it 'dropped' over the horizon of the west. Perhaps not, as has so often been stated, 'as above, so below', but rather, 'once above, now below'.

The pyramid and ritual

We cannot prove Bauval's theories about the layout of the pyramids one way or another, as the evidence does not exist. But what about his ideas regarding the purpose – that the Great Pyramid served as a temple? Do we have any evidence to support the view that the pyramids were not, as we claim, tombs, but something quite other?

Those who claim that the pyramids were merely symbolic also claim that human remains have not been found within them. Old texts show us that when entered in ancient times, the pyramids did contain human remains.

> The lid was forced open; but within, nothing was found save bones rotted by time.

Since this was not what the seeker was looking for, the remains were discarded as unimportant. Since sarcophagi have been found within most of the pyramids, there is no doubt whatever that one purpose was to place a body there, the body of a King. Could there have been another purpose, though?

The suggestion that the lower chamber of the Great Pyramid was used for the 'Opening of the Mouth' ceremony is perfectly

163

feasible. The *ba* of the dead King could then fly up through the shafts to be reunited with Sirius and Orion. This would be quite in keeping with the textual information we have for the time. However, to suggest that the pyramid was built for this purpose is another matter. The ceremony, which was carried out on the body of a dead King, lasted only a few minutes. To suggest it was worthwhile to build an edifice 481 feet tall for this purpose alone seems completely improbable.

Regarding Bauval's temple theory, it has to be said there are no recorded temples for the Old Kingdom period. Could it be that we have been looking for the wrong shape – that temples in later times had the large sloping walls on either side of the entrance called pylon gates, and columned halls, but that in the Old Kingdom, they took the form of a pyramid?

Excavations at Hieraconpolis and Abydos, where traditional early layouts of temple enclosures have been identified, demonstrate that temples have always been of a similar shape. But let us look at the evidence. If the Great Pyramid had indeed been built for religious reasons, then the alignment of the ventilation shafts shows beyond a doubt that the focus was on the stars. The notion that once a year, a King should enter the pyramid and conduct secret ceremonies in the chambers by which he 'fertilized' Sothis/Isis through the appropriate shaft to ensure the return of the floods later in the year does seem possible at first glance. But the 'evidence' shown was taken from illustrations in the royal tomb of Tuthmosis III in the Valley of the Kings, done more than 1300 years later. This would be akin to a historian declaring that the Norman conquest of England would have been more effective and speedier if the troops had taken a train from Dover! Anachronisms are historical falsehoods. As we have seen, though, the change of state religion during the reign of Cheops meant that his sons and successors all ruled as 'sons' of Re, and the Pyramid Texts showed that they believed they united after death with the barque of the sun as it moved from this world to the next and not, as their

This tiny ivory figurine is the only surviving image of Cheops, although some authorities are now questioning its authenticity

The Great Pyramid shadows its companions, occupied by Chephren and Mycerinus, and dominates the horse and rider at its foot

The Pyramid of Meidum was the first true pyramid attempted by the Egyptians. It was built during the reign of Snofru but was never completed

The Bent Pyramid of Dahshur, also built during the reign of Snofru, was constructed on a base of sand. Its lower corners later started to collapse under its great weight

The exposed south face of the Step Pyramid of Netcherikhe at Saqqara shows clearly the lines of the original *mastaba* and its extensions

The Fifth Dynasty Pyramid of Unas had its facing stones robbed in antiquity, leaving only the core of sand and rubble. This has collapsed completely and it now resembles a sand dune more than a pyramid

My twin daughters, aged eleven, give scale to the facing and core blocks of the Great Pyramid. While the facing stones on which they stand are huge and carefully cut, the core blocks behind them vary considerably in size – many of them are quite small

A few facing stones survive at the base of the Great Pyramid. The fine, compact stones are enormous and sit together snugly, unlike the core blocks above and behind them

The Ramesside Osiriform statue lies unfinished in the southern granite quarry at Aswan. It is still part of the bedrock and gives clues as to the working methods of ancient sculptors and stone workers

The mysterious series of cylindrical holes on the Giza plateau once held capstans, used to move huge stones easily

This stone horizontal support beam in the temple of Abydos shows the hieroglyph for the letter 'a' , an arm, which has been interpreted by some as being a 'helicopter' used to transport stone!

This reconstructed plain wooden box now lies in Cairo Museum and contains Queen Hetepheres' magnificent set of silver bracelets. The original box was more ornate, but collapsed entirely

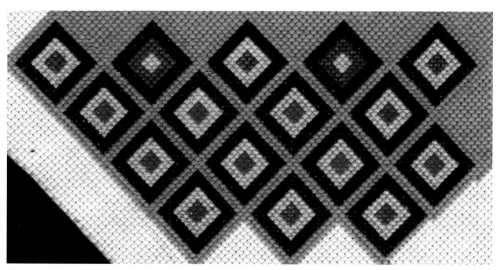

Reconstructed textile (cross-stitched by the author) shows the brilliance of colour and pattern on the fragment of beadwork found in the tomb of Queen Hetepheres. The original crumbled into dust. It was probably originally a *heb-sed* cloak . This unique reconstruction is the first-ever glimpse of what such a cloak must have looked like

The head of the Sphinx at Giza has been recut. The residual paint on the face, together with other facial features, indicates it was remodelled in the Eighteenth Dynasty.

This damaged head is that of Redjedef, heir and successor to Cheops. It bears a close resemblance to the face of the Sphinx (above)

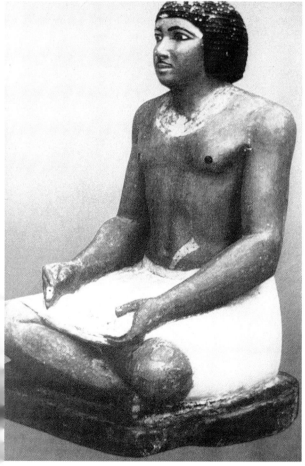

Although we have little idea of what Cheops looked like, this pair of statues shows his brother Rahotep, and his sister-in-law Nofret. The statues, found at Meidum, are typical Fourth Dynasty carvings, and the colourful image of Rahotep is probably very similar in appearance to Cheops

This finely painted statue of a seated scribe bears the features of Crown Prince Kawab who died too soon to inherit the throne from his father. There is a strong family resemblance between him and his uncle Rahotep (above)

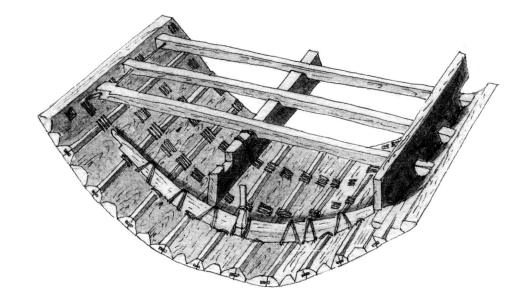

A cross-section of the construction of the hull of the Cheops' boat shows its complexity, despite the simplicity of the materials used – just wood and ropes

This reconstructed ship was once used by Cheops during his lifetime. Today it stands in a purpose-built museum below the Great Pyramid predecessors had believed, ascended to join the stars. In other words, even if, against all evidence, the Great Pyramid had been conceived as some kind of temple, it was too late. Once Cheops was dead, its stellar function had no relevance whatever to society and it would have been sealed anyway.

Of the various theories on why the pyramids were built, some must be discarded as unlikely. They could not have been modelled on the shape of rays of the sun, as the first pyramids long preceded any link with solar cults. Similarly, they were unlikely to be temples: we have evidence from the First Dynasty and even earlier that temples always followed the same design. We cannot concentrate on the Great Pyramid alone and dismiss all the others in the argument, as there is a clear progression of design and thus a continual concept behind them from the very start. The reason behind pyramids needs to extend to the earliest, not just the largest.

There seems to be only one answer. The pyramid form has to be a symbolic mound, representing the place at which creation took place – the peak or pyramidion. It must represent the source of creation itself, and thus the epicentre of power enabling the rebirth or re-creation of the dead King in another world.

This being the case, every pyramid should theoretically stand alone, which makes the suggestion that the Giza layout duplicates the belt of Orion also improbable, since there could not be three mounds symbolizing creation. Since they were designed at one time and probably built alongside each other, it is more likely that each was considered the centre of its own enclosure. Yet the layout of the Giza plateau is strange and unique. There are, as yet, no reasonable answers as to why, if it were not a copy of Orion's belt, the third pyramid should be so much smaller than the other two, unless, as in other aspects of pyramid building, the architects finally realized that the height of the finished pyramid was determined by the size of the base and the angle of the corners. It may be as simple as this – that they wanted to build the shape, but to make it smaller and easier to attain.

The evidence shows that during the lifetime of Cheops, for reasons now lost to us, there was a radical change in religious thinking. We do not know if Cheops embraced the new ideas, but it seems unlikely because his name is never found with the title 'Son of Re', as are the names of his sons.

It would seem that new ideas swept through Egypt during the Fourth Dynasty. Perhaps these were based on logic, on the observation that at night, the sun clearly went somewhere else until dawn. At any rate, old ideas were forgotten.

Few fundamental religious changes happen quietly and without opposition. Although Snofru ruled many thousands of years ago, from his viewpoint Egypt was already an ancient land with long-established traditions. The removal of the old pillars of belief and the advent of an entirely new system must have felt threatening. Moreover, the ascendancy of Heliopolis challenged the supremacy of the Egyptian King. The King ruled alone, and had contact with the gods. To accept new ideas which emanated from people outside the royal family seems unthinkable. It was akin to the Egyptian King declaring that he and his predecessors had been wrong for generations.

History has an uncanny way of repeating itself. So – could it be that the later religious movement of Akhenaten, who worshipped the god Aten, was simply a replay of the Fourth Dynasty revolution?

The naming of Cheops' sons after the new god, Re, is highly significant. Someone within the royal family went along with these new ideas. Since Cheops is not listed as a Son of Re, it was unlikely to be him, so all indications suggest it was one or more of his wives. Significantly, we do not know the name of one woman, the mother of Redjedef. We do know, though, that Henutsen, mother of Khaefre, or Chephren, named all her sons after Re and thus probably belonged to this new revolutionary group. So did this change start from within the heart of the royal family? And if it did, then once again, it points irrevocably to the influence of the royal women. They carried the bloodline of the throne, so the Kings owed their crowns to them. If the Kings also now owed their belief system, the very nature of royal life after death, to the influence of their wives, then our view of the Fourth Dynasty Kings changes slightly.

I stated above that we have no idea how incestuous inbreeding affected the Kings. Could it really be that, like the ineffectual Ptolemies, these Kings too were flawed, and that their lives were ruled by powerful women? Was Cheops' so distant and aloof because he wanted to preserve the illusion of his divinity, or because his ineffectuality made it vital to shelter him from public view?

Whatever the fundamental reason, the change in state religion in the middle of the Fourth Dynasty could only have happened smoothly if it came from the royal palace itself. If, as seems likely, this meant not Cheops but his wives and sons, then this is clearly another indication that trouble was brewing within the palace.

CHAPTER SIX

How to Build a Pyramid

C heops remains a shadowy character, just beyond the reach
of archaeology. The Westcar Papyrus recalls him as a
greedy monarch, trying to gain wisdom for himself which
would give him, so he thought, even more control over the
people and the world over which he ruled. At the same time, he
is depicted as suspicious, testing those brought before him and
totally lacking in any trust. Herodotus's view of him is of a
tyrannical despot. This is the image which remains in people's
minds even though it was transparently based on little other
than gossip and rumour. As we saw in the last chapter, indications could suggest either that he was ineffectual as a King and
sheltered from public view; or, more likely, that he deliberately
kept himself at a distance from the world in order to preserve
and enhance the divine image. This would have been especially
important if he wanted to inspire the country to pull together
on his behalf. As we have seen, although relatively few people
actually worked on the pyramid itself, most of the country
worked at full production levels to ensure that the building
programme could be maintained.

By definition, however, Herodotus has to be wrong when he
says that Cheops reduced the country to beggary through his
building. Cheops, by employing so many people in various
support departments on behalf of the state, gave them all

security, prosperity and a common purpose. Even though the workload was immense, people would have had little reason to complain. The alternative, that they worked alone to feed their families, was harder and far more precarious.

The successful completion of the Giza pyramids, whatever their theological purpose, proves that the country must have been undergoing times of reasonable prosperity and good floods. If the inundations had been poor, crops would have been low, men would have been poorly fed and there would have been trouble. Even allowing for the probability that pyramid workers would scarcely have gone on strike, by the same token a worker paid badly in poor or little food would not have been able to work effectively, the rate of progress would have slowed and the pyramid would not have been completed. If crops had been poor and Egypt had had to import to make up for local deficiencies, then we would have more records of international trade. Where such records exist, they show the usual image of Egypt as the casual exploiter of neighbouring countries' mineral assets. There is no record of active military intervention during Cheops' reign, nor, among the titles of his relatives in the *mastabas* around his pyramid, do we see many titles associated with a large army. Yet from excavations we have evidence of enormous bakeries, fisheries and butchers, all running at full speed and capable of feeding a massive enterprise like pyramid building. It is interesting to realize that for every support worker employed in producing goods for the builder, there was another family to feed – the support worker's. To support one man working on the face of the pyramid may add four, five or more others to the 'payroll'. This was not a cheap scheme to run, and demonstrates beyond a doubt that the administration and production levels of Egypt at this time were at their most effective.

The image that results, then, is of peaceful prosperity on a single task, the completion of the pyramids. It appears in the midst of all this that Cheops as an individual scarcely existed. He became the royal cipher around which the daily world of work centred. He would not need to be visible as a man to inspire the work on the plateau.

The continual, permanent pyramid-building industry meant that pyramids were not, as has been previously supposed, designed and built with a particular King in mind. It was not a case of a King being crowned and then a pyramid being designed and built for him. The work of Meidum and Dahshur shows that pyramids were rising in different places at different stages of completion, and gangs being moved from one site to another as the workload changed. This being the case, if three pyramids were in various stages of completion at any one time (and this seems to be the rate, judging from Dahshur and Giza), and allowing 20 years to complete each one (we have no other guidelines than this), then there would have been a pyramid ready for occupation every six or seven years. This means that even short-lived Kings would have a burial place almost ready when they died. This is the only way such a system could possibly function.

The opposite face of this, in the case of Snofru, was that he lived so long that he had a choice of burial site. It seems that Meidum was never occupied. It was probably too far away from the capital, in any case. It also seems that the Northern Pyramid of Dahshur was complete in time for his death and burial, thus also leaving the Bent Pyramid empty. Undoubtedly, if his successor, Cheops, had also been short-lived, he may have been buried in one of the empty ones. But the choice of Giza as a brand-new site, with designs for the largest and finest pyramids ever built, totally eclipsed the earlier ones. And fortunately, Cheops, even though an elderly man at the time of his coronation, survived for long enough to see the first of the Giza pyramids completed.

Now we have examined who built the pyramids and why, we must focus on the biggest problem of all – how exactly were they built? Did it take superhuman powers? Even extraterres-trial assistance?

As always in archaeology, the truth is far more prosaic. There have been many theories, but none of them seem to fit. Yet the answer, as always in these cases, is remarkably straightforward. Like most simple explanations, it is staring everyone in the face, although no one has yet understood it.

We have been looking at pyramids inside out.

Herodotus's levers

The method employed was to build it in steps or, as some people call them, tiers or terraces. When the base was complete, the blocks for the first tier above it were lifted from ground level by contrivances made of short timbers. On this first tier there was another which raised the blocks a stage higher still, and then yet another which raised the blocks even higher. Each tier or storey had its own set of levers – or it may be that they used the same one, which, being portable, they shifted up from stage to stage as soon as its load was dropped into place. Both methods are mentioned so I give them both here.

Once again, Herodotus makes it clear that the information he was recording was that which was told to him. Remember, at least 2000 years had passed between the building of the Great Pyramid and Herodotus's visit, and this in a country where history was of no interest whatever. There is no chance that accurate information was passed down for Herodotus's benefit. We have seen that pyramid building was a highly skilled and developed industry which did not spread beyond the Nile Valley at the time that pyramids were being built. Since pyra-mids were admired and regarded as things of wonder, one needs to ask why no other neighbouring country ever copied the Egyptians. It would seem logical that the knowledge the Egyptians had won through trial and error and bitter experi-ence would not be passed to others simply for the asking. We have also found that the architects and builders, through review and analysis, subtly improved their work at every stage of development. If the knowledge they developed did not pass at that time to neighbouring countries, then what chance would there be of such privileged information being passed casually after 2000 years to a passing foreigner on holiday in Egypt?

Today, many people accept Herodotus's account as basically true and then try to work out what exactly he was talking about. What were these 'contrivances', for example? But perhaps we should, instead, be wondering whether they existed at all. It is evident that when Herodotus was there, before the arrival of Alexander the Great and Egypt's absorption into the classical world, many people were still fascinated by how the pyramids had been built. Herodotus's guide passed on speculations about the techniques involved. It is also evident, since he speaks of 'both methods', that no one at the time really had any clear idea of how it was done and that they were trying to explain the method from their own viewpoint. Thus, even from the simple basis of analysing what Herodotus said, we can see it was based on pure speculation and no knowledge.

The main problem that everyone in the 4th century BCE was trying to work out, according to Herodotus, was how the stones got from the ground and on to the pyramid. There was no discussion, for instance, about difficulties posed by the shape of the pyramid itself.

The shape of a pyramid is totally predictable. If you want to get from the floor towards the sky, then there are few ways of doing it. If you are working with cuboid blocks, then it is easier to start with a square or rectangle than with a circle at the base. As you go upwards, you have only two choices – to continue straight up, or to canter the walls inwards. If you continue straight, you get a tower. This not only uses an extravagant amount of stone, it also makes lifting the stones higher more difficult, because you have to lift them vertically at some point. If you canter the levels inwards, you end up with a pyramid. All that a pyramid proves is that, for some reason, the Egyptians desired above all to create a form which could reach as high as possible into the sky.

The pyramid, therefore, is not a deliberate design concept pioneered by the ancient Egyptians. It did not inspire the pyramid form of South America, despite a longing to prove a link there. The last Egyptian pyramid was built in the Twelfth Dynasty around 1800 BCE; the South American pyramids belong to the current era, a gap of at least three thousand years. It is simple. Mathematically, a pyramid is the most logical and easiest method of using square blocks to get as high off the ground as you can, bearing in mind that the top half of a pyramid contains only an eighth of the total stone.

The problem, then, is not the shape but the method of raising the stones. Herodotus mentions two methods: ramps and levers. Surprisingly, when he mentions ramps, he explains that they were used to drag the stone on to the site rather than to take them up on to the pyramid, like a causeway. A stretch of stone was completely levelled, running from the *re-esh*, the man-made harbour, up to the site where the pyramid was to be built. He does not suggest they were used to carry stone up on to the pyramid. Yet today, ramp theories dominate the field of stone raising in Egypt. Speculation always centres on the shape, number, direction, size and slope of the ramps, rather than whether they actually existed.

Mark Lehner has identified a ramp like the ones Herodotus speaks of in the area of the workmen's settlement. It had a mud-brick base, over which a thin, compressed layer of smooth river mud was laid. Into this, narrow slats of wood were set at intervals, like railway sleepers. To move stones, water was trickled on to the ramp, liquefying the mud and making the slats slippery. An image which seems to confirm this was shown on a carved relief in Deir el Bersheh in the tomb of Djehutihotep. It shows a colossal statue being dragged into position by men pulling on ropes, with the statue seated on a flat-bottomed sledge. On the front of the sledge, a man is shown pouring out a liquid on to the floor under the sledge. This was previously thought to be milk. Milk would certainly be a superb lubricant, since the globules of fat floating in the liquid would be evenly distributed under the sledge.

A ramp of Lehner's design was re-created in the *Secrets of Lost Empires* television series, which I have mentioned elsewhere, when a team backed by NOVA attempted to build a miniature pyramid at Giza as an attempt to re-create the old methods. The ramp had water poured on it and was found to be extremely effective, making the blocks relatively easy to move and to manoeuvre.

But Herodotus does not specifically mention that ramps were used to build the pyramid itself. Instead, he states clearly that levers were used, since he presumed that the ancient Egyptians did not have pulleys. In one of my previous books, *Exploring the World of the Pharaohs*, I showed images of pulleys used in the rigging of the earliest ships. From these it is self-evident that the ancient Egyptians knew the basic principle of a pulley, which was to divert the angle of the pull rope.

There seem, then, to be two basic ideas. Either ramps were added to the pyramid up which the stones were dragged, or the stones were lifted from one tier to the next. All that remains is to decide which method was used, and how. Miroslav Verner has recently compromised by suggesting that they used both together, and that there was no one method of lifting the stones, but that the Egyptians used anything they could get their hands on at the time. Although attractive, this idea seems too confusing and chaotic.

In experiments on the NOVA pyramid carried out by Lehner, he tried to replicate the use of levers to raise stones from one level to the next. It was a failure. It was not only an extremely slow process, but an exceptionally dangerous one as well. If the piles up which the stone was slowly levered collapsed, the stone would easily tumble down. It was a slow and frustrating task even when carried out almost at ground level. To repeat this 200 or 300 feet up the side of a pyramid would be nothing short of suicidal: the feet would have had little to stand on on the previous level, and it would be crazy to lean backwards to gain more leverage, as the builders would fall off the side of the pyramid.

So can archaeology help to solve the problem? The remains of wooden 'rockers' have been found at the pyramid sites. These are sledge-like platforms with curved bottoms. If the rocker was lowered on to one side, a stone could be slid on to it. If it was then tipped the other direction, the stone could be slid into another place. This would effectively move the stone only about 2 feet, scarcely worth either the technology or the effort. A stone on such a rocker could, it is true, be moved from one place to another and then tipped to offload it. However this would be hard to balance during the moving process as well as extremely wearing on the small amount of wood under the rocker which touched the ground at any point: it would quickly grind it flat under the weight of the stone. So although these must have been used, it would not be for lifting the stones into place from one level to another.

The ramp theories

Some people have interpreted Herodotus's ramps and levers in a different way. It has long been suggested that the ramps led up the side of the pyramid in some way, so that the stone was brought up to the platform-like top of the partly built pyramid, and that levers were used to 'jolly' it along into place.

This theory is supported by the Rhind Papyrus in the British Museum, one section of which gives methods for calculating the amount of bricks needed to build a ramp with a slope of 1 in 8. By taking various measurements and following a prescribed series of calculations, answers would be given in bricks needed, or the number of men required to move them – a very practical, if extraordinarily complex, series of arithmetical sums.

Yet there are no remains of tall ramps to give us clues as to how they would be placed against the pyramid.

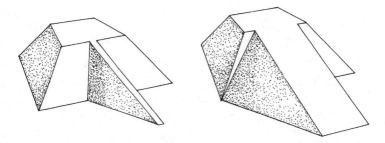

Using straight ramps: left, narrow and right, broad

The most obvious choice, using the least amount of material and the easiest design up which to move stones, would be a straight ramp. Lehner has found the remains of such a ramp against the south side of the Great Pyramid. However, as the levels rise, maintaining a 1 in 8 slope means that the length of the ramp, and the whole surface, would have to be increased.

Lengthening the ramp while still maintaining the angle of rise would mean adding large quantities of material

The smallest increase at each level would thus use vast amounts of materials as the full length of the existing ramp has to be raised. To maintain the 1 in 8 slope to reach the maximum height of 481 feet would result in a ramp so long that it would have to reach the other side of the Nile from the plateau!

This clearly would not work. Dieter Arnold suggested that the straight ramp would be formed straight over the working surface of the pyramid, so that eventually the upper part would form part of the core of the pyramid.

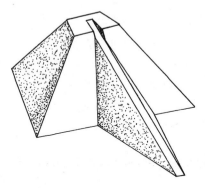

An integrated ramp, according to Arnold, would cut into the core of the pyramid

This would only shorten the run of the ramp by a few feet however – not enough materially to change its length, especially at the top.

A much favoured design is a winding ramp. This would be fitted to the sides of the pyramid and curl up steadily around it.

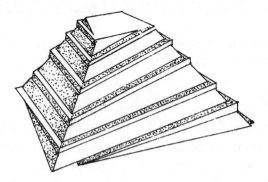

A single winding ramp would start from just one corner of the pyramid

Other suggestions include a complex series of ramps starting from each corner and each making its own way up to the top.

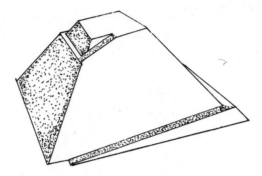

An alternative winding ramp would start from just one corner of the pyramid

Alternatively, the ramps might have zigzagged back and forth along one wall of the pyramid.

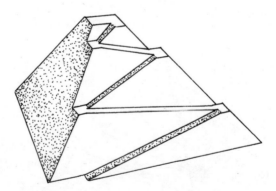

A zigzag ramp winding up one single face

There is one basic problem with them all. None of them would work!

The problems with ramps

The pyramid form seems a simple one – a square base with four inclined faces rising to a peak, which stands exactly above the centrepoint of the base.

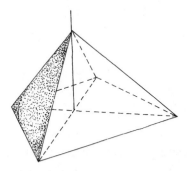

The apex must be over the centre of the base or the pyramid will lean

But this is harder to achieve than it may seem at first glance. As we have already observed, the eventual height of the pyramid is decided by two factors: the size of the base and the angle of the sides.

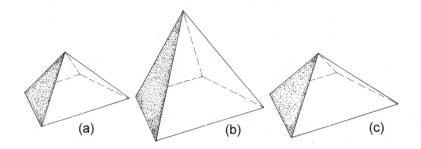

The height of the pyramid is determined by (a) the size of the base and (b) and (c) the angle of the base

However, during the building process, any number of things

might change the finished result. For example, every layer of stones added must precisely line up with the corner of the previous layer. If there was any twist in the layers, the corners of the pyramid would be irregular.

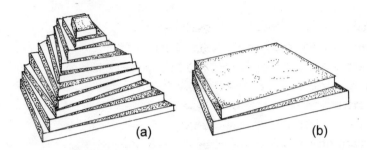

(a) (b)

If the layers are not exactly square to each other (b) then the resulting pyramid will not have straight corners

If there was even the slightest difference in the four angles of the corners at the base, the apex would not be over the centre of the base and the pyramid would lean to one side.

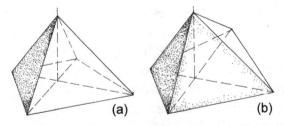

(a) (b)

If the apex is not in the centre of the pyramid, it will appear to lean (a); while if the base is not square, the whole building will not align (b)

If the angles of the faces were not maintained exactly as the pyramid rose, the sides would 'bag' out, or sink into concavity.

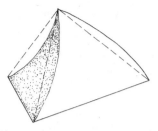

The sides must be absolutely flat, not concave or convex

In order to establish that the corner angle was rising up perfectly straight and the faces were flat, only one method would work: the stonemason had to be able to 'sight' the outside constantly. Ramps wrapped around the pyramid, no matter in what direction they moved, would remove this essential view. No matter how superb the architect or the mason was, the effect after the ramps were removed could be disastrous.

And there is, in any case, a way to prove that ramps could never have been used at all.

Let us return to the mathematics we examined in Chapter 4. In this, we calculated that to use 2.5 million stones in 20 years, 125,000 stones needed to be put into position each year. We also saw that the stones needed for the first two levels were one entire year's quota of stones. In the second year, another two levels would be completed and a start made on the next layer. As the pyramid rose, the number of levels required to be completed would slowly increase. In the top half of the pyramid, these layers would rise up extremely rapidly.

The average stone, so it is said, is a 3-foot cube weighing around 2.5 tons. To move such a stone on a sledge would thus need a ramp 6 feet wide in order to get the sledge around the corners of the pyramid. Given that the sledge also had to be pulled and manoeuvred by a gang of men (or even a draught animal, as some have suggested), then to turn a corner safely without fear of the sledge, stone and pullers falling off, 6 feet would be barely adequate.

In fact, it is not adequate at all. Working on the premise of a curved or zigzag ramp – it makes no difference – we can see that the ramp would have to be twice the basic width of 6 feet. Why? It's the only way empty sledges and pullers could make their way back down alongside the full sledges. To build a ramp 12 feet wide against a slope of 50° 51′ 40″ would mean it would have to be 9 feet 9 inches high against the side of the pyramid wall. The external edge of the ramp would also have to be reinforced to take the weight and the constant traffic at the edge, since the edge would have to be in constant use and under great weights applied to it. Once again, working 200 or 300 feet up a pyramid is a different matter from working at ground level. Although to the ancient Egyptians, Nubians were to an extent a replaceable resource, these were trained men, and their loss would be hard. The proved provision of a medical service which was capable of setting broken bones easily or, in one case, amputating part of a limb, suggests that the Egyptians valued their men highly, and an accidental death would have been upsetting to all on the site.

At the foot of the pyramid, ramps would not be needed for several years as the levels rose up so slowly. After three years, the pyramid would still have only six complete layers, or be 18 feet high, and it's easier to drag a stone up on a rope than to go to the time and trouble of getting the men and materials to build a ramp. But further up the pyramid, to build a ramp 12 feet wide to reach a new level with a reinforced edge, while adjusting it to maintain the 1 in 8 slope, would take weeks, since the material had to be brought up from below. The entire ramp would have to be filled with ramp-men carrying mud-bricks and mud mortar, stones and wood, while the builders sat at the bottom and waited. As each level grew smaller, so fewer men could actually work on it. The time wasted by them having to wait for the ramp-men to finish would be more than the time needed to complete a level of stone.

In addition, as the size of the pyramid diminished towards

the apex, building a ramp 12 feet wide at a 1 in 8 slope over increasingly shorter distances on the sides would mean that upper layers of ramps would actually have to be built across part of the lower spiral of ramp, which would then narrow the ramps and make them unfit for their purpose.

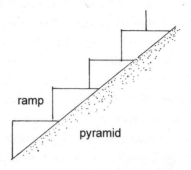

Towards the top of the pyramid, a winding ramp would start to encroach on the lower levels, thus narrowing the space for moving stone

No matter how you examine the situation and no matter what the shape of the ramp, they simply look unworkable. This is regardless of the fact that a 12-foot ramp would have extended the sides of the pyramid from 756 to 780 feet (with a ramp at each side). This would mean a 3 per cent increase in the sides at the base, which would continue to increase as the pyramid rose. Towards the top, as the sides of the face reduced to 24 feet, it would make a 100 per cent increase. This would result overall in a 10 per cent increase in the total amount of material needed to complete the pyramid. The 10 per cent extra material within these ramps would later have to be dismantled and the material disposed of somewhere off the site. This is a vast quantity of material and work to have to organize after the pyramid is completed.

It could never have worked.

In the temple of Karnak, which was the major state temple in the New Kingdom, behind the southern front pylon (gateway) are the remains of mud-brick edifices which are generally stated to be the remains of such a ramp. In fact, they are unlikely to be any such thing, but let us for the moment assume that they are. The temple was the home of the great god Amun, visited daily either by the King or by his appointed representative. It functioned daily for at least 1000 years and probably for much longer. If workmen could not be bothered to remove ramps behind a pylon in such a place, given that they would be seen every day by the King himself, then where would be the incentive to dispose of ramps around 100 pyramids which stand out in the desert and were occupied only by the dead body of an ancient King? These external ramps would totally hide the shape of the pyramid beneath. Why not leave them in place as an architectural item? And can we really suppose that every pyramid, even those not completed, would systematically have had these huge ramps demolished, without leaving even a single small heap of rubbish somewhere nearby?

It makes no sense whatever. There has to be another explanation.

The facing stones

The Giza pyramids were built with a soft core of limestone blocks, but were faced with compact, hard limestone brought from across the river in Tura. These facing stones, unlike the locally quarried soft stone, took longer to cut and work and were substantially larger than the core-blocks, but once faced, maintained a brilliant white sheen that would have been almost blinding under the hot sun.

Herodotus mentions them in his account.

The finishing off of the pyramid was begun at the top and worked downwards, ending with the lowest parts near the ground.

The Tura coating was formed with stones several times the size of the core blocks. Those which remain today, at ground level, measure more than 6 feet along the upper edge and, accounting for the finished slope, some 7½ feet along the underneath level. Despite Herodotus, these had to be put into place from the bottom upwards. Starting at the top would mean inserting stone 7½ feet long above one's head.

So the stones were put into place from the bottom upwards, and according to Herodotus's account, were levelled from the top downwards, their faces chiselled to form a flat, shining surface. But again, this would not have worked. To level the face from the top downwards gave the masons no points of reference, no line of sight, except upwards, on stones already faced. Rubbing or chiselling the stones in order to make them align accurately both above and below, and from side to side, would be possible only from the bottom upwards, not from the top downwards. The stonemason needed to be able to 'sight' the line of the slope and the corners. If the stones are first laid to the top and then smoothed downwards, the mason can only predict the slope below him; and the line achieved above can never be amended if it twists, bellies or sinks, as it is then smooth. If the facing stones are laid from the bottom upwards, and smoothed as they are placed, then the mason can follow the slope using line of sight and can lower down on ropes to make

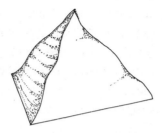

The facing stones must be level and flat, or the pyramid will be twisted and distorted

amendments. So how exactly were they finished?

The facing stones actually define the finished shape of the pyramid. They mark the all-important diagonal edges. If this line were out of true, the pyramid would appear twisted.

They also must be true and flat from one level to the next or the faces of the pyramid would bulge. In fact, the angle of the rise, at the bottom corners, is defined entirely by the cutting of the facing stones.

Looking at pyramids the right way out

Although we know of 100 pyramids in Egypt, there are few real pyramids left today. This may sound startling, but it is true. A pyramid is made of two elements: the facing stones, which are fitted to each other so exactly that there is not room to slip a piece of paper between them, and which defined the completed pyramid shape; and the core, which is largely rubble infill. All we have left is the core.

So what is left to us at Giza is therefore not a pyramid at all, but just the rubble infill which was left behind after the facing stones were stolen. Only in the top section of the pyramid occupied by Chephren, and the coating of the Bent Pyramid at Dahshur, can we see part of a true pyramid as it was designed.

This is far clearer to understand with later pyramids. The pyramids of the Fifth and Sixth Dynasties at Saqqara were built in a more hasty and shoddy manner. The core was not stone, as at Giza, Dahshur and Abusir, but sand and rubble, whatever loose material came easily to hand. The facing stones of these pyramids were removed by robbers, presumably to be reused in later buildings. This has left little more than sand dunes which are barely recognizable as pyramids at all (see photo).

The problem is this. If you look at the remains of the Pyramid of Unas, for example, you would need to be told that it was a pyramid at all. The outer face is gone.

Let us consider how this pyramid was built. You would not

even start to consider the manner in which men tried to raise stones up the outside of a pile of sand. It is quite obvious that the sand could never have been placed there first. Instead, the external facing had to be placed into position first and afterwards the infill was poured in behind it, by men carrying the sand up in baskets.

The sand formed the core only, and was substantial enough to maintain the weight of the finished building. It served only to ensure that the outer face would not collapse inwards. Once the facing stones were removed, the soft sand core then slurried downwards to form a low dune.

Think about it: it is not possible to suggest that the sand was placed there first, that stones were dragged up it, and that the facing stones were then added last. This notion is simply inside out. Why, then, do we look at the infill of the Giza pyramids and try to work out how stones would have been carried up them?

It is true that today, we see steps formed by the core-blocks in the pyramids of Giza. But this is accidental, left purely because the Giza pyramid builders decided to infill the core with stone and not with sand. If they had been built like the Fifth Dynasty Pyramid of Unas, all that would be left today would be the biggest sandcastle in the world! With the Unas pyramid, the infill collapsed because it was soft; at Giza the infill stood firm because it was of stone. But just as the sand of Unas is not the pyramid, what remains of the Great Pyramid is nothing other than infill.

We know that pyramid-building technology advanced stage by stage. There is no evidence anywhere of a sudden, radical change in method. We need to understand the method used to build all pyramids, not just the Great Pyramid. Whatever method was used for the smallest is likely also to have been used for the largest.

When the architects and designers of the Fifth Dynasty Saqqara pyramids reviewed the pyramids built in the Fourth

Dynasty at Giza, they would first have to identify the greatest problems which they had faced in order to try to improve things. Their major aim was to build the best building they could in the least time, with the fewest men and minimal problems. The improvements they might consider may be structural, such as checking the solidity of the base; mathematical, such as changing the angle at the base and increasing or decreasing the finished height; organizational, such as changing the location of food, drink or sleeping provision; health, such as improving medical support systems; or design, such as changing the materials. They would have to review the process at every stage to do this – to check the qualities of stone they had to quarry and move; the men and infrastructure it took to lift and place these stones; and the time it then took between the quarry and the pyramid. It seems that the building of the Giza pyramids must have cost a great deal in terms of time and manpower. How, then, to improve this? Since the core would never be seen, then why go to the inordinate trouble of using good limestone at all? Why not simply use the sand from the desert; it would be easier, lighter, faster, less labour intensive and yet just as effective?

Until, of course, the facing stones are stolen! Although such foresight would be unlikely to be a factor in their planning.

Try, if you can, to imagine the Great Pyramid as it was during the process of being built. If, during the reign of Cheops, you had lived in the nearby workmen's village, you would have looked up and seen not a pyramid as we do, nor a honey-gold stone building which dominated the sky, but a platform, faced all around with brilliant white stone. The men doing the building would be scurrying around the top of the platform not up and down the sides. The principal aim was to place and shape the facing stones. What was put behind them could be anything you liked. There would never have been any steps visible, except for the crude facing stones until they were smoothed. The steps are only in the rubble infill.

Today, we look at the inside, but they would have seen only the outside, and it is this which we must try to encompass in our ideas of how the pyramids were built.

If you examine any one section of the face of the Great Pyramid today, you will observe several things (see photo). The stones, for a start, are by no means all 3-foot cubes, but are of irregular size and shape. Although some have been cut, the cutting is crude. There are many smaller pieces pushed into spaces to level them and fill in the gaps. These small stones are not modern but have been there since the pyramid was built. Many of the stones are bigger, longer, or shorter than others. You should also note that, in defiance of commonly held beliefs, there are indeed gaps between the stones – huge, irregular gaps and big holes, in fact. Again, this is logical. This was never intended to be seen. The facing stones and the granites which lined the inner passages and chambers, and which would have been seen, were finished in a different way.

The Egyptians would never have expected the crude stone infill to be seen any more than the Fifth Dynasty builders would have imagined that we would be left with a sand dune. They would have believed without question that the white facing that was the pyramid could never be destroyed. They were not to know that, over the process of thousands of years, all varieties of peoples would come and use the pyramids as ready-cut quarries.

With this knowledge, we can now examine, stage by stage, how any pyramid would have been built, not just the Giza pyramids of the Fourth Dynasty.

The process of building

Laying out the site
After the debacle of the Dahshur pyramid, which was built on to a bed of sand and so developed cracks, the first aim was to choose a solid stone base. Another priority, it would seem, was

189

to choose a place which was naturally higher than surrounding land, so the finished buildings would be looked up to. The site had to be close enough to the river to allow the easy arrival of stone from Tura and Aswan. It had to be close to the capital, where the royal family, who supervised the work, all lived. Once you consider the requirements, it can be seen that Giza was absolutely ideal in every respect.

Sonar tests carried out within the Great Pyramid have shown that the first level of stone was not laid on a pre-flattened surface but on a natural mound of rock. The natural peak of the plateau was never levelled but was left as it was. There is a logic to this: after all, why spend time cutting stone away only to replace it immediately?

Leaving the mound in place caused problems, for this means that the base on which the pyramid was to be built was neither flat nor level. Ropes could not be used to measure lengths, as the ground was not flat. The most important parts of a pyramid to get accurate are all at the base. The bottom level of stones needed to be truly flat, not just on the surface of the plateau, which may have been inclined in one direction.

This was easily achieved by building a low wall all around the area, within which the base of the pyramid would be laid. This was then flooded with water. Into the water, across the full area, vertical wooden stakes were placed. The water-line was then accurately marked on each. This served as a gigantic three-dimensional spirit-level. Once the stakes had all been marked, the wall was breached, the water drained away, and finally the wall was removed.

Some colleagues have suggested that the water-level could be marked on the wall itself. This would not work. To drag stones on to the site and ensure they were level would mean crossing the wall – a big impediment. It was vital that the wall, once the level had been taken, was fully removed. In addition, over a base 756 feet square, it was also absolutely vital that the level was maintained all over and not just around the outside.

Once again, a water-level on the inner face of a wall would only give you a perimeter level, not an overall level.

The marks on the stakes could then be joined by light ropes or string as needed. This would create a visible web. The lines could then be removed as stones were placed into position, and then retied as stones for the base were dragged into position. The lowest level of stone had to be fitted exactly to this level to be certain of an entirely flat base.

Astronomical observations probably made possible the true north–south positioning of the square base. Since there was then so little ground light, the stars would shine clearly. The Egyptians excelled at observing the heavens, and thus would be able to pick out certain stars and groups of stars. Due to the movement of the earth, during any night the stars would appear to wheel about the heaven, from horizon to horizon. If a wall was built, in any direction, and a vertical stake was placed several feet away, the observer could place an eye against the stake and wait for the appearance of any one star over the surface of the wall. The exact position of the rising star on the wall would then be marked. As the hours passed, the observer would wait and watch until that same star sank behind the wall again, and once more the position would be marked. Finding the central point between the two marks on the wall, a string would be run from here to the vertical post. This marks true north–south.

Then the corners of the pyramid would need to be fixed.

First, posts would be fixed firmly into the ground at each end of the north–south line. If a rope is attached to each post in turn, then an arc can be drawn along the ground. The two arcs from the posts will cut each other at two points. If these two points are also joined across by a marking line, this will be absolute east–west and will form exact right angles with the north–south line.

These two lines marked the central line from the middle of each face of the pyramid. The four posts which marked the ends of the lines would then all have two ropes attached to

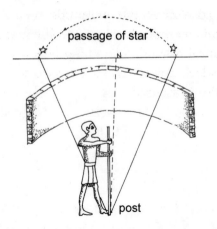

Establishing north–south using a rod, a wall and the movement of the stars at night

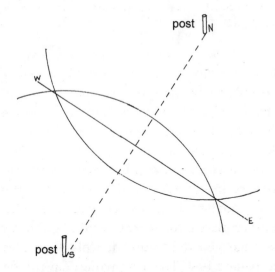

With north–south established, ropes create arcs which work east–west where they intersect

them. These would be extended sideways until they met at a corner. By checking the angle of these joinings carefully with a set-square (examples survive as part of carpenters' sets of tools), the four corners of the pyramids would be laid out precisely. Since this method does not involve measuring across the top of the central mound, something which would alter the lengths if diagonals were used, then the accuracy of the lengths of the sides would be assured.

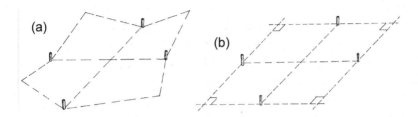

With the axes laid out, the angles of the base must be created at rightangles. If they are not exact, the result will be irregular (a); if correct, there is no need to measure diagonals, as all the sides will be straight and equal

The first layer of stones would then need to be laid. Only this one layer was vital to the success of the whole enterprise. This would be established first using core stones. They would need to be cut to the exact size of the base they had to cover. The core blocks would be dragged up the causeway and laid into position, taking note at every point of the exact heights marked on the water-markers. In some places, the stones needed would be thin or even may not have been needed at all, where the ground ran high. In other places, the stones would be far in excess of the 3-foot average generally quoted. Only the outer ring of stones would be laid first. This ring would have to be worked by stonemasons to get it absolutely accurate. Inside this ring, core blocks would be tumbled without any care or attention to achieving good bonds between them while observing the flat level. This section, after all, would never be seen, and as long as the stone was solid enough to stand more stones on top for the next level, there would be little problem.

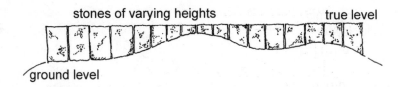

Establishing a true first level on an uneven base simply meant varying the thickness of stones used

Architects, meanwhile, would have had to work out the position within this square where the tunnel for the descending passage to the lower chamber would be cut. The mathematics for this would be extraordinarily complex to ensure that the angle was exact and the lengths accurate. However, as this had been done on previous pyramids, the blueprint to achieve this presumably already existed. The stone removed from this tunnelling would simply be piled into the pyramid base; any rubble would work for the core. The descending passage had to be extremely accurately measured, for once the rubble of the first level of the pyramid rose around it, the angle would have to be followed exactly up through the levels of rising stone to the outside face. Panels of relatively thin granite from Aswan were used to line the passage, each made with tenons at the back to lock into holes in the limestone and keep them in place. The joints of these were carefully rubbed to ensure accurate joins and a neat face.

Under the ground in the lower chamber, stonemasons lying on their bellies used blocks of volcanic stone to chip away the softer limestone bedrock. The din and the dust must have been indescribable, the pounding creating a constant fine limestone dust which filled the air, the eyes, the nostrils and the mouth.

Outside, once the outer level had been finally established, the first level of facing stones would be added. These were, remember, the actual pyramid, and these too would have to follow that first line of outer core stones. To ensure a good finish, the

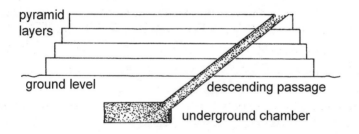

The descending passage had to be cut in correct alignment through layers of stone as they rose

ground outside the core blocks already laid would now have to be adjusted to allow for exact 3-foot facing stones to be placed. In some places, where the core blocks were thick, base stones would have to be added outside upon which the facing stones were placed. In other places, where the core blocks were thin or non-existent, they would have to cut out stone to a depth of 3 feet. Once this had been done, and the ground beyond the core stones was exactly 3 feet all the way around, the facing stones would be added.

The limestone, although compact, was still chalky and easy to work. Once the facing stones were lying next to each other on the ground, a long bladed copper 'saw' would be inserted between the two blocks. This was more akin to a long palette knife; one was found in a First Dynasty tomb at Abydos, and they are pictured in reliefs, paintings and tomb models. This would quickly grind away any unevenness until the finished joint was perfect.

Once these were all in place, then skilled stonemasons would lie full length along the tops of the stones and begin to dress the faces and corners. The angle at which they dressed these stones would be the final angle of the pyramid corners. Accuracy was vital. This stage could not be rushed. It was important to establish an absolutely flat surface across the tops of the facing stones. This would allow further levels to be cut to exact sizes

195

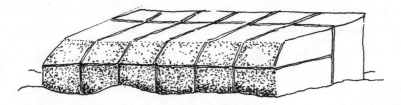

The first layers of facing stones precisely mark the angle at which the pyramid wil rise; they were finely ground to sit exactly next to each other

so that the pyramid would rise slowly and accurately. The level of these stones, the accuracy of their shape and their joints, the fineness of their face – all these would guarantee that the rest of the pyramid would rise exactly as planned, so long as, on every level, the stonemason, by lying on the surface of the facing-stones, could get an accurate line of sight below him.

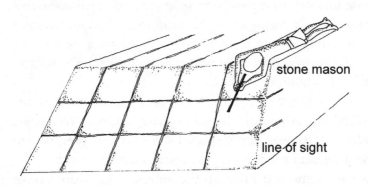

A stone mason lay on the top layers of facing stones to align the sides and corners exactly, to ensure all was flat and true

Quarrying

The majority of the stones were quarried on the edge of the Giza plateau itself. This had one big advantage: they would not have to be moved far. This is undoubtedly where Herodotus's and

Lehner's ramps came in. Long gentle ramps, rising from the lower ground of the quarries on to the causeway, would allow the stones to be moved quickly into place at the foot of the pyramid.

The proximity of the huge workmen's village meant that the builders would be on site as the sun rose. The whole area would ring from dawn's first light with the sound of hammers. These, made of either stone or, more rarely, of hardened copper, would be used to strike sharp flint or stone wedges into lines across the rock surface. One swift blow of the hammer along the line of wedges, and the stone would shear away.

If you closely examine any face of the pyramid (see photo), you will observe that the rock varies from area to area. In some places, the stone is firm and barely weathered; in others it is badly pitted, its face so apparently frail it looks as delicate as a cobweb.

The quarries would have been worked one area at a time. As the stone was dragged up and used, whole areas of the pyramids were formed from panels of rock which were reassembled in the same order into the core. The stones were wildly different in size, their edges crudely cut. Where a large gap appeared or a stone wobbled, the space was filled in with potsherds, rubble, piles of sand, whatever came to hand.

Over on the east bank, stone from Tura was cut with much greater accuracy. Although the same strike and split technique was undoubtedly used, the resultant stone would then have to be worked to form exactly proportioned rectangular cubes.

In Aswan, some 500 miles to the south, stone would have been stockpiled, probably for months, awaiting the right moment to be shipped. The fine granites were only used to face the areas which could be seen, the insides of chambers and passages. Yet the stones were huge. The ceiling beams for the King's chamber, for instance, each weighed around 80 tons.

How did they cut this granite? Although dolerite pounders (a hard volcanic stone, harder than granite) are found around the sites, they were undoubtedly not used in the early stages of extraction as they would have caused chips to break away almost at random.

There are two main quarries in Aswan. The northern quarry, open today to tourists, was worked until relatively recent times: modern workings are often pointed out to groups as being ancient. The quarry is dominated by a huge abandoned obelisk, undoubtedly cut in the reign of Ramesses II on account of its uncommonly massive size. The obelisk was left unfinished, as it cracked during extraction.

The southern quarry is far more informative. Although this is still a working quarry and thus is generally closed to visitors, I have been able to explore the site. Unlike the northern quarry, this one has areas of ancient workings which have simply been abandoned. Perhaps the quality of stone in one patch became inferior, so the quarriers moved on. As a result, whole areas have remained untouched since ancient times. There are several abandoned pieces in this quarry also. In one part stands an ancient sarcophagus, its edges smoothed and yet still part of the granite bed from which it was formed, never split away. In another part lies a statue in the form of Osiris, part-formed, staring at the sky and, like the sarcophagus, still part of the granite seam from which it was being formed (see photo). These two pieces, plus the obelisk in the northern quarry and other workings in both, all show small rectangular, concave areas on the surfaces of the stone which can only have been formed by rubbing or abrading the surface. It is clear that striking the stone would have had little effect. The workers seem to have rubbed the stone slowly, probably using handfuls of sand mixed with a little water to form an abrasive paste. It was slow and tedious work, but seems to have been effective. Granite working was a highly skilled job and went on year round, with stones being stockpiled for future use.

From the same granite quarry, a separate area was being worked for Cheops to produce his sarcophagus – that most precious object which the Egyptians called the 'Lord of Life'.

The granite used for this was the most prized stone of all, as it was used for the most precious object. The work was done by the finest craftsmen using their eye and years of experience. Despite this, as W.M.F. Petrie later wryly observed, there were more errors in the measurements of the sarcophagus than in the sides of the pyramid itself!

Moving stone

As many museum keepers have found to their cost, moving huge stones is not easy. If you were to remove Egyptian statues and other pieces out of a gallery and into a native Egyptian context – in a temple or a pyramid complex, for instance – they would look small and dreadfully insignificant compared to their massive surroundings. Yet to move these takes lots of planning and lots of heavy machinery. Often gallery floors have to be underpinned to allow them to take the weight of the pieces involved. If these pieces cause us trouble, then how, 4500 years ago, long before mechanical lifters existed, did ordinary men manage to move such massive stones?

From the start of the Old Kingdom, the moving of huge stones over vast distances became an Egyptian skill, and it still baffles us today. In 1815, Giovanni Belzoni, while attempting to move the head of a statue of Ramesses II from a temple on the west bank of Luxor for the British Museum, managed with great difficulty to drag it through column bases (he had to cut off pieces from their corners to get the head past), down the river bank (he used ropes and rollers) and finally to the gang-plank of the ship. Once the head reached this spot, however, the ship naturally upended and the prize was unceremoniously dumped into the Nile. Fishing it out and devising lifting frames to allow it to be placed in the centre of the deck took many more weeks of work.

Similarly, when trying in the 19th century to work out how to move a relatively small obelisk which had once stood in the temple of Heliopolis to London, the only solution was to encase it completely in cast-iron sheets, create a deck on one face, and launch it as the *MS Cleopatra*. In a storm off Biscay, the terrified crew, uncertain about the sailing characteristics of an ancient obelisk, abandoned ship. Luckily, the *Cleopatra* still floated and was reboarded later!

If moving stones causes us so much trouble, then how much more complex would it have been for the ancient Egyptians? Surprisingly, it may actually have been easier, since they were aware of the characteristics of the materials they were working with, knowledge and skills we have since lost.

One problem has long played on my mind, however. As I have noted, in the northern quarry at Aswan, an unfinished obelisk still lies in the trench from which it was slowly and painfully extracted. The obelisk lies approximately northwest/southeast. A short distance away from it, the land is flat and leads down to the fertile belt and the river. The Nile-side wall of the trench in which it lies is only about 3 feet thick. I want to know why. Why was it not removed altogether? This would have made it far easier for the workers to get access to the obelisk and remove it later.

To cut an obelisk, a trench had first to be cut down each long side. This meant that the stone workers sat, legs pulled up in front of them or else crouched on their knees, in the narrow trench on each side of the emerging obelisk, rubbing the face of the granite hour after hour. When the desired height was achieved – which was the width of one of the faces of the obelisk – they had to start burrowing underneath the obelisk from each side. This would have been a precarious job; and the measurements from each side had to be exact to ensure they would meet in the middle.

Yet they had also to be certain that they did not meet, but left a ridge or spine of rock for the obelisk to rest on. Leverage to either side would then crack the obelisk from this narrow ridge. It would also, however, mean that the obelisk would then tilt towards one side of the trench or the other. The abandoned obelisk weighed an estimated 1100 tons. Whichever way you look at it, once this weight of stone had tilted and come to rest against the side of a trench, not the finest tools or fingers could have been inserted between the obelisk and the wall. How, then, was the obelisk to be removed? If the side wall had been cut away first, the obelisk could have been rolled, with restraining ropes to control it, towards the river's edge. But left as it is, within a narrow trench on each side, then even if ropes were inserted first into holes pierced through the spine, the obelisk would have to be first lifted upwards and then moved sideways purely to get it over the wall. Again, why?

The power of ropes

The Egyptians used hemp ropes. Many actual examples have been found from ancient Egypt, as well as images within tombs of ropes being made. The diameter of the ropes varies, from small cords to great hawsers, 7 inches in diameter. Fragments of rope regularly turn up in excavations on every site, including Giza. The Royal Naval College at Dartmouth in Devon had more reason to understand the natural qualities of natural-fibre ropes than most organizations, since for centuries they were used on masted sailing ships to raise and lower sails.

One of the intrinsic qualities of all new natural-fibre ropes is that they shrink quickly. As they shrink they exert huge forces on anything to which they are tied. New ropes shrink the most and fastest, so in the Navy, as in other organizations, new ropes would have to be soaked for some time before use. Ropes that have been previously shrunk will still shrink, but to a lesser extent. If a fresh rope were used tied to the beams of a masted ship, then as the seawater wet them, the shrinking process would be so powerful that oak beams would snap like matchsticks. Today, with the use of man-made-fibre ropes, the problem is not so obvious and this quality has largely been forgotten.

In Egypt, both on the plateau of Giza and in the stone quarries of Aswan, large cylindrical holes have been bored into the surface of the rock. These, about 4 inches in diameter and 6 inches deep, were deliberately made and precisely cut in order to hold something. The holes, on average, are about 5 yards apart. On the Giza plateau they form a line eastwards from the base of the pyramid alongside the causeway (see photo). In Aswan, they are about the same distance apart, about 5 yards away from the obelisk in the northern quarry, and in a straight line.

Clearly they must have been meant for some kind of wooden posts, since this was the only material with such a diameter available during the Old Kingdom. But what were the poles for? Stadelmann suggested that they were used for the ceremonial tent, as shown in the reburial of Queen Hetepheres and, perhaps, shown in several illustrations. However, this seems unlikely. The posts found in the Hetepheres shaft – the shaft leading 100 feet below the Giza plateau to the burial chamber – which Reisner and others propose were used to support a tent were slender. The shaft also included limestone bases which had holes cut in them, and which matched the diameter of the poles. The poles on the 'bed canopy' (see Chapter 8) were supported on horizontal beams. The holes on the plateau, moreover, cover more than 43 yards; allowing for an approximate 5-yard spacing between poles, and with poles of 4-inch diameter, this would be a giant marquee rather than a tent. And why should anyone have wanted to erect a 'ceremonial tent' in a granite quarry where the same holes are also found?

If the posts struck into these holes were long, they could have been flagpoles. But again, why at a 5-yard distance from each other, and why in a quarry? If short, then with a 4-inch diameter they could only be designed to take weight – not the sort of thing you would use, for instance, to hold a rope fence.

In other words, they would be capstans. Capstans designed to have ropes tied to them. Ropes which would shrink if wet.

The Egyptians were always remarkable for finding solutions to problems which would cause them the least effort. To drag a piece of granite large enough to span the roof of the main chamber in the Great Pyramid, or an obelisk, would require several gangs of men. So we need to take a close look at both these gangs, and the granite.

Men, it is known, will pull at different rates – in fact, it would be impossible to find a number of gangs who, if pulling on a rope, would pull exerting exactly the same force each. Granite is not, as many people suggest, solid; under the microscope it is spongiform, with minute air spaces between the granules which form the rock. If a long piece of granite, whose thickness is less than its length, is dragged by a number of gangs, then inevitably the force each team exerts will be different, and the granite will twist slightly and then crack. It would take weeks, if not months, to extract a granite beam for a pyramid chamber or an obelisk from a quarry bed. To see it successfully extracted and then cracked the moment the dragging began would be disastrous. To drag a piece of granite without cracking it, the force exerted along each rope *must* be identical.

The only conceivable way this could be achieved would be to tie a new hemp rope securely around a capstan post at one end, and round the granite at the other, and then throw on a bucket of water. As the ropes shrink, they exert exactly the same pressure on the rock, and the rock would gracefully rise from its bed without a man in sight. Once the rate of shrinkage started to settle (and from the distance between the capstan holes, this would appear to be around 5 yards), new ropes would be tied to the next capstan along and the process repeated. This would mean that the teams could literally sit back and drink a beer in the shade while the stone moved itself – a truly delightful situation!

In the granite quarries, holes would be made to pierce the 'spine' base of the rock under the obelisk or beam at regular intervals. Ropes would be tied through these holes and around capstans, probably two or three ropes to a pole. This would spread the weight across a larger number of ropes. At a word, water would be poured on to the ropes and leverage on the side of the obelisk would crack it free. Since the shrinkage is almost immediate, the obelisk would then not swing against the walls of the trench but would be supported by ropes. The shrinkage would cause the obelisk to rise free of the trench. Again, if we use the 5-yard distance as the average shrinkage of the rope, this would bring the obelisk clear of the trench.

On the Giza plateau, this method would not be used for anything but the heavier stones – the granites and the sarcophagus. The capstan holes are placed exactly to drag the stones up the causeway.

Shipping stones

Moving stones across the ground was only part of the problem. The granites, the more precious stones quarried in Aswan, had to be moved on to the building site using ships. The problem faced by Giovanni Belzoni, mentioned earlier, demonstrates how difficult it is to load and unload ships with massive stones.

The Egyptians used the river for transport, trade and communication since the start of the history of their civilization. Even in the times of empire in the New Kingdom, there were few roads. Those that existed were within towns, but between towns there was only the river. As a result, the people became consummate riverine sailors, although whether or not they ever deliberately ventured far into the open sea is open to question.

We know the names of many different varieties of ship, although few of them can we also describe or identify, or understand their purpose. Images of stone-moving ships exist, among other places, on stone of the Unas causeway at Saqqara, where ready-cut and carved columns are shown strapped to the deck of a ship, and at Deir el Bahri on the west bank at Luxor, where a curious image of an obelisk-carrier appears to be a tall vessel with four decks.

The interpretation of Egyptian art is always a problem, in that perspective was never deliberately used. If a table, for instance, was rectangular, then it was drawn as a rectangle with objects drawn upon it in profile, a technique that Heinrich Schaefer called 'childlike'. In the instance of the Unas ship, the deck is shown fully but gives no clue about the shape of the hull beneath. The side view of Hatshepsut's obelisk carrier is equally problematic, as we do not identify the Egyptians as makers of multi-decked craft, while at the same time both the positioning of an obelisk on to the top deck of a tall vessel, and its subsequent stability, make it seem impossible. One suggestion is that the craft was wide rather than tall – a multi-hulled vessel created by four ships tied against each other, or a raft.

Quarry inscriptions from the Old Kingdom onwards demonstrate that sailors bore military titles – that it was, in effect, a duty of the army also to move around in ships. Crews of 60 men were divided into four gangs of 15 each. These were responsible for shipping the stone, not cutting it, nor, probably, for either loading or unloading it. Pictures of ships being loaded and unloaded in the tomb of Paheri in El Kab show special crews of men being used for harbour work.

So the problem that still vexes logic is how exactly would the ancient Egyptians have loaded huge granite blocks, such as those used to line the main chamber of the pyramid, on to a ship? Several solutions have been proposed. Among these is the use of a dry dock. This would involve filling in the area around a ship with earth or rocks to allow the stone to be dragged on to the deck of the ship. But this seems too time-consuming for the amounts to be shifted. In addition, the ship would then have to be dug out again afterwards and refloated. Another possibility mooted was that the ship was steered into a narrow harbour with a jetty each side; the hull was filled with ballast and sailed under a series of wooden beams straddling the two jetties; the stone was dragged on to these beams; the ballast was unloaded, allowing the hull to rise; and the beams were slid out, one by one, allowing the stone to lie on the deck.

In a demonstration of these ideas, both failed. In the first case, where mud was used to form the dry dock, it became apparent that when multiplied to life-size, the infill would be impossible for any team to drag heavy stones across. In the second case, the ship sank!

It is clear from dates cited in quarrying and building texts that a lot of stone was shipped from the quarries to the sites during the height of the annual inundation. This seems sensible, since the quarries are in the south while the building sites were in the north, so the course of the river could be followed. One possibility never tried nor really suggested is perhaps the simplest of all. One thing we know clearly about the ancient Egyptians is that they would never use exertion when there was an alternative; for instance, they threshed using oxen dragging palettes behind them instead of using flails. Since every quarry is sited directly adjacent to green areas covered by the flood, the logical thing would be to load the stones needed on to rafts which lay on the grass verge. By definition, once the floods came the green area would be flooded, thus floating the raft. The floodwater would then swiftly transport the stone downriver. In the height of the flood (and it would have to be high to raise the rafts), the river would be deep enough to avoid sandbanks completely. The only problem, so it seems to me, would be stopping it at the other end!

Raising stones

The stones for the core, as we have seen, vary considerably in size. Although some of the base blocks are huge, this was only for the one level, in order to achieve a truly flat surface. The facing stones are less than 3 feet thick, and these would define the thickness of the core blocks behind them. Towards the top of the pyramid, the core blocks grow smaller and smaller, until at the top they are usually small enough to be carried by one man.

The process of building thus far is very clear. On each

platform, formed by the raising of the levels of the core blocks, the first stones to be put into place would be the facing stones. These would be placed with the bottom of the new facing stone exactly level with the top of the previous layer. The face would then be smoothed down, probably initially by pounding it gently with dolerite blocks but then, as the level of the bottom joint grows closer, by smoothing with a sandstone or limestone flat block. The stonemason, lying on top of the block, would have a clear sightline down the entire face below him. One area of one face would be left as steps, probably three facing stones wide. We shall see the reason for this later.

The stones would reach the platform in one of two ways. The easiest way, used for most of the pyramid, was to drag them on sledges up through the passages already finished. These gave easy open access to the platform surface. On the platform, during the hottest part of the day, temporary covers – the 'ceremonial tents' of most texts – would be erected to afford some shelter. Workers may have taken it in turns to accompany the empty sledges to the bottom at set intervals to allow for drinks, food and toilet necessities. These, prepared in the settlement and brought to the foot of the pyramid, would save having to take more to the platform than was necessary.

At the heart of the pyramid, space would be allowed for the main chamber. This was initially left as a large open space. Huge granite blocks had to be brought to line the floor area first. These could be brought up using capstans on the platform surface and shrinkage ropes, which slowly dragged the stone on a sledge up the polished face. Water or fine sand poured down under the sledge would make this easy. The stone would quickly be brought to the top level of the facing stones of the platform where work was being done, where rockers would be used to collect it from the higher blocks and slide it to the lower level needed.

In 1986, the density of the inner sections of the pyramid were tested and 'anomalies' were found adjacent to the Queen's chamber. Bore holes through the granite linings allowed the drills to enter first through white limestone; then into sections filled with sand; and finally into another section of limestone. The following year, a Japanese team from Tokyo established with similar tests the likely presence of another tunnel entrance into the pyramid.

The truth is that we have no idea whatsoever what lies within the core beyond the granite-lined passages and chambers. The tests prove beyond doubt that more tunnels, later filled in with sand and loose material, exist beyond the chamber walls and within the core. All of the tests have been carried out from the passages and the chambers and thus only give information about the lower half of the pyramid. Above the level of the main chamber, we have no information. It seems reasonable, then, that a whole series of work tunnels were left open to allow the stone to be carried out on to the upper platforms, which were later backfilled quickly using sand.

The passages within the pyramid were, in truth, ramps, and yet part of the structure. There was never any need later to dismantle anything – the ramps formed the core itself.

Finishing the facing stones

As the workers approached the top of the pyramid, a new approach had to be made to complete the facing stones. Mark Lehner observes that there is a discrepancy in the levels of the facing stones at the top of the pyramid of Chephren – they mismatch by several millimetres.

As the top was approached, to allow space for the work tunnel to emerge on the pyramid meant that in the last two or three levels all four faces could not be completed in the usual manner. Only one face could be finished properly, with its two corners. Stones into the sides, the two front corners and the last facing block would have to be pushed into place from the inside, with the face already worked. If the facing stone was pushed a fraction too hard, there would be no way of pulling it back; and this appears to be what happened.

The capstone
The positioning of the final capstone has caused more discussion than any other stone in the whole building. In one extreme instance, it has been suggested that it was placed using a helicopter! This wonderful suggestion came as a result of examining hieroglyphic inscriptions. One version of the letter 'a' is a forearm from the elbow downwards, showing a hand with the thumb slightly raised ⟶◻. In some cases, the artist folded the thumb slightly downwards, back on to the hand. This was interpreted as being a fuselage, cockpit and tail of an aircraft! In one instance, in Abydos, a vertical crack in the wall crosses one of these letters and also crosses the horizontal frame of the whole text. By judicious use of digitization of the image to darken outlying areas, a 'helicopter' appears!

Obviously we can dismiss this form of technology, delightful although the mental image might be.

We have traced the rise of a pyramid, and the smoothing of the facing stone at every level as the pyramid rises. I suggested earlier that a series of three or four facing stones would be left unpolished in the centre of one face. These would form a staircase, and it would be up it that the capstone would be carried.

Several examples of capstones have survived. The finest, from the pyramid of Amenemhet III, in the Liverpool Museum, has carved images on its four faces. A simpler one, found adjacent to the southern South Saqqara pyramid of the late 12th Dynasty, was actually cut into two pieces, a base and a small peak. Recently a limestone one has been found at Giza for one of the small pyramids adjacent to the Great Pyramid. Each of these capstones has a slightly convex underside. It follows that the final facing stones on the pyramid would be smoothed to make a compensating concave surface, so when the capstone was put into place, it sat there firmly. It also allowed it to be pushed in to place from one side, certain that it would not, if pushed too hard, fall straight down the opposite face.

Although the capstones are large, their peaked shape means they are only a quarter of the weight a full stone of the same dimensions would be. They could thus be placed on a trestle and either carried to the top or, more likely, passed up the staircase which was left from one group of men on one level, to the next higher up.

Once in place, as has been observed on the capstones and in texts, the whole could be gilded to catch the rays of the sun. It only remained, then, for a stonemason to return to the top and systematically smooth out the last facing stones. And the pyramid was completed.

Often, the simplest suggestions are the most effective. Following Herodotus's commentaries, for centuries scholars have apparently been misled into increasingly complex ramp theories. As I have shown, every examination of these theories reveals they could never have worked.

All archaeology must be based on evidence. The clearest evidence is found in the internal structure of the sand-filled Fifth Dynasty pyramids, which demonstrate that the shape of the pyramid was determined by the facing stones and not the core. In the Great Pyramid as it stands today, we are not seeing a pyramid at all, but merely the core infill. This, taken together with the finished pointed shape, has deceived scholars into seeing a pyramid as a series of steps up which stones must be taken externally instead of the platform it would have been during the building progress.

The procedure I have outlined is simple and yet totally revolutionary. It explains easily how a pyramid the size of the Giza pyramids was built.

The evidence is there. It simply needed to be read correctly.

PART THREE

THE STRUGGLE FOR THE SUCCESSION

Evidence from the Plateau

—

The building of the pyramids of Giza dominated the reigns of the Fourth Dynasty Kings.

When Cheops ruled, undoubtedly two, if not all three, of the main pyramids were starting to rise on the Giza plateau. If the King had died early, the pyramids built in his father's reign stood empty, and could have been used as a tomb. After all, the stone monsters of Giza deserved a great King, not one who died too soon.

Cheops the man hid behind the organization of the State. Since cult temples of traditional design have not been identified from the period, we are denied even the formal inscriptions and reliefs which could have told us more details about his reign. A fragment of relief from his causeway shows that the King celebrated his *sed* festival. This jubilee festival was celebrated, it appears, at the whim of the King. Some books state categorically that it only occurred in the 30th year of a King's reign. While this may have been true for Kings of the 18th and 19th Dynasties, it is an inaccurate generalization.

We also know from inscriptions of his reign in countries both to the north and south that Egypt was maintaining a trading presence strong enough to ensure a continual influx of those extra goods that Cheops needed, and which Egypt's plenty could not supply.

Cheops married at least two and probably more of his sisters and through them was blessed with a large family, many of them healthy sons. But as we have seen, discord grew. The role of King was by now so established and so powerful that it was only natural that the sons would all want a piece of the action. Yet the old ways maintained; and the sons of his primary wife, the Royal Daughter Meritetes, dominated the other children solely by birthright. For the sons starting to grow old who had been born to other, lesser, mothers, what hope was there? Their tombs, clustered around the foot of the Great Pyramid, show that many of them received titles from their father. Some, though few, may have had a measure of authority. But of what use was that power, as long as Cheops maintained his distance and ruled alone, with Crown Prince Kawab waiting in the wings?

It is true that the role of Vizier was handed out, like second prize, to other sons. But the office was empty of real power. Even the building of the pyramids, although supervised by the King's sons, was so well organized that it left them little to do. Their father, one day, would die and be buried in one of them. But what would happen then? The rights of Kawab were unassailable.

Since Cheops was already elderly when he came to the throne, it is likely that his mother, the Royal Daughter Hetepheres, was very old indeed. We know that she survived to see him crowned, as on her furniture she bore the greatest title any woman of Egypt could ever bear – Mother of the King. A King, after all, might have many wives and daughters, but only one mother. As yet we do not know where she was buried; probably alongside her husband Snofru at Dahshur. Sometime afterwards, in the middle of the reign of her son, it seems that her burial was robbed. It must have been a bitter blow for her son. At once a new burial was arranged for her near his own chosen place, the Great Pyramid.

In this third section we shall look for more evidence of Cheops, this time from Giza itself, from the tombs and monuments that lie nearby.

CHAPTER SEVEN

The Lost Queen

M ost discoveries of major finds in Egypt happen through scholarship combined with detective work. This research can take years, and usually happens far from the desert sites and often within the ivory towers of academe. First there is the meticulous sifting of records, then the noting of discrepancies, of realizing that something is missing, and finally, the start of the search. Very rarely does the ground voluntarily offer up some new discovery of its own accord. But this happened on 2 February 1925, on the Giza plateau.

Discovering anything major at Giza seems unlikely. During the 4500 years which have passed since the pyramids were built, the site has been trodden by millions of feet, of hundreds of passing generations. It is hard to understand that when Ramesses II was ruler of Egypt, the pyramids and their surrounding tombs were already more than 1000 years old, and already great antiquities to which ancient Egyptians went as tourists and left graffiti in hieroglyphs. When Cleopatra ruled Egypt, the pyramids were older to her than she is to us. Once the Greeks elevated the status of the pyramids to Wonder of the World, everyone beat a track to see them. The Arabic rulers systematically explored them and spent years, where no entrance was apparent, trying to break in to get the treasures that they were convinced were hidden within.

This amounts to 4500 years of concerted looting. Is it any wonder, then, that once scientific Egyptology began, there was little to be found but the detritus left by those passing visitors and tomb robbers? However, by the start of the 20th century it became apparent that this well-known site had never been systematically explored, numbered and mapped. There may have been little left, but what little there was needed to be recorded before it, too, vanished without a trace.

In 1902 George Reisner was given the concession – a licence allowing him, and no one else, to dig the site – to start the mapping off. Head of the Hearst expedition mounted by the University of California, Reisner was an American professor of Egyptology, and had been trained to be both observant and meticulous. By nature a quiet and shy man, he was also hard-working and thoroughly dedicated to his field. Reisner had to agree with the usual terms for the period: that any random, unimportant objects belonged to the expedition; that from any collection found, the pieces should be presented to the Cairo Museum for them to take their pick first; and that, in the rare instance of an intact tomb being found, the collection as a whole should remain in Egypt.

The method in which this concession was granted, however, was extraordinarily strange even for those times, and could certainly never happen today. Three separate groups had requested the Antiquities Service for permission to work during the same season on the same site at Giza: Reisner with the American Hearst-funded expedition; Ernesto Schiaparelli, on behalf of the Museum of Turin, with an Italian team; and George Steindorff for the German Sieglin expedition on behalf of Leipzig University. All three were intent on gaining permission to excavate one particular area, the unexplored western cemetery behind the Great Pyramid of Cheops. Despite the problems, and to save offending anyone, a solution was proposed by the Antiquities Service. Giza was large enough for several groups to work there, so the Department of Antiquities decided to be fair and rather than award the concession to just one team, called all three men to a meeting at the Mena House Oberoi hotel, adjacent to the site, to decide who should work where.

In the western cemetery behind the Great Pyramid, the largest *mastabas* awaited clearing. There was the probability of important finds here. Unable therefore to decide between themselves, the three Egyptologists simply took a ruler, and on a map, divided the whole area except for the western cemetery into three exactly equal sections. A plan of the area of the western cemetery itself was then torn into three equal strips and put into a hat, which Mrs Reisner was invited to draw, amid greatest solemnity, to decide who should excavate where. George Reisner took the northern section, Steindorff took the centre and Schiaparelli took the south.

The three men then divided the rest of the plateau easily and with gentlemanly agreement. Chephren's pyramid and complex were taken by Steindorff, Mycerinus' pyramid and the associated necropolis by Reisner. The area to the east of the Great Pyramid was divided diagonally with a ruler, the southern section, including the Sphinx and the Valley temple, was taken by Schiaparelli; and the northern section, with the three subsidiary pyramids, was given to Reisner.

As a result, in a pleasant afternoon meeting over tea, sandwiches and cakes, the four and a half millennias'-worth of royal burials at Giza were allocated with the judicious aid of a ruler and a hat, to the three leading excavators of their time.

Three years later, however, by 1905, Schiaparelli, who had achieved little on the plateau except sporadic and unsystematic digging, was persuaded to give up his concession. After private discussion, he agreed to hand over all of his share to Reisner and the Americans.

By 1905, Reisner had one-third of the western cemetery and the whole of the eastern cemetery of Cheops' pyramid, effectively taking over the greatest part of Cheops' complex except for the small section controlled by Steindorff. In 1911, Steindorff handed his concession to his German colleague Junker. The outbreak of the First World War, involving the countries of the two Egyptologists, did not affect their affable work relationship: they were united by their love of Egypt. By the mid-1920s, nationalism in Egypt was running high, especially after the debacle of the tomb of Tutankhamen in 1922. There was an increasing outcry in Egypt for Egyptians to participate in their own excavations. After pressure, and with great reluctance, the German team handed over the eastern section of their concession for Chephren's pyramid to an Egyptian University group headed by Selim Hassan.

In 1905, Reisner moved from the Hearst expedition to work instead for Harvard University and the Boston Museum of Fine Arts. In the first years of his work he had concentrated on the seemingly informative and little-known western cemetery, the original aim of his bid for the site. However, their northern strip proved frustratingly slow as it was virtually impossible for them to find areas in their own patch for spoil heaps. There seemed little of interest to be found. In 1903, Reisner had 'purchased a light railway' to use on the site to carry away the spoil altogether from the site.

In the 1906 season, Reisner redirected his efforts towards his concession of the Mycerinus pyramid instead, but by now pressure was growing on him to join an international team to begin surveying Nubia. After the opening of the relatively small British dam in 1902, there had been an intensive call by the Egyptian government to build an enormous new dam in Aswan which would stop up the Nile completely, giving Egypt year-round control over water instead of relying on the annual flood; and, almost incidentally, would destroy over-night almost the whole of the land of Nubia. Although this was little more than a plan at that time, Egyptologists began to understand that time was against them. Most archaeologists active in the field, including Reisner and his team, were drafted in to help to explore and map Nubia, ignored thus far, before it vanished completely. The work was hard, and Reisner's heart lay in the north, in Giza. After putting in two seasons in Nubia, in 1909, he resigned from the team so he could return to Giza. But to his dismay, he was sent instead by Harvard to Samaria.

The only solution, it seemed to him, was to split his time between the two areas. During the winters he worked indefatigably at Giza, spreading his work, season by season, between the western cemetery of Cheops and the Mycerinus enclosure, while adding to it excavations at the Fourth Dynasty site of Zawiyet el Aryan. The rest of his time he spent outside Egypt. He managed all of this by delegating management of various areas to colleagues, so work could continue even when he was not there.

Throughout the years of the First World War, Reisner excavated the Giza site, clearing *mastabas* methodically, employing meticulous systems of recording the finds. Systematic archaeology in Egypt was only just beginning to replace the earlier methods, which had concentrated solely on making spectacular finds. The methods used by W.F. Petrie and Reisner attracted less attention from the media, but yielded lots of missing information about ordinary Egyptians and their technology. They concentrated on retrieving the tiniest fragments, working slowly and methodically and allowing nothing to escape their attention.

Work in the Nubian royal tombs of Napata occupied him from 1920 until 1923, by which time he was able once more to return to Giza, and turn his attention instead for the first time to the massive cemetery which lies to the east of the Great Pyramid. Here were some of the largest tombs, built for Cheops' closest family.

So by 1925, work had been carried out on the plateau at a tremendous pace for 23 years. Reisner had an established trained corps of assistants, mappers and photographers, all trying to make sense of the destroyed *mastabas*.

From 1902 to 1905, Reisner had taken his own photographs around the site, developing them himself every night in his makeshift darkroom. There was only so much, though, that one man could do. Assisted from the start by Said Ahmed Said, one of the young Egyptians working at Giza, he began to train him to take over. From 1906 onwards, Said trained a string of young Egyptians to follow him. Their job was both to take photographs needed and also, using the same tripods, to set up and use theodolites to measure the contours of the site.

In February 1925, one of this team was working directly to the east of the Great Pyramid. Here stand the three subsidiary pyramids. G1a, G1b and G1c, ascribed positively by Reisner to three of Cheops' queens. This first identification of the small pyramids was made by Herodotus, who recorded:

> No crime was too great for Cheops. When he ran short of money, he sent his daughter into a brothel, with instructions to charge a certain sum, although they did not tell me how much. This she actually did, but she added a further deal of her own. With the idea of leaving something behind her after her death, she asked for each customer to give her a block of stone, and with these stones, so we are told, the middle pyramid of the three which stand in front of the great pyramid was built.

This is nothing more than myth, of course. The smaller pyramids contain almost a million stones. So if this were true, this unnamed lady must have been quite a worker!

In fact, the internal chambers within the subsidiary pyramids are tiny, far too small to contain even the smallest Old Kingdom sarcophagus which has survived. Perhaps the chamber may have been used as a sarcophagus in its own right, with the coffin simply placed within. Inscriptions nearby do link the sites with the Fourth Dynasty queens, but all of these date from the late period onwards when cults were set up there for the souls of the Queens. This may have depended on no more than the legends of that time, echoed in the writing of Herodotus. At any rate, since the women of Cheops' family are represented by huge *mastabas* in the eastern field, it is increasingly hard to ascribe the subsidiary pyramids to the royal wives.

East of the subsidiary pyramids lie a pair of enormous *mastaba* tombs, each subdivided into two smaller tombs, the northern one belonging to Queen Hetepheres III and Crown Prince Kawab, and the other to Nefertkau and Khufukhaf.

In February 1925, at a midpoint between the subsidiary pyramid G1a and the *mastaba* of Hetepheres III, one of Reisner's Egyptian photographic assistants was desperately trying to set his tripod straight. The position he needed to take was just to the south of the causeway which led to the pyramid. The limestone plateau was uneven and solid, and try as he could he was unable to set all three feet of the tripod down flat. In frustration, he banged the tripod down. Looking down, to his surprise he saw a small piece of brilliant white plaster. Plaster should not have been there on a limestone bed. He called Reisner over. Within a few minutes they had uncovered a large, flat area of infill and started to clear it.

The shaft

Within moments, Reisner knew he had found something unusual. From the very start, he called it his 'secret tomb'. Although at Giza there were often burial shafts and chambers below the *mastaba* tombs, to find an entrance in the bare rock with no superstructure was unprecedented. The plaster formed a raft just under the surface of the sand, a large white area in an area of golden stone. It bore no sign of entry by robbers so from the start, expectations of finding something intact were high.

Underneath the thick ancient plaster was a gentle staircase of twelve steps filled with rubble, apparently leading into a shallow tomb. Suddenly, at a depth of about a metre, it turned a sharp angle and opened out instead into a vertical shaft about 1.5 metres square. Like the stairs, it was filled with rubble but plunged straight down into the heart of the limestone plateau. Clearing the shaft took many days. In the side walls, crude cuttings were found at regular intervals to serve as hand and foot holds for the ancient workmen who had laboured down this deep shaft.

At a depth of about 25 feet, they encountered an entrance in a side wall, seeming at first to be a doorway, plastered over like the surface opening. When the plaster was cleared, they stared into a small recess, which contained two intact wine jars, the horned skull of an ox, and three leg bones. The food had been wrapped inside a reed mat, although this fell apart as it was exposed to the air. It seemed to be an offering made during the infilling of the shaft.

At around 56 feet below the surface they found many small fragments of gilded wood, the largest of which appeared to be a slender, fluted column, together with a few copper fittings. These fittings, when cleaned, were found to have been formed by soldering together several copper pieces using silver solder. Silver was an exceptionally rare material in ancient Egypt, far more rare than gold, as Egyptians were unable to smelt silver separate from the other elements with which it was naturally found. The use of silver as solder is totally unattested before or since. The fragments came from a canopy or support, which Reisner later declared to have belonged to a tent used during the burial ceremony. Further down the shaft, at a depth of 72 feet, were found eight limestone bases into which the fluted columns fixed. Reisner deduced that these were the supports for the canopy found further above.

At almost 79 feet deep, at last they found the bottom of the shaft, with a doorway to one side. The doorway led into a chamber, last entered 4500 years ago.

The chamber

The first sight inside must have been a great disappointment. Only three years earlier, the tomb of Tutankhamen, found in Luxor in the Valley of the Kings, had revealed great treasures when the door was first broken down. Inside this chamber, there was gold, but it lay apparently haphazardly on mounds of dust and broken wood. The contents of what had once been an intact tomb had crumbled into tiny fragments of wood rotted by damp. A few larger sections and pieces of gold could be seen in places. The chamber itself was crudely cut and uneven, its walls not square and the floor uneven and sunken in one corner. It was later found that one section of the floor had been dug out to a depth of more than a yard. Presumably a lower level had once been planned and then abandoned. The walls were undecorated. There appeared to be doorways cut into two opposite walls; later, these would both turn out to lead to cuttings less than half a yard deep. Clearly a far larger tomb had been originally planned, but the plan had been abandoned with the first chamber only roughly hewn, and the part-finished work of the stone-cutters was crudely filled with debris and then plastered over. The room itself was a pitiful sight, far from the lavishly finished chambers of some tombs.

To the left of the door stood the one complete item in the whole room, an alabaster sarcophagus, on top of which were piled poles. These had once been made of wood, covered with heavy sheets of gold. Dampness and time had caused the wood to rot away, although the gold retained its original shape. On the floor, amidst broken jars and dishes, there were recognizable shapes. Here was a chair leg; there a rectangular-shaped section of gold. It was instantly apparent that this was the tomb of an extremely important and wealthy person. But for the moment, the prospect was a daunting one.

At this point, many archaeologists would have been tempted simply to leave things as they were; or to carry out a simple rescue operation of the larger pieces, sweeping the dust and debris away. Reisner seemed more optimistic than most. He announced his intention to clear the chamber with the utmost care, recording meticulously in his reports the exact location of every single tiny fragment, no matter how small. In his first report, he 'makes the seemingly rash statement that from the records it would be possible to replace every object in the tomb in its former position should anyone be so unreasonable as to make such a demand'. It seemed impossible, not unreasonable, that the exact positioning and design of every item could be understood from such a mess. But Reisner had the faith – and the patience. The team took over 1700 pages of notes, plans and diagrams, and took almost 1100 glass-plate photographs, painstakingly recording even what appeared to be the most insignificant pieces. The recording alone took them three seasons, from 1925 until May 1927.

By the end of this almost irrational task, Reisner was proved to be correct. He was finally able to reconstruct two complete sets of furniture from the tomb, one for his own funding museum of Boston, and the other, with the original gold fragments, in Cairo Museum. It was the gold pieces which finally told the name of the owner. It was Hetepheres, the wife of Snofru and the mother of Cheops.

The objects

The layout of the chamber
Reisner was eventually able to fulfil his promise. Not only was he able, from his records and the layout of the tomb, to reconstruct exactly the furniture that had belonged to the great King's mother, but more importantly, he was able to prove

exactly where, in the tomb, each piece had once stood and exactly how it had collapsed.

Inside the doorway on the lefthand side was the alabaster sarcophagus, with what appeared to be poles on top of it. These poles proved to be from a dismantled wooden frame which Reisner later identified as a 'bed canopy'. Pushed tight against the side of the sarcophagus had once stood an armchair, one of two chairs in this tomb, the oldest to survive from the ancient world. Its arms are carved with delicate tracery in the form of entwined lotus and papyrus plants, the symbol of united Egypt. The second armchair stood at right angles to the first one. Behind this second chair had been a bed, its mattress sloping down towards the chair back, and on top of it had been placed a carrying litter. Standing up between the armchair and the foot of the bed had been a tall, cylindrical leather case, top and bottom made of discs of gilded wood, inside which had been some staffs or sceptres. Between the bed and the sarcophagus, there had lain a long, narrow, rectangular box, its sides and top elaborately inlaid. Inside this box had been a second smaller box, which held a wonderful group of inlaid silver bracelets. Behind, at the back of the small room, had stood a small cosmetic chest and a gilded headrest for use with the bed. Behind all of this there had stood four larger boxes, probably containing linen. It was all the equipment a Queen would have needed in life as in death.

Several problems, however, still concerned Reisner greatly. The chamber was tiny, originally packed tight with the objects, and in a very poor state of completion when it was filled. Was this, then, the way that the mother of Cheops had been buried? In comparison with the burial chamber of Tutankhamen, now being made public for the first time since its discovery, this room seemed mean. The sarcophagus was damaged. Slivers of alabaster from it were scattered all over the floor in different places. More importantly, the equipment seemed to be all in the wrong place. It seemed to have been put in backwards! By rights, the sarcophagus should have been placed inside first, the furniture added later and probably her personal possessions, the smallest pieces, last of all. Yet the sarcophagus was next to the door, the last thing pushed into the tightly packed room. What could have possessed the ancient Egyptians to bury such an elevated person as Hetepheres, 'daughter of a King, wife of a King, mother of a King', in such an illogical manner?

The chairs

Not enough wood fragments survived from the debris to establish beyond doubt what varieties of wood were used for any of the furniture. Most of the pieces were edged with narrow, inlaid strips, some gilded, some of ebonized wood, each inlaid with the name and titles of the long-lost Queen. These strips defined the shapes of the pieces and their size, making the reconstructions accurate and never guesswork.

The chairs were both provided with lions' legs, with the front and back legs different, just like a real lion. This style, although attested in fragments of legs found on sites of earlier date, were the first complete ones to be found used in a chair. The use of lions' legs for chairs continued throughout ancient Egyptian history. There were no clues as to how the back and the seat had been made, whether of wood, inlay or rushwork. For the purposes of reconstruction, plain pieces of wood were used.

Near the chair that stood close to the sarcophagus, Reisner's team found a panel of inlay which, when put back together, formed the first real image of the lost Queen. Like most Old Kingdom images, her jaw, shoulders and body frame are bulky and square, and her limbs heavy and well muscled. Although there were no inscriptions associated with the image, it shows her wearing the bracelets which were found nearby in the bracelet box. Reisner felt that the inlays 'do not seem to provide a very appropriate design, particularly in the size and proportions of the preserved parts, for the back of the chair'. On the other hand, very similar images were found on the back of Tutankhamen's golden chair. Less elaborate images, although of similar size, decorated the backs of chairs in the intact tomb of Yuya and Thuya, found in 1905 in the Valley of the Kings. These had been given to the deceased by their granddaughter, the Great Royal Wife Sitamun.

This chair originally, then, may have had both gilded frame and legs and a brightly coloured image of Queen Hetepheres, wearing the jewellery of which she was clearly immensely proud, fitted on the back. This was in keeping with the ancient love of colour all around them; the piece must have been beautiful indeed.

The bed

Like the chairs, this was the earliest such piece to have survived in enough detail to be reconstructed, even given the damaged nature of the wood. The bed, in the traditional manner of most Egyptian beds, was fitted with the legs of a bull, again gilded and, like the chair, made as back and front legs. The mattress base sloped downwards towards the footboard. The provision of a footboard was more useful than our modern headboards, which serve no real purpose. The footboard was made for you to place your feet against while sleeping, to prevent you from slipping off the bed, while at the same time preserving a remarkably healthy head-raised position in sleep. The footboard was elaborately inlaid in a delicate feather pattern interlaced with colour rosettes, which formed borders around the edges.

Again, like all Egyptian beds, it was narrow, designed only for sleeping. The matching headrest, of gilded wood, was undoubtedly used by the Queen during her life to sleep on. There has been much discussion over the use of headrests, as it is generally assumed that the sleeper placed the back of the head on them, an extremely uncomfortable position giving immense strain on the back of the neck and upper spine. A small figurine, now in the Metropolitan Museum of Arts in New York, shows that the sleeper, in fact, lay with the cheeks against the headrest. The stem of the headrest was thus designed to match exactly the width of the owner's shoulder, and when lying down, the spine was thus kept completely straight, while the elevated stem allowed a flow of air to the back of the neck. This was not only a healthy way to sleep, but also extremely comfortable and cool in a hot climate.

It is always surprising to me, in looking at the reconstructions in the two museums, how little interest the furniture of Hetepheres arouses in the average visitor. After all, a bed is a bed, and thus too familiar piece of furniture to warrant a second look. It is easy to glance at it, recognize it and move on to something more visually stimulating – a nice piece of jewellery, for instance. It is an interesting fact, in Cairo Museum, that while the room displaying Tutankhamen's treasures is always so full there is barely space to breathe in comfort, let alone move, the room with Hetepheres' furniture in it is almost always empty.

It should be understood that these pieces were never cheap or disposable furniture, but the masterpieces of their time. At this early date, few people outside the palace had any furniture at all. People sat or squatted on the ground, and slept wherever they could find a space. While images existed on tomb walls of beds during the Old Kingdom, this was the first chance we had to find out, in three dimensions, what one looked like. Thus this bed is of huge importance, not only for Egyptology but for archaeology in general. The concept that the Egyptians had worked out the healthiest position in which to sleep 4500 years ago shows how far Egyptian society had developed in knowledge and understanding. In addition, for the romantic in every archaeologist, it is impossible to look at the bed and not picture the Queen lying there so very long ago.

The boxes
Four boxes, which as noted apparently once all contained linen, were stacked on the floor at the back of the room. They may have possibly once held clothing belonging to the Queen, although this had perished almost completely. On top of each stood another box, these upper four containing pottery. The organization had not been a good one. As centuries passed, the walls of the upper boxes began to perish, so that the pots they contained slipped sideways. Again, as time progressed further, the weight of the pots on the decayed wood caused the top boxes to break apart, throwing the pots out. Some smashed on the floors, others fell on to the nearby bed, causing it to collapse bringing the carrying-chair which lay on the bed on to the ground with it. Many of the broken pots smashed open on top of the linen boxes below them, spilling the linen on to the ground.

The pots had once had contents ranging from edible to perfumed oils, wine and beer. At some point of destruction, as the top boxes fell apart and the jars crashed down, the fluids within them had spilled on the boxes and linen below them and then over the floor of the room. Ancient Egyptian jars were always made with unglazed sides, so their contents tended to evaporate quickly. On the other hand, as these jars were sealed into an airtight room a hundred feet below the surface of the ground, the evaporation rate would have slowed to a halt. The jars, if not full, would have had enough liquid within them to cause major problems. This liquid falling on to old timber would have accelerated the progress of the destruction. Had the boxes containing pottery been placed on the floor instead, with the boxes of linen on top, then the resultant damage would have been much less.

The inlaid box
Next to the sarcophagus and behind the armchair placed in front of the door lay the finest piece of furniture in the room, a

long rectangular box, shallow and narrow. Once, its lid had been heavily inlaid, its sides plated in heavy gold. Over the years, in a process probably accelerated by the spilled liquid, the wood had completely rotted away. All that was left were edges of the two ends, showing the original length of the box; gold from the sides which had collapsed outwards; and the inlay, which had fallen on to the objects the box had once contained. The damage had been made worse because when the box had been laid on the ground, it had rested on some unevenness in the floor which left it tilted. When it collapsed, the inlay had fallen unevenly.

Restored, it was found that the lid had once had a broad inscription, inlaid with faience pieces, which ran horizontally the full length of the box and contained the Queen's full names and titles. The edges of the box were inlaid with exactly the same feather and rosette border design which was on the bed's footboard. It was very clear that these were made as matching pieces of furniture.

To everyone's surprise, the box seemed to have contained a strange collection of odds and ends. At one end was a large wooden box which contained the Queen's bracelets. All around this box, copper implements had been pushed – razors, tweezers, small bowls and a ewer. Tiny chippings of alabaster from the sarcophagus had also got into the box, evidently from the sarcophagus. It was immediately clear that this was not the original purpose of the box. Reisner suggested it had perhaps once held linen from the 'bed-canopy' or other items of clothing. It still bore the remnants, at one end, of an elaborate piece of beadwork (see below). When placed in this small chamber, it had evidently been used for carrying a variety of small objects retrieved from somewhere else. The chips from the sarcophagus suggested these pieces had been collected, perhaps even swept up, from the floor of another place. This was, then, not the original burial place of the Queen, but perhaps a reburial.

The carrying litter

Although we have many pictures of dignitaries being carried in
such a litter from reliefs on the walls of the *mastaba* tombs of
Saqqara, this was the first ever opportunity to examine an
actual example, albeit reconstructed. The litter originally lay on
top of the bed. When the bed collapsed, the weight of the litter
made the damage to the bed worse, but somehow cushioned
the fall of the litter. The wood for the litter was surprisingly
well preserved, probably explained by the fact that it was saved
from the wet floor by the bed which collapsed beneath it.

The whole was covered heavily with gold, with the edges
lined with ebony strips listing the Queen's titles in gold letters:

> Mother of the King, the one who sees Horus; the one who is in charge of
> the encampment, she whose orders are followed, the God's daughter of
> his own body, Hetepheres.

The litter was carried on two poles, capped at each end with
gilded palm-tree heads. The four corners of the base had staples
affixed, in order for ropes to be tied securely from front to back
and side to side to strengthen the bottom joints. The floor of the
carrying litter is completely flat, and would thus have been
extremely uncomfortable if used for hours on end, as the knees
of the person being carried would have to be drawn up towards
the chest. Illustrations of carrying litters in use are not very
informative, as they show a sideways view which hides the
inside of the litter. However, illustrations of chairs from all
periods clearly show them fitted with loose cushions which
cover the seats and extend over the back of the chair. If cushions
were used to upholster the litter, this may have made it more
acceptable for long distances.

Being carried in a litter such as this was a sign of very
elevated rank, even though the person carried was open to
view. This is made clear from an extract from the Westcar
Papyrus, in which Prince Hordjedef, one of Cheops' sons,

travelled to the region of modern Meidum to collect a magician to impress his royal father (see also page 80).

> After the ships had been tied up to the bank, he travelled overland seated in a carrying litter of ebony, the poles of which were of sweet-smelling wood.

The identity of *sesnedjem* or 'sweet-smelling wood' is a matter of some contention, but in all probability it was cedar.

On the homeward journey, the Prince assisted the very elderly magician, and out of respect for his age, declined to travel by litter.

> The prince Hordjedef offered him his arm and helped him to stand. He went with him to the riverbank, holding his arm.

The bracelets

The box containing the bracelets was originally covered on all faces with heavy gold plates, incised with patterns making it look like mats wrapped around the box. These pieces of gold, in too fragmentary a condition to be reused, have been left out of the reconstructions and today the box appears simple and plain, made of bare wood.

On one piece of the gold plating, the words 'the Queen's rings' were written in hieroglyphs. Inside were marks where once, two tapering cylindrical shafts of wood had run from side to side in the box to hold two matching sets of bracelets. The box had clearly been specially designed just to hold these pieces. Each shaft had once held 10 bracelets of graded sizes. At first, they were considered to be anklets, but not only are the diameters too small to be placed over the foot, but the narrowest would also be too narrow to fit any ankle, while taken as a group they would have extended far up the calf. They were designed to be worn instead on the arms, all at the same time, grading from the elbows down to the wrists on both forearms.

233

The image of the queen, probably from the chair (see above), shows her wearing them in this way.

The bracelets were of pure silver, continuous bands, hollow on the inside face, the convex outer face inlaid with turquoise, camelian and a few small pieces of lapis lazuli in the form of delicate butterflies. Several of the bracelets were too decayed to be saved.

Neither the material nor the design is Egyptian. Clearly these pieces had come to Egypt from elsewhere, probably as gifts for the mother of Cheops. Chromospectographical tests today might prove, from impurities, where the silver was mined. According to recent investigations by P. Nicholson and I. Shaw, *Ancient Egyptian Materials and Technologies*, Cambridge University Press, 2000, these bracelets seem to have escaped attention. Other items of silver which have been tested show them to have been high in impurities (gold or copper) and thus probably native Egyptian, or almost pure silver and imported.

Were the origin of the bracelets to be established, whether of materials or design, the information they would then provide could be exciting. Egypt during the Old Kingdom (see Chapter 2) is generally believed to have existed in splendid isolation from its neighbours. This cannot have been the case; traded goods would have been vital for Egypt's development. The gift of such precious bracelets, so treasured by the Queen that she is even depicted wearing them, might establish Egypt's trading partners. One high probability, given the design of the pieces, is that they came from the region of Anatolia, later the land of the Hittites, and were exported through Byblos. The port of Byblos maintained such close links with Egypt at all times, even when neighbouring city-states rebelled against Egypt, that it is tempting to see it as an Egyptian colony. So far it is unclear how far back we can trace this link; but the origin of these bracelets may well confirm this and take Egyptian-Byblos links back to the early Old Kingdom.

Beadwork

Thanks to Reisner's determination to recover everything, even the tiniest fragments of detritus were recorded with absolute care. Inside the large inlaid box, a piece of beadwork had been pushed into one end. The exact position of thousands of tiny ring-beads was noted, even though the linen threads which had once connected them together vanished long before. Although the beads' colours had faded, enough remained to show that the piece as a whole had once had a blue background, so beloved by Egyptians of all periods, with a diamond pattern and a small central diamond on each. (See photo.) Most of these diamonds were black, two beads wide, enclosing an area of yellow, with a three bead by three bead square of red beads in the centre. Above them, forming a border, were diamonds again with the black enclosing areas of yellow with blue squares alternating with blue with yellow squares. The overall effect was dazzling (see photo).

Enough survived to give a 6-inch square, although it was clear from a scatter of beads around that the piece had once been substantially larger, many beads probably having decayed totally. The pattern was observed on belts found dating from the Middle Kingdom, but these were long and narrow, which this piece was not. Reisner eventually concluded that it was perhaps the bodice section of a dress. However, another possibility was overlooked. This same diamond design is found in many of the short cloaks worn by Kings celebrating the *sed* festival. It seems to me more likely that this was once such a cloak. The weight of the beads would have made the garment heavy, the beads flashing and the colours brilliantly eye-catching. The border would have formed the edges of the garment which would be worn over a short kilt. We know from broken fragments from the vanished causeway of Cheops that her son celebrated a *sed* festival. Perhaps this was his cloak.

The bed-canopy

Like most of the other items of furniture in the tomb, the wood of the canopy had decayed badly. However, as the sections were larger than the more delicate walls of boxes and frames of chairs and bed, enough survived to show the complex joints and other interesting features. Most of the pieces had been covered in thick layers of gold, so much so that these survived as shells, testimony to the wooden frame they had once covered.

The sides were formed by tent-pole design columns, fixed at the top into a roof-frame, and at the bottom into beams which sat on the ground. The shafts were sheathed in heavy gold. The tenons at top and bottom were individually sheathed in heavy copper, as were the floor beams. The copper lining of the tenons suggest that these were designed to be put up and taken down regularly. If they had been made to be permanently fixed, they would have been glued or dowelled into place. Copper linings were fitted only on to parts of timber that were intended to be movable, such as door hinges. The heavy copper wrapping of the floor beams, fixed on the underside and wrapped around the bottoms of the sides, was also clearly intended to stop the timbers rotting because of damp: it was designed to sit on damp ground and not a stone floor.

The corners of the roof frame and floor beams were also attached by mortice and tenon joints, and again, sheathed in copper to make the whole easy to dismantle and erect. At each corner of the floor and roof sections, copper hooped staples were hammered into place enabling the joints to be secured more firmly to make the corners more stable. Reisner suggested this might be achieved with rawhide, as similar chariot joints were secured in the New Kingdom. However, it is also equally likely, given the similarity of design of this furniture and the woodworking associated with the Cheops boat (see Chapter 10), that they were secured with ropes. Once again, this would have been easy to fit and then take down, while giving the whole stability once erected.

The frame had been used, probably often. One of the cross-timbers which formed the roof had broken in antiquity, then mended using a plate of copper wrapped around the fracture and hammered into place using small copper nails. Once again, such a fracture could not have happened if the frame had been permanently assembled, as the secure corners would have made any movement of the roof timbers impossible. Nor can it have been broken as it was placed in the tomb, for the repair was an old one as the wood it held was patinated with copper oxide. Once again, like all the sheathed tenons, such a break could only have been made by the sections being taken apart and fastened into place. Copper hooks were hammered into the frame at the top corners and along the outer edges of the floor beams. These were clearly designed to hold a cover in place.

Reisner postulated that the sides had once been draped with linen hangings, and that the inlaid box (see above) had contained these bed hangings. 'The whole canopy must have formed a curtained space where the queen's bed and perhaps other furniture could be placed, partly for the sake of privacy and partly for protection against insects.'

This view seems subjective and very much of its time, when richer people still had four-poster beds complete with drapes, or when travellers to the Raj covered their beds against mosquitoes with fine muslin. In fact there is another, more likely, logical and astonishing conclusion. It would appear that this was a full and matching set of royal camping equipment! It is clear from several later inscriptions that when the Egyptian King went abroad on military campaigns, the court went with him; and that, once on site, they established an encampment whose layout mirrored exactly the layout of the palace back at home. This included, surprisingly, the royal ladies!

Luxor temple, reliefs of Kadesh.

  Time Ramesses II, year 5

    Arrival of the (wife) of the King (life prosperity, health), at the (?), the

mother of the royal children, together with ... (Tuya?) the King's
mother ... moving to the west side of the camp (to avoid) the enemy.

One tent from ancient Egypt has survived. Although on display
upstairs in Cairo Museum, it stands within a glass case which
has been made to fit it exactly. From the outside, it appears to be
a rather uninteresting coloured box. I have known people to
stand by it, leaning bags against it, totally unaware that there
was anything at all inside the case! The tent was found in 1881
in the tomb of Queen Istemkheb on the west bank of Luxor,
together with the royal mummies removed from the tombs in
the Valley of the Kings, which had been placed in her tomb in
ancient times to protect them from robbers. The tent is, surprisingly, cuboid and not, as we would recognize, with a gabled
roof. It was made entirely of leather squares, dyed red, green
and yellow and stitched together. The entrance is not, as we
would have it, cut into the side faces, but opens up between the
corners, where two corners have not been fastened together.

This tent cover would have to be placed upon a frame, and
the frame of Queen Hetepheres fits the bill exactly. By leaving
two corners of the tent unstitched, one wall could then be rolled
up and tied to open up the tent along one face. According to the
one illustration that we have of an encampment, that of
Ramesses II at Kadesh, such a tent is shown surrounded by an
external protective wall of shields. These would not mark the
outside of the camp, but rather a boundary between the rest of
the camp, around the four sides, and the private royal enclosure. The canopy, as we have seen, is deliberately designed to
be taken down and put up with ease, and the parts, tied
together, would easily be carried from site to site. The copper
sheathing of the bottoms of the floor beams was designed to be
placed on a damp field or area of ground, while the matching
furniture would provide an elegant and sophisticated set of all
the equipment a Queen would need. The matching boxes with
jars and linen would provide ancient 'suitcases', while the

carrying litter shows that the job of some trusted infantryman would include carrying the Queen from site to site. We know, again from details of military texts, that the Egyptian army abroad covered around seven miles a day until the final encampment was reached; and this progress, no doubt, would have been limited greatly by the carrying of the Queens and their equipment.

The funerary equipment

Once the debris was recorded and collected, attention could be finally turned to the sarcophagus. Despite what has been suggested in many books, Reisner held out little hope that it would contain any human remains. The sarcophagus was chipped in many places, and chips in the inlaid box proving that the damage had happened much earlier, in another place. It could also now be seen that the lid on the side next to the chamber wall showed extensive damage along the joint between it and the trough.

To the right of the entrance door a patch of plaster was observed in the wall. Once the facing was removed, a narrow niche was found high up, its top flat with the ceiling. In this was found an alabaster container sitting on the decayed runners of a sledge. When the cover was eventually removed, the box was found to be divided into four compartments, one dry but the other three filled with a liquid which turned out, eventually, to be a brine solution in which were the removed viscera of the Queen. This proved beyond doubt that Hetepheres had been fully mummified, the first and earliest evidence that mummification using evisceration had begun in Egypt.

The examination of the sarcophagus was carried out with due ceremony before an invited audience. To everyone's disappointment and mystification, when the lid was raised, the sarcophagus proved to be completely empty. There was no evidence of a body ever having been in it, although the damage to the lid suggested that the body had been destroyed in the robbery at its previous site.

It was an anti-climax to an astonishing discovery. To have seen Hetepheres, the mother of Cheops, face to face would indeed have been the final triumph.

The explanation

It was clear from the very start that this was not a burial, but a reburial. The reverse order of the objects within the chamber suggested to Reisner that the original burial chamber, probably at Dahshur near the burial of her husband Snofru, had been attacked by robbers. When the damage was discovered, the tomb was systematically cleared and the objects immediately transferred to Giza. Here they were lowered into this new chamber in the same order in which they were removed. Thus, the last objects placed in the original burial would be the first removed and first into the new tomb. This would mean that the sarcophagus, the first thing in the original burial, was placed last into the new tomb, next to the door.

Evidence of the earlier robbery was apparent everywhere. The sarcophagus had been forced open roughly, chipping both the trough and the lid. Chips from the sarcophagus, thrown around the floor, had been casually swept up and pushed into the inlaid box. Smaller objects had also been collected together and placed randomly in the inlaid box to carry them from the original site to here.

So where was the original site? To date it has not been located. The sarcophagus alone is too large to fit into the chambers of the so-called Queens' pyramids. It is more likely that Hetepheres would have been buried alongside the pyramid of her husband, Snofru, and would thus have been at Dahshur. Perhaps one day it will be found.

Reisner created a reasoned explanation of events as they must have unfolded. Towards the end of the reign of Cheops – the 23rd year seems likely – robbers violated the tomb of the

King's mother. Someone had to inform the King, presumably one of his sons. Cheops immediately ordered the reburial of his mother's body and of all the grave goods which had survived the attack, although no one apparently dared tell him that his mother's body had been destroyed. Four and a half thousand years ago, a macabre charade was played out upon the sand close to the completed pyramid which Cheops would soon occupy. He witnessed the transfer of his mother's goods and mourned as her sarcophagus was lowered into the deep shaft. As the shaft was filled, he placed an offering of beef and wine in a niche for her *ka*. But he never knew that the destruction had been more complete than it seemed, and that the sarcophagus over which he mourned was empty.

The question remains: who would have dared to enter the original tomb? It could scarcely have been at the foot of a deep shaft as the reburial was placed. How could robbers, openly and systematically, have dug down into a rubble-filled, 100-foot vertical shaft with no one looking? The robbery of an ordinary burial was probably commonplace. But the burial of the great Lady Hetepheres is another matter. Placed inevitably close to the burial of her husband, was security, then, so lax that only a few years after her death and burial, a group had managed to steal into the royal burial enclosure and have enough unguarded time to remove the Queen's body and destroy it? The robbery gives us some more information about the reign of Cheops. It shows that, apart from the organization of the building works, which relied on Imhotep's original plan, security in Egypt during the time of Cheops was extremely lax. It also suggests that people were not as religious as some suppose. To break into a tomb and rob it is a fearsome task; to take out and destroy the body of a recently dead Queen proves that the robbers had both time and determination, linked with some certainty that they would not be caught. It may be argued that since the furniture and jewellery survived intact, the robbery was interrupted. But this is impossible. The sarcophagus would have been placed at the back of the original tomb chamber.

Or could the destruction of the body have been deliberate? What if this were the whole aim of the original plan? We already know of divisions within the royal family. Was this, then, some form of revenge upon the old lady after her death?

As for the goods within the chamber, perhaps during her life Hetepheres had accompanied her husband and her son on campaign, sleeping within her coloured tent on some foreign field. The title on the furniture states that the tent was in her charge. It would have been delightful to have found the original burial intact. What else would it have contained? Since the furniture within this burial is clearly a matching set, it is hard to believe that everything was destroyed except for a completely matching set of camping equipment which, for inexplicable reasons, survived intact. It seems much more likely that this does indeed represent a complete burial set, together with the required food and drink offering.

Probably, if Reisner is right, the boxes containing the heavy jars were placed on the floor of the original tomb with the linen chests on top of them. During their removal to Giza, the order was reversed. If the jar-boxes had not fallen apart and spilled their contents everywhere, perhaps the objects might have remained in a better condition. As it was, their survival at all is little short of a miracle. In any case, the tomb and its reconstructed contents are as much a tribute to the finest archaeological method by a great Egyptologist as to the lost Queen herself.

CHAPTER EIGHT

The Sphinx

The Great Sphinx, a colossal limestone statue of a lion with the head of a man, has stood guardian over the pyramids of Giza for 4500 years. Its face is carved with the image of Cheops' son and heir, Chephren.

This statement is an easy one. But how true is it? Is it actually 4500 years old? And does it really bear the face of Chephren? The riddle of the Sphinx today has changed in nature from the time of the Greeks. Today, many people question when it was cut, and by whom.

The view over the Giza plateau 4500 years ago used to be very different from the one we see today. Today Cairo, the largest city in Africa, dominates the east bank. A permanent pall of traffic haze hangs over the city streets, as it is also a heavily polluted city. The west bank is often almost obliterated from sight.

The ancient pyramid site remained unchanged for many centuries. Glass slides and postcards only a century old showed a different view of them even then. The pyramids, although more than a mile from the river on the west bank, at that time dominated the city view, clearly visible and majestic despite the distance. In the days of inundation before the opening of the dams, the Nile spread its fingers right to the edge of the pyramids, creating a closer link between east and west banks.

Today, a view of the pyramids is scarcely possible from Cairo at all, except on a very clear day, and then only from the top floor of one of the many luxury hotels which cluster on the east bank of the river.

In the days before high-rise buildings and pollution, when Cairo's sprawl was limited to the east bank and Giza province on the west was truly an independent area, the view of the pyramids also included that most mysterious of statues, the Sphinx, called in Arabic Abu'l Hool. For centuries, the Sphinx has divided Cheops' world of the dead on the plateau from the world of the living down by the river. Looking patiently towards the eastern horizon, it has witnessed more dawns than almost any other monument in the world. It was already ancient when the Greeks came and wove stories about it.

But exactly how ancient is it? Recent research has tried to indicate that it is even more ancient than Egyptologists have claimed, that its origins date back long before Cheops built his pyramid on the plateau. So what is the truth? Could Cheops and his architects have chosen the site because the Sphinx already stood there, ancient even in his day? Or as the pyramid rose from the plateau, was the view before them clear to the Nile? When exactly was the Sphinx cut? And why?

Which came first – pyramid or Sphinx?

The design and layout

From the central pyramid of Chephren, a causeway runs eastwards down to a Valley temple at its foot. Alongside and to the north of this temple stands the Sphinx, flanking the causeway. It is not a statue at all in the accepted sense of the word, since it does not stand free but is still part of the bedrock from which it was carved. To fashion the lion's body, masons and sculptors cut a trench into the rock to work the freed stone, and thus it lies below the line of the plateau. Only the head, worn and battered, stands proud of the sand around it.

The Giza plateau today appears as one huge burial site, covered almost at random with ruined tombs and dominated by three pyramids which stand side by side. This is a false impression: it was not designed to appear this way. In ancient times, it was subdivided into a series of independent enclosures, each surrounded by large stone walls. The walls have long since disappeared – undoubtedly, like the facing stones of the Great Pyramid, used as instant quarry material by later builders in Cairo. Only their foundations indicate where they once stood.

Once, the road from Cairo to the pyramids was empty and majestic. Today, it is dual-carriageway filled from dawn to dusk with cars nose to tail, overheating, pushing for space and all honking their horns. Even the camels in front of the pyramids have grown accustomed to it all, waiting to take tourists on their mandatory ride, as they watch the traffic jams bemused. The impression that Giza is all one huge site is accentuated by the modern metal enclosure fence out to the west of the pyramids which surrounds the whole area. Visitors, whether in car, coach or on foot, now have to check in here and buy tickets before they can enter what is an enormous funerary compound. A tidy car park has had to be created alongside the Great Pyramid.

At the new entrance gate, guards issue and check tickets and limit the amount of road traffic which can enter and leave the precinct. Forty years ago there were no such controls. Cars and lorries without number used to thunder down a modern tarmac road across the centre of the area, running between the pyramids of Cheops and Chephren, connecting the main Cairo road to the village of Nasret es Sammaan. Although it seems unlikely that they could have caused damage to the pyramids, the threat to the Sphinx was always there. Today it is at least safe from losing its head through the danger of the unexpected vibrations from traffic.

Chephren's causeway, up which stones were once dragged from the nearby quarries, today stands open to view, a rough

245

stone track among many ruins. But when the pyramids were completed in the Old Kingdom, this causeway was entirely covered over from *re-esh* to pyramid, like a tunnel across the surface of the sand. There would have been one for each pyramid, hidden behind the enclosure walls. These walls would even have hidden from sight all but the upper portion of each pyramid with its gilded pyramidion at the peak. The eastern side of the walls, facing the river, were fronted by a row of granite-faced temples. From archaeological digs, we know that there was once a lake in front of them, reflecting the massive square, red façades.

So an ancient visitor would have seen a lake, faced by temples and walls which hid almost everything behind them. Each pyramid stood within its own walls like a private city. No roads ran anywhere near the sites, just faceless desert.

To the north of the lake there was a large village settlement where the pyramid builders and their families used to live. There were even cemeteries here for workers. This, at least, has scarcely changed. Today, the modern village sprawl of Nasret es Sammaan stands on top of the last ancient settlement and offers up its shops for the hot and thirsty visitors, just as its ancestor did in the times of the ancient Greeks, when Herodotus came here to see the sights. Small shops permit tourists to sit under shady awnings while the owners persuade them to buy souvenirs, ranging from postcards (sold together with the right number of stamps for airmail, very enterprising!) to camel whips (of limited use outside the Sahara, but an interesting wall decoration), fly-whisks and sun hats (much more useful for the traveller going up the Nile) and of course the ubiquitous sheets of papyrus, here often sold in packs of 10.

Surprisingly, this town has probably not changed a great deal over the centuries, even perhaps back to the times of the ancient Egyptians themselves. We know, after all, that Herodotus was shown around by a guide; and the best guides to this day come from Nasret es Sammaan. Even the houses are probably of similar design. Random excavations here have uncovered countless souvenirs from ancient tourists – *wadjat*-eyes, figurines. So little has changed except the names and the clothes of the travellers.

To the south of the lake there was another settlement, entered through a massive gateway and hidden, like the pyramids, behind high walls. Inside these walls, vast quantities of food and drink were once prepared and served daily to the loyal building workers of the King who toiled on the pyramids. Anciently, the smell of bread and beer and the smoke from a hundred fires and ovens would have filled the air from dawn to dusk, tempting the tastebuds. Today's travellers are confronted by the smell of kebabs and shawarma, a concoction of chopped beef, tomatoes and onions in a hot chilli sauce – and even McDonald's. Despite this, a time traveller's overall impression would not be so very different.

In the times of Cheops, those who were allowed to step into the temples behind the lake and to walk behind the walls left the living behind, with their noise and smells, and entered into the silent and tranquil cities of the dead. Tunnels, walls carved in raised relief showing events from the lives of each King, led from behind each temple to the face of the appropriate pyramid where daily offerings of food and drink were secretly left before a statue of the King, painted, inset eyes glinting, uncannily lifelike and terrifying. Outside the walls of the causeway but within the enclosure walls of the compound lay neat streets of rectangular limestone tombs, *mastabas*, their roofs flat so as not to divert the eye from the pyramid at the heart of it all. The *mastabas* closest to the pyramid were the largest, the massive burial places of the King's most important children.

Further down the slope, arrayed in neat ranks, were the tombs of lesser officials. In death, as in life, your status was defined by how close you came to the feet of the King. In front of the tomb entrances, statues of the dead sat as impassively as the owners had once sat around the King in life. The doorways to the tombs, closed with decorated wooden doors fastened with bolts, were surrounded by carvings, images of the deceased and texts telling of his titles, and were all coloured red-brown, black and white. Although the tunnels and halls beyond would be meticulously swept clean, around the tombs, sand would blow, gather and drift.

Down by the lake there were once four temples by the water's edge, three leading to the pyramids and the fourth, between the temples of Cheops and Chephren, leading to an altogether different compound. Over the walls of this temple rose the top of a brightly painted, gigantic stone face of a man.

The Sphinx compound

The Sphinx stood within its own stone enclosure wall. Although the area within the walls was less than a tenth the size of that of the adjacent pyramid-cities, the statue within dominated it entirely. In front and between the outstretched paws of the Sphinx stood the massive standing form of a pharaoh. As I have mentioned, the body of the statue stood within a trough cut into the limestone, although the great head stood proud, well above the height of the body. In ancient times, virtually nothing would be seen of it from the outside. To the left, or south of it, the causeway/tunnel of Chephren added such height that the top of the tunnel would have been the same height, if not higher, than the head of the Sphinx. To the right, or north, the wall rose high up.

Visitors to the area would have entered a large temple, four times the size of the temples in front of the pyramids and filled with chambers and passages. In here they could make an offering, probably sold to them outside before they came in.

In most ancient Egyptian temples, the focal point was a sanctuary at the rear of the building. This contained a shrine or a small niche which featured a cult statue, standing on a plinth. The sanctuary was closed to all but a few visitors, either a

248

server or the King himself. This temple was a slightly different experience for the visitor. Having made his way to the darkened rear of the temple, he would then face massive closed doors. When the doors were flung open in front of him, he would have been almost blinded as he was confronted by the gigantic painted face of the Sphinx, standing out in the full glare of the sun, a hundred times taller than any other temple image. The body of the Sphinx would never be seen as it stretched away behind the figure. Under the front paws of the great lion, extra rock had been cut away so that to all appearances it sat, like any other cult statue, on a plinth. It was, indeed, a sight created to overawe and amaze.

The visitor would probably never realize that the statue was part of the rock itself. Its antiquity would have been of no interest. It was the image of God, of the phases of the sun, and for them its meaning was more important than its age.

The passing years

It does not take more than a decade in Egypt for the encroaching sands to move in and cover up human achievements. The fine sand is insidious. It flows and puffs in on the slightest breath of the wind and accumulates at first as little more than a fine, gritty layer under the feet. If it is not swept away constantly, it will not take more than a few months to accumulate in corners, and then for floors to start to vanish under the undulating powder. It does not happen in a single day or night; you scarcely notice it happening. But without constant vigilance, it will inevitably take over.

The necropolis of Giza would have been well served with mortuary offerings for several generations. Although the descendants of the *mastaba* owners may have forgotten them within half a century, it would take longer than that for the cult of the Kings to die. Yet the covered causeways meant that removal of sand from the outside tombs was unnecessary. The causeways eventually would become tunnels below the sand, which would then have gone unnoticed.

The back of the Sphinx, lying in its trough, would have received no attention at all even in its heyday. It was of no importance: the head and face were everything. It would have taken only a few decades for the sand to start to pile up behind the head, but for the overawed visitor, the effect would have been unchanged.

The end of the Old Kingdom undoubtedly sealed the fate of the cemeteries of the old Kings. The overturning of values, the rethinking of the nature of Kingship, all would have made the pyramids seem as false and aggrandized as their owners were in the eyes of the newly enfranchised people. Their cults were quickly forgotten, Giza was abandoned to nature and the sand inexorably piled up. Even the temples started to crumble, or their stones were used for new building works elsewhere. As the stone walls around the enclosures were moved away, the sands would have started to cover everything.

More than 1000 years later, Egyptian Kings of the New Kingdom, determined to show off their athletic abilities, left the palace of Memphis to drive their chariots around in the desert and shoot at targets or wild game. The Kings of the 18th Dynasty, around 1400 BCE, were proud of their physical prowess. Their chariots, drawn by a pair of fierce stallions, would be fast and hard to control. The warrior princes and Kings needed to practise their balance, practise the shooting of arrows at high speeds, to gain admiration and save their lives in battle.

They seemed drawn magnetically to Giza, which by now was covered thickly with sand. They were probably lured there by the pyramids which dominated the plateau, but also by the lone head which stuck up out of the dunes. They arrived with their courtly followers, who came partly to assist them and partly to given them an enthusiastic and appreciative audience. King Amenhotep II got them to set up thick copper targets behind the stone head jutting out of the sand and, galloping at full speed, would let loose arrows which struck the copper so hard that they emerged out of the back. It was no mean feat.

The Sphinx, its body obliterated, stared impassively at the east. Amenhotep II ordered a temple built to the northeast of it for reverence to the old figure, not knowing of the older temple complex hiding below the sand. Here he set up a new cult. His son, the young Prince Tuthmosis, came here also, to copy his father's exploits. One day, in the full heat of noon, he fell asleep in the cool shade of the Sphinx's head, below the chin. He had a strange dream. The god Re-Horemakhet appeared to him and spoke to him in a clear voice. He called him his son. 'I am your father, you are my son. I have been awaiting you for a long time.' He demanded that the Prince clear the sand around his body.

In a daze, the Prince obeyed the dream. For the first time for over 1000 years, the body of the Sphinx, nestling in its stone trough, stood open again to the sun, freed from its sandy prison. Tuthmosis, now King as Tuthmosis IV, made his own personal offerings and recorded the dream on a stone which he erected between the paws of the Sphinx, on the bedrock. Like his father, he too built a temple to the Sphinx, although his was alongside and to the north of the ancient one, now uncovered but in ruins.

As time went on, even these temples were abandoned and once more lost under the sand. As the Greek and Roman Empires came and went, the Sphinx once again jutted its worn head from the sand. Only in the last 150 years has the whole been re-excavated. Today, though, we are careful to sweep away the encroaching sand.

How to date the Sphinx

It is very strange that when Herodotus visited the pyramids at Giza, he did not mention the Sphinx at all. People have speculated endlessly about this omission. The most common suggestion is that the head had by this time completely vanished from view under piles of sand. This seems improbable since there are graffiti written in Greek along the side of one of the Sphinx's paws. In seems that the statue had been dug out again at some point. One highly likely possibility, raised by Dr Alan Lloyd in his commentary on Herodotus, is that Herodotus never actually went to Giza at all but relied totally on the accounts of a guide he considered to be accurate.

In 1816, an Italian sea-captain named Giovanni Caviglia was the first in modern times to dig out the Sphinx again. He located the Dream Stela of Tuthmosis IV between the Sphinx's paws. It seems that he copied out a great part of the text, although he was unable to read hieroglyphs, as in 1823, in *An Account of Some Recent Discoveries in Hieroglyphical Literature*, the co-translator of ancient Egyptian hieroglyphs, Thomas Young, used the text from the stone as one of his examples for reading.

Prior to the text's translation, it was generally thought that the Sphinx was perhaps of Middle or even New Kingdom date – at any rate, it was thought unlikely to date before 2000 BCE. Sphinxes lined the routes to most temples, and these were of Middle Kingdom date or later. There were no attested older Sphinxes. The Dream Stela changed this, for it told how the Sphinx had been dug out by Tuthmosis IV around 1470 BCE. The text even then was very badly damaged. In 1842, during the Prussian excavations of Karl Richard Lepsius, a more accurate copy of the text was made. For the first time it was copied by people who could read it. The text, published in his classic work *Denkmaeler aus Aegypten und Aethiopen*, became a 'standard' version for study. In 1904 Kurt Sethe, Professor of Egyptology at Göttingen University, travelled to Egypt specifically to copy hieroglyphic texts. These formed the basis of his almost comprehensive publication of texts of all periods, the *Urkunden*. The Dream Stela appeared in Volume IV.

By the time Sethe inspected the Dream Stela, however, many

sections recorded by Lepsius had fallen off. The granite stone, standing on the bedrock, had suffered badly from dampness rising from the water table, close to the surface of the plateau. Water, permeating the granite from the bottom upwards, caused salts to be exuded on to the surface. This causes the surface first to 'bubble' and then to flake off entirely, taking the inscription with it. Many of the lower sections had fallen off between the time of Caviglia's copy used by Young, and Lepsius' copy of 1842. The 67 years from that time to the time of Sethe had seen further destruction. Lepsius recorded about the top half of the text intact. By Sethe's time, it was down to about a third.

Young had observed, and Lepsius had copied, the last half of a cartouche on the last line of text then visible. The cartouche, the rope-ring which enclosed a King's name, had only the second half of two signs visible – a ⌒or *kha*; and ⤝. The only royal name which this could fit was that of Khaefre, or Chephren. Since the Sphinx actually stood at the foot of the causeway which led up to the pyramid of Chephren, this seemed to fit. As a result, it was now, for the first time, declared to be of Old Kingdom date, of a time contemporary with the building of the second pyramid, and bearing the image of Chephren.

By the time Sethe checked the text against Lepsius' copy, the small section of cartouche had long since vanished entirely. We thus have only the previous records to be assured it was there in the first place and that it had been recorded correctly. Moreover, excavations which had cleared the two New Kingdom Sphinx temples of Amenhotep II and Tuthmosis IV seemed to back up this story. The great Sphinx, it seemed, was as ancient as the Giza pyramids.

In 1949, Selim Hassan, Egyptian Professor of Egyptology, published his *magnum opus*: excavation reports on the Sphinx enclosure. Both the excavation and the publication were masterly works which are unanimously accepted today by scholars as the definitive account of the background of the Sphinx. In it Hassam points out several interesting features. Between Cheops' enclosure wall and that of Chephren had once run a broad ditch, designed to carry away rainwater. When the Sphinx's body had been carved from the trench which surrounded it, the ditch ended up directed straight into the new trough. The Egyptians had thus had to block up the ditch at the Sphinx end with blocks of granite to prevent the trough around it flooding. This proved beyond question that the ditch had been there before the Sphinx was cut out. Since the ditch separated the two pyramids, obviously the pyramid enclosures had to have been made before the Sphinx. This was confirmed by the discovery of rock-cut tombs in the north and south walls of the trench cut around the Sphinx, all of Fourth Dynasty date. Once again, this means that the trench was in place just before the tombs were cut. The Sphinx, he concluded, was cut after the layout of the pyramid enclosures but before the end of the Fourth Dynasty. This seemed a reasonable conclusion.

Hassam observed, moreover, that the ancient Sphinx temple which had once stood at the front of the Sphinx had been cut from limestone taken from around the Sphinx's body to create the trough. The sides of the trough bore clear signs of horizontal and vertical lines where blocks of stone of similar size to those used in the core of the pyramid had been taken. It seemed that the trough had been used as a quarry.

The head of the Sphinx is formed of a hard, fine-grain stone which had weathered well. The body, on the contrary, was cut into a lower, very soft stratum of rock which did not weather quite so well. Another, harder layer of rock was encountered underneath the soft stone body. The result was that the base and the solid head were made fragile by the eroded soft rock of the body in between.

Once, the front lion's body, with its legs extended, had supported an integral carving of a King, shown standing. Over the passage of time, this statue had disappeared totally, leaving nothing but a few lumps in the stone, although medieval illustrations showed it to be still in place at that time. The Sphinx's beard has also long since dropped off and pieces of it have been taken to various museums. The beard would once have been joined to the body with a 'skin' of stone; the tip of the beard would have met the top of the statue, so between them, the beard and the statue would have supported the head almost totally.

The disappearance of these supports, plus the crumbling state of the body and neck, meant that the head was precariously balanced. Over centuries, the combined action of wind and sand had eroded the body very badly, undercutting the head around the chin. Modern concrete, used to infill the broken headdress and the area underneath the chin and front of the neck, gave some support to the head. At the time the concrete was added, though, it was observed that the head had undergone considerable repairs as far back as the Romans. The Roman cement had accidentally made the situation worse, as it seemed to draw water up through the stone towards it.

When the neck was repaired, a substantial break in the rear body towards the back haunches was also infilled with cement. During the two world wars, additional brickwork supports were added temporarily, just to make sure that no explosion could cause the head to be dislodged completely. These were removed afterwards.

All of the evidence seemed to fit an Old Kingdom date. Clearly the Sphinx had been carved in the Fourth Dynasty. It could not date later than that because of the ditch and the rock-cut tombs.

The Dream Stela also once bore the name of Chephren, the King who owned the pyramid and causeway against which it sat. The face was thus declared to be the face of Chephren, created in his honour about 2550 BCE. The harder rock of the head, so prominent above the body, it was believed, probably inspired the cutting of the whole. It was the core of an outcrop of limestone used for the building of the pyramids. In the Fourth Dynasty, someone had decided that instead of removing this last outcrop of rock it would be carved into a royal head. Later, the trough was cut into the bedrock in order to form the body. It seemed a straightforward answer.

But there remained one huge problem. The archaeology proved beyond any doubt that the Sphinx could not have been built after the Fourth Dynasty. But then voices of dissent began to be raised. The archaeology did not prove that it could not be older. So was it not possible that it was, in fact, far older?

The new theories

In 1934, the American medium Edgar Cayce went into a series of trances centring round ancient Egypt. Cayce, it was claimed, actually spoke in ancient Egyptian, speeches that were taped and kept for future research. He claimed that in 10,500 BCE, at the end of the last Ice Age, the rising waters of the world's oceans had submerged an entire continent called Atlantis. This civilization had been described extensively by the classical writer and philosopher Plato, so Cayce's referral to it seemed to make sense. Cayce said that in a previous existence, he and a small group of survivors had arrived safely from the lost civilization of Atlantis into the Middle East, whence they had all gone in different directions. They took with them the benefits of their civilization to introduce culture and wisdom into an otherwise troglodytic world.

The Atlanteans, he said, brought with them knowledge so advanced that the Middle Eastern cultures were not ready for it. Regarded as gods, the Atlanteans hid their knowledge away in 'Halls of Records'. The ancient race then died off, leaving the Egyptians none the wiser. Then, Cayce said, one man found the records and learned from them the lost wisdom of the Atlanteans. With this, the Egyptians were able to write hieroglyphs and build pyramids. This, of course, accounted for the sudden leap forward made by the Egyptians and their apparent superiority over all other nations at the time.

Cayce claimed that although the 'Records' had been studied, they had been reburied. One of these lost Halls of Records, he predicted, would be found under the plateau of Giza before the end of the 20th century. During his life, Edgar Cayce founded a research institute, the Edgar Cayce Foundation, designed specifically to train people to investigate his claims. It is no surprise, then, to know that in the mid-1990s there was a flood of books and articles in all aspects of the world media, aimed at finding the predicted Hall of Records in Egypt in time to match Cayce's prediction.

The modern Egyptians were inundated with appeals to dig for the lost chamber, but they remained remarkably sanguine about the whole affair. While allowing non-intrusive investigations to be carried out to see if passages or chambers might be located under or around the Sphinx, they were equally determined that the process of scientific archaeology could not be served best by excavations prompted only by the trances of a psychic.

As a result, to increasing panic as the end of the millennium approached, it was now claimed that the lost Hall of Records was hidden below the Sphinx. Sphinxmania reached new heights. In the event, the new millennium dawned with no hall having been found – hence the cries of 'conspiracy' among the supporters of the theory. They believe that the chamber is there; that Egyptologists know it is there; but that we cover it up as well as denying them the chance to prove their point.

New evidence was now brought in to try to back up the claims. Robert Bauval's aforementioned theory about the alignment of the pyramids matching the belt of Orion added fuel to the controversy. Bauval's calculations showed that the ventilation shafts of the Queen's chamber of the Great Pyramid, because of precession, or the 'wobble' of the earth about its axis, only lined up directly with the constellation in exactly

10,500 BCE. This accorded with the idea that the plan for the pyramids and the shafts had been among the lost texts. The author Graham Hancock then went on to suggest that the Atlanteans had left 'messages' and halls of records for man-kind in many different locations, from the stone circles of Stonehenge to the Cambodian temple of Ankhor Wat. Why the 'message' should have been different in different places is, as yet, unanswered.

Another notion was that 10,500 BCE saw the constellation of Leo rising on the horizon. Now, the constellation of Leo has exactly the same shape as the profile of the Sphinx; and since, as has been indicated, the Sphinx is the first lion *couchant* ever made in Egypt, therefore, they reasoned, the Sphinx must also have been carved at this time by the Atlanteans to celebrate the new era. This would have made the Sphinx thousands of years older than the pyramids.

For some years, Hancock et al. suggested that the pyramids themselves were also built around 10,500 BCE, but later accepted that this could not be correct and that the traditional Egyptological dating had to be right. The reason, though, for the ventilation shafts to be pointing to a constellation only visible in 10,500 BCE was 'proof', it was declared, that the ancient Egyptians had found some of this lost knowledge and were applying it in the Fourth Dynasty.

More support was found in the Inventory Stela. This carved stone was found at Giza by Auguste Mariette, the French Egyptologist, in 1853, in the 21st Dynasty temple to Isis to the east of the Great Pyramid. It caused a sensation when its inscription first appeared in translation.

Long live – Horus, Medjer, King of Upper and Lower Egypt, Khufu, may he be given life.

He founded the temple of Isis Lady of the Pyramid next to the temple of the Sphinx of Horemakhet behind the temple of Osiris Lord of Rostau. He built the pyramid next to the temple of this goddess; and

258

he built a pyramid for the King's Daughter Henutsen next to the temple.

According to this, the Sphinx was there *before* the pyramids. It fitted in nicely with Cayce's statement. The Sphinx was, it was suggested, a monument built by the lost civilization of the Atlanteans around 10,500 BCE, as a message to mankind that they had been there, and as a marker to the lost Hall of Records.

The text of the Inventory Stela accorded nicely with the Cayce-based prophesies. Unfortunately, the language, the style of carving, the layout and the vocabulary used on the Inventory Stela all prove beyond doubt that it was a very Late Period text, or, in terms of its content, an outright forgery. However, since the contents were useful, they have become for many the backbone of the 'early Sphinx' theories.

A final scientific support, it was believed, was added by the geologist Robert Schoch, who examined the Sphinx and the trough in which it lay in 1996. He observed vertical markings in the rocks at the side of the trough caused by rainwater running down the sides. As he stated, it was known that Egypt and Giza especially were dry and that the last substantial rainfall which could have caused such damage happened – you guessed it – in 10,500 BCE, at the end of the last Ice Age.

It all seemed so neat. Cayce would have enjoyed it.

In fact, none of this evidence really stands up to any close examination. It is all circumstantial and based on taking an hypothesis and then finding evidence to back it. Let us examine all the points, one by one.

Robert Bauval's suggestion about the ventilation shafts pointing to the Orion constellation at an earlier date does seem true: the shafts certainly do point in the general direction of the constellations. However, this point was made by Egyptologists long before he took it up in the Cayce discussions. It was already known and accepted that the shafts were directed towards the stars. What is more, it is very clear from many fundamental errors in pyramid building, not only in the Great Pyramid but in earlier prototypes, that their Egyptian designers were on a steep learning curve, and that their designs were being constantly reviewed and adapted with every subsequent pyramid.

Bauval is a highly qualified engineer, and in one respect he cannot be faulted. The ventilation shafts are limestone-lined. This lining, forming a channel only 8 inches square, rises from the main chambers inside the pyramid to the outside walls. The angle at which the limestone channelling had to be cut is extraordinarily complex, as it had to be calculated to rise from the chamber; to cut through an area of rock; to rise at an angle opposite to the angle of the sides of the pyramid; and to erupt on the surface of the pyramid at an exact given point. The thought processes and technology that caused this to be made so accurately are staggering. But understanding that this was the first pyramid in which it was attempted, it would be highly likely that by the time the shafts emerged out on to the facing stones, there might be a slight error in lining up with the constellation as intended. Interestingly, similar shafts were started within Chephren's pyramid, but were abandoned unfinished. Perhaps the inaccuracy of the first trial in Cheops' pyramid decided them to give up the idea altogether.

The idea of the appearance of the constellation of Leo above the horizon around 10,500 BCE is also a delightful one, but the argument is a nonsequitur. There is no evidence whatever to tie the Sphinx in with the constellation of Leo anywhere, except in the minds of those who would like to point out the coincidence. Coincidence is all that it is. There is no evidence that the ancient Egyptians 'saw' either a lion or a Sphinx there. There is also, in fact, evidence of Sphinxes long before the Great Sphinx. And there are also Egyptian lion statues far older than the Sphinx.

The Inventory Stela was carved about 2000 years after the Great Pyramid was built. It was a piece of propaganda written by the local priests of Isis in the Late Period to assert that their temple was older than the pyramid. Similar forgeries are known elsewhere from the same period, most notably the so-called Famine Stela on Seheil island in Aswan. The Inventory Stela was undoubtedly carved for a purpose. Perhaps there was a dispute over the antiquity of the Isis temple and someone wanted to 'prove' its age. It is certainly very badly written, almost scratched, on the stone, and the lines of hieroglyphs are irregular and sloping. It bears all the marks of being the hasty work of an educated individual who was completely untrained in stone carving, working around 600 BCE. The 'facts' it contains are fictional, and about as convincing as the existence of Harry Potter's Hogwarts School and Platform 9¾ (although there are probably people out looking for them, too).

Robert Schoch is an eminent geologist, and the statement he has made about the water drain marks on the sides of the Sphinx's trough are unequivocal. His reputation is such that it would be foolhardy to make such a statement, were it not so. However, his statement concerns the marks and not the dating. In fact, Giza is wet, and very often it is extremely wet. It may not rain often in Egypt, but in the winter months gentle showers are frequent. Once a year, usually in January or February, there will be an annual downfall of such ferocity that I have frequently sat in the Mena House Oberoi hotel, looking out at the water flowing over the pyramids, and mused on the cascade effect it causes as it runs in torrents down the sides. In the hours after the storm, huge puddles gather over the surface of the desert and water flows into the *mastaba* tombs, many of which are entered through descending steps. Cairo, the most polluted city in the world, generates acid rain. *Ergo* drain marks are only what would be expected and are probably relatively modern. The drainage channel, cut between the external walls of the Pyramids of Cheops and Chephren, prove beyond all doubt that the same thing happened at the time the pyramids were built.

In summary, the main impetus for all of the new theories

261

was the vision and prophecy of Edgar Cayce. And as Hawass, Chief Inspector of Antiquities of the Giza plateau, has pointed out, dreams and visions are scarcely the basis for a scientific excavation.

The face of the Sphinx

The American writer John Anthony West, who is often at the centre of controversial new Sphinx and pyramid theories, pointed out two problems he had with the Sphinx a number of years ago. First he pointed out that while the Sphinx looks fine and in proportion from the front, from an aerial view the head is far too small for the body. He suggested it must have been recut by Chephren. Secondly, he argued, the face of the Sphinx in no way resembled Chephren, as archaeologists like to claim. He suggested that this also pointed to the fact that the Sphinx was far older than Egyptology claims.

In recent years he has filmed controversial sequences, included in a number of programmes, where images of the head of Chephren from his famous diorite seated statue, found in the Valley temple at Giza, were overlaid on top of other images, reduced to the same size, of the Sphinx. He then asked a forensic pathologist if in his expert view, the two faces were of the same man. The forensic pathologist was adamant – they were of two completely different people as none of the notable points on the face actually coincided between the two.

Once again, his expert view cannot be contradicted. The faces are different, indeed. The more accurate question to have asked would be – how do we know the face of the Sphinx is that of Chephren at all? The answer is – that we do not. The suggestion that it was the face of Chephren came from two pieces of evidence: the first, that the Sphinx guards the causeway leading to the pyramid of Chephren; and the second, the existence of the now-vanished half-cartouche bearing Chephren's name on the Dream Stela.

Like most arguments over the Sphinx, neither of these two points of evidence is entirely satisfactory. Just because the Sphinx is at the foot of the causeway does not mean to say it relates to Chephren's pyramid in the slightest. It could have been placed there purely because the rock most suitable for it was there.

The second point is clearly false. The entire inscriptions might, for instance, have read 'the Sphinx, which bears the image of King x, stands guard over the pyramid of Chephren'. Or something similar. Without the rest of the text or any earlier copies which might tell us more, we have no way of telling. The name could simply be a red herring.

It is clear, though, that West has a point and that the head is far too small for the body. It does indeed seem to have been recarved. On the basis of his evidence, it is suggested that the Sphinx was actually carved around 10,500 BCE, at a time when rainfall was heavy, and was later recarved in the Fourth Dynasty.

Against this, the position and layout of the original Sphinx temple shows conclusively that those who visited the site were shown the head and face where a temple figure should have been. From the front, the head, shoulders and paws are perfectly in proportion. It is only the length and size of the body that cause difficulties.

So whose is the face on the Sphinx?

The stylism of the head

There are several ways in which a date can be obtained in archaeology. Absolute dating, which might render a date of, for example, 2743 BCE, is a minefield, and without more information for the present is impossible. Comparative dating is easier. This enables us to fix a date to a period, such as Old Kingdom; to a dynasty; or to the reign of a King. It can be done using texts (references to an event, for instance); to images (a painting, relief or statue which bears inscriptions giving a date) or by use of salient points on the image which fix it beyond doubt to a certain period.

This last method is a skill rarely taught even to professional Egyptologists, but tends to be acquired over years of practical experience. However, I have taught such skills over a number of years, enabling people to identify pieces for themselves. This is valuable, since museum labels have often been written by non-specialists and thus may be misleading. There is, and never can be, any substitute for the skilled eye.

For most people, ancient Egyptian art is easy to recognize. Quite apart from the simplistic view that all work is done in profile and that curious poses of arms and legs are evident (not true – this belongs more to music hall than to ancient Egypt), to most people it all looks the same, although being recognizably Egyptian and not, say, Sumerian or Greek. In fact, we have Egyptian objects spanning a vast span of time. Unlike classical archaeology, whose heyday lasted only a few centuries, Egyptian art begins before the dynastic period, probably around 4000 BCE, and continues until the arrival of the Arabs in 641 CE. So dating a piece is vital – to say 'ancient Egyptian' is not sufficient.

The faces of statues can be most informative, and there are easy ways to distinguish the age of a piece. For instance, Old Kingdom faces are square-jawed and plump-cheeked, with small, wide-set eyes and a relatively small mouth, simply executed. The eye is strongly curved on top and almost straight underneath. The eyelids are marked with a double line above. The eyebrows are generally realistic, implied but not heavily marked.

A New Kingdom face, on the contrary, is of a slimmer build, with the chin more pointed. The eyes are very wide, sometimes almost almond-shaped. The curve of the eyes is as pronounced underneath as on top. They are set close together across the bridge of the nose. The mouth is wide and often has a double line to outline it. The eyebrows are broad, raised bands, heavily delineated. Most important of all, the lines of eye-paint round the eyes are often drawn out almost to the side hairline. This 'typical' Egyptian eye is peculiar to the New Kingdom.

An examination, then, of the Sphinx's face will reveal something very odd. The face as it is is an amalgam of two sets of features. The eyes are not level; one is higher than the other, while the mouth droops slightly at one side. The chin is broad and square, typically Old Kingdom. The eyes, on the other hand, are wide, more New Kingdom in style, while the eyebrows and the painted lines to the side cannot in any way be anything other than New Kingdom. It would seem, from a close inspection of it, that the original face was Old Kingdom, but that it was recarved in the New Kingdom.

This would mean that the alternative thinkers are correct. The Sphinx has indeed been altered. But it is not, as they believe, an ancient statue of 10,500 BCE recarved in the Old Kingdom, but a Fourth Dynasty original recarved in the New Kingdom. This seems conclusive, although like most points, some may try to dispute the stylistic evidence. It would be helpful if there were corroborative evidence.

And there is.

The Dream Stela

Since the first translations of the Dream Stela text, the content has been largely accepted. As we've seen, Tuthmosis IV, while still a Prince, dreamed a dream of Re-Horemakhet, the spirit of the Sphinx, in which the god told him that if he would remove the sand which had covered him, he, god, would give Tuthmosis the throne. Since the sand was cleared (the stela stands on bedrock), this means Tuthmosis fulfilled the dream and thus gained the throne.

However, as I pointed out in my previous book, *Tutankhamen: The Life and Death of a Boy-King*, the text actually says no such thing. Advanced groups of students working on the text in my classes quickly understood that the words '*if* you clear the sand *then* I shall give you the throne' do not actually occur anywhere within the text at all. It is beyond any doubt that Tuthmosis was the eldest, possibly the only son of Amenhotep II and thus would inherit the throne in any case. The Dream Stela seems to have been placed there not because Tuthmosis wished to justify his hold on the throne, but because on a distant, hot day, a Prince came face to face with god and heard his voice! This would be sufficient for anyone to mark such a miraculous event.

The group reading the text from Kurt Sethe's copy, however, quickly encountered problems. Sethe, working from previous translations, had decided that the text was in fact a long poem. As a result, he took a text which ran in long horizontal lines from right to left; and in his 'copy' chopped it into small fragments which read from left to right. As a result, he introduced an element of doubt into the copy on which we worked. Attempts were made, not fully but reasonably successful, to find a sharp, detailed photograph of the text to compare with Sethe's copy. It was also decided, for the sake of accuracy, that Sethe's line divisions had to be ignored.

Reading ancient Egyptian is not as hard as it seems. On the other hand, as I have been reading it since I was nine years old, perhaps I am not the right judge! However, the pictorial signs each stand for a 'sound' or group of sounds; or else are 'determinatives', a picture which tells you what the word is about.

For instance,

□ is the letter 'p'

◠ is the letter 't'

The word is *pt*, which we pronounce *pet*.

The ▭ is a determinative which is a stylized view of the sky.

So *pet* means sky.

There are no punctuation or upper-case letters. So our real problem is deciding where one word ends and the next begins.

Usually, it is very clear, but sometimes it can be open to doubt.

In the advanced groups, we decided never to use a translation until after we had sorted out the signs and the probable readings of them. This is fairer. A scholar working alone will, if stuck, turn to a previous translation to understand how someone else read the signs. With a group of people, all of whom could read hieroglyphs to some extent, there was always fierce discussion about the grouping of signs. No one allowed anyone else to take anything for granted. The result was startling.

The text reads:

Along the top line, the lion should be an image of the Sphinx, but this sign, which occurs here and nowhere else, is not represented in hieroglyphic fonts.

The accepted translation is:

> May the good god live, son of Atum, protector of Horakhte, the living
> image of the Lord of All, a sovereign created by Re, potent heir of
> Khepri, beautiful of countenance like his father.

The problem lies with the end of the top line. Here, Sethe has taken the image of a king bearing a mace and staff; the sun; the eye, and the zigzag and has made it into a phrase, 'a sovereign created by Re'. The next phrase, using all the signs down to the seated picture of a god on the second line, reads 'potent heir of Khepri'.

This translation cannot be justified in any way. According to Egyptian rules, a sentence starts with a verb, then has a subject and then an object. The way Sethe has divided his lines, the first section has subject, object, verb – an order which can never, ever happen.

It was clear that the signs had to be regrouped. In this case, the 'sovereign' and the sun-disc became the determinatives of the 'Lord of All'. Immediately, the whole sentence changes. The correct translation actually reads:

> The living image of the Lord of All which the heir created *when he carved Khepri, beautiful of face, like his father.*

The heir, of course, was Tuthmosis. Khepri, an aspect of the sun as he rises over the eastern horizon, the area to which the Sphinx points, was a pseudonym for the Sphinx.

Tuthmosis, the text says clearly, carved the Sphinx's face to appear like his father.

The Sphinx is an image of god whom Tuthmosis encountered in his dream. Associated with all aspects of the sun, it faces the eastern horizon to welcome the dawn of every new day. According to artistic, archaeological and textual evidence, it was carved in the Fourth Dynasty from an outcrop of good rock left after stone for the core of one of the pyramids had been quarried. The body was carved from a softer stratum of rock in the bedrock. Over centuries, the body has alternately sanded up and been cleared by successive rulers. During this process, the soft core of the body has been eroded by sandstorms and attacked by rain. During the 18th Dynasty Tuthmosis IV, copying the example of his father Amenhotep II, hunted regularly by the Sphinx, and on one occasion, dreamed that he met god. As a result he ordered the face to be recarved 'in the image of his father' and erected a cult temple alongside.

The original face of the Sphinx was of Fourth Dynasty date; and it was recarved and repainted in the 18th Dynasty renovations. But John Anthony West, who found that the original face is not that of Chephren, is indeed correct.

It is the face of his little known half-brother or brother, Redjedef.

The Sphinx gives us the next clue to the story of Cheops. The trouble in the royal family was about to erupt.

CHAPTER NINE

The Heir of Cheops

Cheops, remember, came to the throne an elderly man, husband to several wives and father to many children. Although we know relatively little of his reign from contemporary documents, the evidence which can be gained from the necropolis of Giza tells us as much about the man as the King. We know that even before he became King, the pyramid-building industry, started by Imhotep in the Third Dynasty in honour of his King, had become almost a production line. The previous pyramids built at Dahshur had been faulty because they had been built on a base of sand. The builders were not going to make that mistake again, and so turned to Giza, where a huge limestone plateau made it possible to build pyramids and their surrounding necropolis on a grand scale. In doing this, they may or may not have designed a chain of three modelled on their limited sight of the belt of Orion. Since the King's spirit at the time was associated in life and after death with the constellations, it seems a reasonable thing to have done. However, it is also clear that although we see Giza as one single site, when it was planned it was actually four distinct and separate sites. This would suggest that the three pyramids were not aligned originally.

Around the Great Pyramid, the northernmost one, large tombs already started to rise at the start of his reign, at the same time as the pyramid was being laid out. These were destined to be used for members of his close family.

The family was surprisingly large. Surprisingly because, for several generations, all of the children had married their own siblings, probably in an attempt to keep out other families. There were rivalries between many of the branches. Cheops, the son of a brother-sister marriage and married to several of his own full sisters, may well have suffered from the results of incestuous inbreeding within the family.

The building of the Giza pyramids and the necropolis which surrounded them was a mammoth enterprise, employing in one way or another almost the whole population. Once again, this was reasonable. At this early date, the belief that the King owned everything and controlled everyone was a reality. By employing them on a project which united them all, he fed and maintained them at the same time. The things which they received they had, of course, produced themselves, but they understood that these products belonged to the King. Anything they grew or made they believed belonged to him absolutely and could be handed out by him or not as he chose.

Yet the system almost organized itself. At every harvest, the grain was stored in centralized granaries in several towns, from which rations were doled out monthly. The workshops of various kinds only existed for the King's use. Since shops did not exist, then all products of these workshops were directly at the disposal of the King. The only way that anyone could get linen, for instance, was through the King's boon. It was like running a rather large household, with one single earner who dispensed things as he saw fit. To get the country working on a project such as pyramid building seems sensible. The King was the hub of the wheel in life; it was reasonable to see he remained the same after death. He was thus able to employ almost everyone, reward them through his largesse and still maintain the illusion of his total supremacy in all things.

Using Imhotep's blueprint, the organization of labour, the

provision of food, the management of equipment, the provision of stone, the labour on the building site – all of these, once set in motion, would almost have run themselves under the watchful eye of Cheops' Vizier. In the first section we saw how there was vying among his sons for the role of Vizier. The post swung regularly from sons of Henutsen to descendants of Nefermaat, the son and Vizier of Snofru. It is true, as many scholars have indicated, that these were already probably elderly men when they took the post, so their disappearance caused by death would hardly be surprising. But what is also clear from this is that the post did not automatically pass from one brother of one line to the next, or from father to son, but swung regularly between different branches of the family. In other words, like everything else, it was at the gift of the King.

All life and sustenance came from the King as it did also from the Nile. He was the only truly powerful man in the whole Kingdom. There may have been just cause for this. We know that after the unification, when the family line of Narmer came to the throne, he was unable to assert total control over Egypt. There was constant infighting during the first two dynasties. The reason, as we saw earlier, was that the domination of one family was no guarantee that the conquered families would simply sit back and accept it. If they had been strong enough to oppose the victor in the first place, why not form alliances with others and try again?

The emergence of one single family who kept out all others and placed all power in the hands of the family head was the result. It may not have been ideal – but it worked. Unfortunately, it caused jealousies, as we saw in Chapter 3.

The palace of Cheops

It has long been assumed that the King's principal palace was in the capital, White Wall. Of course, we should never assume; and besides, archaeology down to Fourth Dynasty levels is impossible in White Wall because of the high water table. We shall probably never recover anything of this early date from the palace.

The ancient capital city was some miles south of Giza. This has always puzzled archaeologists. Why did Cheops choose not to build at Saqqara, where previous pyramids had been sited?

Saqqara was the necropolis of White Wall, adjacent to the city. However, one of the disadvantages of Saqqara was that the site, as today, was thick with soft sand down to the bedrock. There are no walls or chasms nearby in the bedrock which could be exploited as quarries. Giza is a fine and solid site. Although we see them as two places, the west bank is in fact one large cemetery site, with Giza towards its northern edge. Because it is so high above the Nile, the sand is fine and left the peaks of the hills clear. There were also vast quantities of easily quarriable stone adjacent to it. The remaining quarries all around the plateau suggest that even then there would have been open walls around the site from which stone could be split away. The limestone at Saqqara is fine and hard and requires more working (although it takes well to fine relief carving), while the stone of Giza is soft, friable and often crumbly. This was of no concern, as it was only to be used for the core.

The problem is that because Giza is remote from White Wall, members of the royal family would have had to live on the site to issue the food and other supplies as needed. It seems we may have solved this problem. Earlier we noted the discovery of a huge, thick stone wall below the plateau to the south. This was entered by a large gateway more than 22 feet tall, and led to a broad, wide, levelled street with what appeared to be storage magazines off to the sides. Each of these had, in places, side benches and remains of different forms of crafts including copper working and potteries. The wall enclosed the great bakeries and fish preparation areas, and undoubtedly, in areas not yet cleared, butcheries and areas for cooking meat.

Lehner remarked that these magazines looked very like those

barrel-vaulted buildings which are to be seen today on the west bank at Luxor in the 'mortuary temples' of the Ramesseum and Medinet Habu. We know that these areas housed miniature cities within their walls, and that each contained a separate building used by the King himself.

It appears probable, then, that he has found at Giza the remains of the first-ever royal palace of the Old Kingdom. Later pyramid sites simply had workmen's settlements nearby; Kahun at Illahun and Deir el Medina at the Valley of the Kings are examples. These sites were built at a later date, when the Egyptians functioned on more democratic lines. In the Fourth Dynasty, when Cheops controlled all, it is reasonable that he should have lived close by, where the palace could issue goods directly.

This can be confirmed by titles found in the nearby *mastabas*. Here, many men are given titles such as 'Overseer of the Estate "Mansion of Cheops"' (Nihetepkhnum); 'Overseer of the Houses of the King's Children' (Sepni); 'Overseer of the Great House' (Abdu); 'God's Washerman' (Senenu); and 'Overseer of the Departments of the Tenants of the Great House' (Sekhemkha). It had always been understood that these titles referred to the distant palace of Cheops in White Wall. The strange thing, though, is that many of them date into the Fifth and Sixth Dynasties, during the reigns of different Kings. Why should the White Wall main palace still bear the name of Cheops? He must have been remembered as the founder of the site and its greatest King.

It now seems far more likely that the pyramid builder decided not only to use Giza for pyramids for the burials of himself and his successors, but actually to live close to the site.

Royal Giza

The recent excavations can now be seen in context. When examining the Sphinx in the previous chapter, I described Giza as it must have appeared at the time of the Fourth Dynasty. We can now add to this.

From the river, a harbour or *re-esh* was built at a level which would be permanently flooded to the foot of the plateau. This would have had a jetty wall all around it, for the immediate access of ships. To the west of the *re-esh* would have been the front wall of the funerary complexes beyond, with four magnificent 'temples'. These buildings, each coated with polished granite, led to cool, columned halls and thence to the cities of the dead beyond. To the north of the harbour lay the workers' village and cemetery, where the permanent builders lived and were buried after their death. To the south stood a great wall, its entrance blocked by a gate more than 20 feet high. Behind this lay the city and palace of Cheops.

Somewhere here, further to the south of areas already dug, will undoubtedly be found the remains of the King's palace itself. Here will be quarters for his wives, the so-called harem. Here also will be the rooms for his children and their children. Palace though it may be, it was also one enormous family home. Perhaps there will also be discovered more images of this elusive King. But it will be satisfaction enough, I think, finally to see the rooms where Cheops once walked as he lived.

The family of Cheops

Within the walls of the nearby palace, Cheops' sons were already grown men, married and fathers, when their father was crowned under the aegis of Ptah, local spirit-protector of White Wall. We know from titles on various artefacts that Meritetes and Henutsen, Cheops' principal wives, were both his sisters. We have the names of several children whom we cannot link to either of these women, so there were clearly other women also, again his direct sisters.

At this date, there was no such title as Great Royal Wife (or King's Chief Wife, as the title should actually read). It seems unreasonable, in some ways, to presume that one of Cheops' wives took precedence over the others. However, we know for certain that Meritetes' sons and daughters not only took the important family names, but also overall authority over the others.

Meritetes' eldest son to survive to adulthood was Kawab, and in time he became a petty ruler within the ranks of his brothers and sisters, as Cheops must have done when he was younger. His statue shows him as a portly man with thinning hair and a look of quiet benevolence on his face, although this may, of course, be pure propaganda. Cheops' eldest daughter was named Hetepheres (known to us as Hetepheres II), named after her grandmother, the sister-wife of Snofru. The next daughter was called Meresankh (called by us Meresankh II), named after her great-grandmother or great-aunt, the wife of King Huni. She seemed of much less importance than her sister, despite the royal name, and married a minor full brother called Horbaf. The two of them later shared a huge *mastaba* at the foot of their father's pyramid. A third daughter was named Meritetes, after her mother.

Crown Prince Kawab is shown in his *mastaba* tomb as paying homage to his mother Meritetes, through whom he had inherited the right to take the throne when his father died. He is shown as a scribe, with papyrus scroll and pens. Snofru, his grandfather, is recorded in the Westcar Papyrus as asking that a papyrus and pens be brought; he was the only King in ancient Egypt shown as being capable of reading and writing. Evidently, from images of Kawab, these skills were expected of all their male children and future Kings. Another fragmentary scene shows him leading cattle. Like the rest of the royal family, he was concerned with the feeding of the palace staff and workers, and cattle were considered, from earliest times, to be the noblest and most prized of creatures.

Of his sister-wife Hetepheres II we know very little, as the rooms she shared with her husband in their giant *mastaba* were later damaged beyond repair, perhaps deliberately, as we shall see. They had a daughter, Meresankh (known to us as Meresankh III). The tomb of Meresankh III has survived well. She is shown in the company of her mother, with her father Crown Prince Kawab standing by. Unusually, she is depicted as having blond hair. This may be a wig, although it is cut short and seems more likely to be her natural hair colour. Nowhere is she shown with any direct brothers or sisters, but seems on the contrary to be an adored single child. The presence of her mother and her father confirm what we know – that the line of right to the throne passed directly from her mother.

Hetepheres II thus gave the right to the throne to her brother Kawab, and then passed it on to her own daughter Meresankh III for the next generation of Kings. This exclusivity gave the women immense power and at the same time made them extraordinarily vulnerable, as we shall see.

We have no idea for the moment whether Meritetes and her children occupied separate areas within the palace. Her full sister, Henutsen, was also wife to Cheops, and gave birth to a number of sons. These all took similar names – Khufukhaf, named for his august father, Akhkhaf, Minkhaf and the son who should probably be called Rekhaf. It seems that this last son, whom we know today as Khaefre, or Chephren (as Herodotus called him), was named for the new solar god whose appearance was just starting to make its appearance felt within the royal family.

It would seem from the names of her sons that Henutsen was not an adherent of Re at the start of her marriage. We cannot know for certain if the naming of a son belonged to the mother or the father. In the case of Meritetes' children, in whom the blood royal ran, the names were probably pre-ordained in that they followed traditional family names. We do know from many texts and images that sons adored their mothers, frequently being the ones to bury them and offer up the funerary cult; and that they bore the name of A son of B, where B was the name of the mother. So it could well be that Henutsen, since her children would never assume kingly power, was given the choice of names for her children, and that by the time of the birth of her fourth son, she had swung over to the new religion of Re.

Rekhaf, or Chephren, would have been brought up apart from the more favoured children of Meritetes. He would have been educated, but also brought up with an awareness of the god whose name he took. There is no indication of any earlier children named after Re. The religious change must have happened just before he was born. So perhaps his loyalty to Re was exceptional, and could account for problems which later befell him.

There was another sister whom Cheops married, and bore him children, but her name is missing. If legend is correct, then the three subsidiary pyramids could well have been for these three wives, Meritetes, Henutsen and the third unknown lady. Those who suggest that one of the three pyramids belonged to Hetepheres, whose tomb was found in 1925, are most certainly incorrect. Her burial place would logically have been near that of her husband Snofru and thus probably at Dahshur. The Westcar Papyrus names an important son of Cheops; Prince Baufre (see Chapter 3). He seems so important that it is feasible that he was a son of Meritetes herself. But we have two other boys, whose names are similar to each other, Hordjedef and Redjedef, who undoubtedly had the same mother and, in the case of Redjedef, this was neither Meritetes nor Henutsen. Another Prince called Shepseskaf may, again by virtue of his name, probably be assigned to the sons of Henutsen.

The succession issue

Throughout the rein of Cheops, although Viziers came and went, Crown Prince Kawab awaited his turn to rule. Perhaps only a few months before his father was to die, however,

Kawab suddenly and unexpectedly died. Dates found around his tomb are from year 24 of his father, the year that Cheops himself died. The death of Kawab, even though he must have been at least in his late forties, must have been a tremendous shock to everyone. There was no appointment of a replacement, so there may not even have been time.

Looking back, we have no indication how he died, except that the chamber of his *mastaba* tomb was unfinished. In all likelihood it had been abandoned, as it might be anticipated that he would be crowned and ultimately buried in a pyramid. It is more than likely that he simply died as a result of illness. It was hard to achieve good ages in ancient Egypt, and Kawab was an old man by general standards of the day. But in the light of what followed, there has to be a chance that foul play was involved.

The death of Kawab, followed so soon by the death of his father Cheops, left a vacancy on the throne. The daughter of Kawab and Hetepheres, Meresankh III, was now a key figure: whomever she married had the next right to the throne, since Hetepheres II, her mother, was now a widow and could not be expected to marry again.

Suddenly, and against the odds, we find Hetepheres II's name linked immediately after the death of Kawab to Redjedef, Cheops' son by his third, and minor, queen. Redjedef had already been married to one of his sisters, a lady called Kentetenka. She suddenly vanished at exactly the right time. It would not be too forward to consider her death as highly suspicious, since it left Redjedef free to take a new wife at just the right time. There was absolutely no reason whatever that Redjedef, a younger son of a minor wife, should even have dreamed of taking the throne himself. His marriage to the widow Hetepheres II was suspicious and, incidentally, completely against the normal way of things. Almost at the same time, her daughter Meresankh III was married to her half-brother, the little known younger son of Henutsen, Rekhaf, or Chephren.

The marriage of the Dowager Crown Princess to, in dynastic terms, a rank outsider is so suspicious that it has been suggested several times that perhaps Redjedef forced her – attacked or raped her. These royal women can thus be seen as both weak and strong. They were weak, in that no woman would be expected to fight back against her husband or to refuse a suitable man. And they were strong, in that whoever controlled this poor woman, still reeling from the death of her husband, took the throne.

What a prospect this must have been! And Redjedef, although he had many other brothers between him and his father's throne, could not resist the opportunity.

Marriage to a widow, although not unheard of, was extremely rare, and certainly would not usually happen within the royal family. Hetepheres II would have been much older than he was, especially since his half-brother, Chephren, married Hetepheres II's daughter. So who should be King now? The man married to the older Princess, or the one married to the younger?

Up to this point, none of the sons of any wife other than Meritetes could have been considered to be a likely candidate for Kingship. Now, as Cheops' body was being prepared for burial, battle lines were being drawn up between two minor sons, whose only claims to power were ambition, an allegiance to the new god Re, and marriages to the Princesses of blood royal.

The plaster infill around the ships of Cheops, which we will encounter in Chapter 10, tells its own story. Into the wet plaster was impressed the stamp of King Redjedef. The throne was taken, against all the usual rules, by Redjedef, claiming the right because of his marriage to Kawab's widow. What rights would Hetepheres II have had? The royal ladies might carry the line of inheritance, but that was all. They could never inherit the throne and rule directly. Women of any class were of lower station than the men around them. In the tombs of their husbands, they would be shown the same size as his servants. So undoubtedly, she would not have had any say in the matter.

Abu Roash

A short time after Cheops died, a new pyramid was springing up for Redjedef, but not at Giza. He rejected those in order to design and build his own. He also turned his back on the pyramids built during his father's reign, and instead tried to turn the clocks back to the times of Imhotep himself.

The pyramid of Abu Roash which he built is barely recognizable today as a pyramid at all. It is the most northerly pyramid ever designed, standing about five miles north of Giza. All that remains of it is a mound of destroyed stone and brickwork, whose underbelly today lies cut open to the skies. Quite unaccountably, Redjedef chose to have it designed on a rectangular base, not a square one. The only other pyramid shaped in this way was the Step Pyramid. The site that he chose was directly opposite the temple of Re at Heliopolis. It is obvious that he chose it because of his loyalty to the worship of the sun-god Re. The limestone mound on which the pyramid was to be built was left standing quite high and then surrounded by outer layers of stone. The stones around the base are very steeply angled at 60 degrees, close to that of the base of Snofru's Bent Pyramid at Dahshur. The stones are also steeply sloped inwards towards the centre of the pyramid, using the force of gravity to keep it together. This is much more reminiscent of the inclines of the layers of stone in Meidum Pyramid, where a central core was 'wrapped around' by lower levels.

Not enough remains of the pyramid at Abu Roash to understand how it would have been built (layer by layer or in wrap-around layers), how steep the sides would have been, and how tall the finished pyramid would have been. The steep incline of the sides has suggested to some that this was going to be a *mastaba* and not a pyramid at all.

The base layers were of granite, not of limestone – almost an inexcusable luxury in a building which would later be covered up with facing stones. Unlike all the other Fourth Dynasty pyramids, which had used working passages leading to burial chambers cut high in the core, Redjedef went back to the old days and ordered a pit cut into the bedrock below the heart of the building. Today the chamber lies open, no more than a gigantic pit more than 66 feet below the surface of the ground, with limestone rafters over the passages and chambers that, once again, were of the same design as those of Snofru.

The whole complex is baffling. For some reason, Redjedef completely rejected the styles of his father and instead emulated his grandfather and great-grandfather. This gives us several clear clues. First, in order to do this he must have had substantial knowledge of the building methods used at Giza, as well as those used by his ancestors, so he could choose between them. This suggests that either he, or someone very close to him, was conversant with the earlier plans and, what is more, with the sites themselves. Before he became King we are barely aware of his presence. Redjedef was never a Vizier. However, all this suggests that he must have been present at the building of the Giza pyramids and have understood the significance of their form.

Secondly, what is certain is that he rejected every aspect of his father's designs at Giza. Given his allegiance to the new god, this suggests that Cheops remained adamantly loyal to the old ways, values and ideas which Redjedef could never accept.

Thirdly, it confirms beyond any doubt that the design of the Giza pyramids was stellar in origin. If we need to find the belief structure which inspired the Giza pyramids, it is to be found here. There can be no suggestion that the pyramids represented the rays of the sun. On the contrary, the possible link between the ventilation shafts of the Great Pyramid and the stars seems increasingly probable. This would have made the Giza pyramids linked beyond any doubt with the constellations, and thus unsuited for Redjedef's leanings towards solar worship.

Fourthly, on a more personal note, it indicates that Redjedef disapproved strongly of his father Cheops and of traditional values. To reject the state religion in its entirety is one thing; to move away from the family burial site is another. There is evidence of an earlier *mastaba* tomb having been prepared for him at Giza, emphasizing that there could have been no anticipation of his getting the throne.

Finally, and perhaps most important of all, it declares his open loyalty to Heliopolis in preference to his family. This implies that he gave ear to people outside the royal family, even to the extent of learning from them or having friends outside the close ranks of his own siblings. For the first time in many generations, the doors to the royal family opened slightly. The fact that the moment he was crowned, he moved his designers away to Abu Roash indicates that this was not a sudden decision, but one which had been planned for some time beforehand. This has two implications. First, it shows that his leanings towards Heliopolis and his involvement with non-family officials pre-dated his coronation and thus happened while Cheops was still King. Since Cheops showed no inclinations towards the religion of Re, and Redjedef rejected outright everything to do with his father, this demonstrates the animosity which must have existed between them, even if, because of Cheops' reclusiveness, it was not overtly apparent. Secondly, it also imputes other reasons for Redjedef's usurpation of the throne when his father died. Opposed to his father during life but powerless to act, Redjedef would have seen it as imperative on his father's death to act quickly. The disappearance of his wife at exactly this moment, and the unexpected alliance with the widowed Hetepheres II, are therefore all the more suspicious. It seems clear that his intention to seize the throne was neither sudden nor forced upon him by others, but rather was planned by him for a long time. Planning of this sort would have involved more people than just himself. The question is – who aided his ambition?

The impact of the seizing of the throne

All the changes must have been explosive for the country. The palace of Redjedef's father Cheops at Giza was still in operation, as we know from the titles of courtiers buried there into the Fifth and even the Sixth Dynasties. The building of the Giza pyramids continued throughout Redjedef's reign, even though he planned to be buried far away at Abu Roash. This would have involved either diverting gangs daily away from work at Giza, or establishing a different workers' settlement at Abu Roash. He would have needed reliable, professional builders, not conscripted labour. He would also have needed people who understood the mathematics and geometry involved in the older designs. All of this must have confused everyone greatly.

There would have been some public expectation that he might still be buried at Giza; so why choose Abu Roash if not to cause conflict? The answer has to be in its position close to Heliopolis. This new King was as much a rebel, if not more of one, as the so-called 'heretic King' Akhenaten 1000 years later.

We do not know who Cheops chose to inherit the throne when he lay on his deathbed. With Kawab gone, there were few of his sons by Meritetes still alive. The most likely candidate was Chephren who, probably shortly before his father's death, was married to the new heiress, Meresankh III, the daughter of Kawab. It is intriguing to examine this marriage. So far as we can establish, Chephren, or Rekhaf as he was more likely to have been called, was not the eldest son of Henutsen. Many of his brothers died before he did, as they were buried in tombs adjacent to the Great Pyramid – that is, during the reign of Cheops. It would appear, then, that with no son of Meritetes alive to succeed, the children of Henutsen were next to be considered. Once again, this all demonstrates the seniority due to birth, and for no other reason.

At what point Redjedef struck, we cannot know. It is certain that he must have had many supporters. But where was Chephren, the heir, while this was happening? We have no evidence that he was out of the country. Yet he seems to have taken no action whatever to counteract the coup. One possibility is that he was still very young. Although Henutsen bore children for Cheops long before he became King, there is still the chance that Chephren may have been born later. Against this is the fact that children matured earlier in Egypt. If Chephren had been born at the start of his father's reign he would have been 21, a grown man in Egyptian terms. Another possibility is that he was forcibly restrained by Redjedef's supporters. There has to be some reason why he was unable to strike sooner against Redjedef.

After the death of Cheops, the body of the old King would have to be taken to be prepared for burial. Plans would have to be set in motion for the funeral in the Great Pyramid. Only when the pyramid was sealed could Redjedef actually receive the crown. And only when he had received the crown would he be safe from the heir Chephren. This would have taken time. If Chephren was forcibly restrained, it would have had to be for several weeks, if not months. Chephren himself would have had his own supporters within the palace. The struggles between the two sides during this period must have seemed akin to a war within the family. The resolution occurred only at the marriage of Redjedef and Hetepheres II. For this reason, many scholars have suggested that the union was forced on her against her will, as we've seen. Certainly, to lose first her brother-husband and then, shortly afterwards, her father, must have been devastating. Perhaps she was in no condition to argue back against a forced union. On the other hand, perhaps it was a willing marriage and she was one of Redjedef's supporters. The marriage changed everything. Chephren lost the throne.

Redjedef officiated at the burial of his father, and it was thus probably he who entered the pyramid in order to carry out the final rite of Opening the Mouth on his father's body. Immediately after the pyramid had been sealed, he would have been taken to White Wall to receive the crown.

The coronation

Coronations, surprisingly, are rarely shown in Egyptian art. On the Red Chapel of the 18th Dynasty female King Hatshepsut, now reconstructed in the open-air museum to the north of Karnak temple, stones show her being received as King. Although this was centuries after the death of Cheops and in a new era, the New Kingdom, the rites of passage of a person or nation seldom changed significantly, since this moment was charged, so it was believed, with divine power. The prospective King was ushered five successive times into the sanctuary assisted by a goddess. In reality, this would undoubtedly have been an assistant, probably a sister or daughter. Once within the sanctuary, the King received a series of crowns, each one confirming a different aspect of Kingship. On each occasion, words would be spoken which became the new monarch's series of five names. The sceptres, wands of power, were accepted each time until finally the regalia, the crook and 'flail', were given.

On one of these occasions, the *nemes* or striped headcloth with its *uraeus* or rearing cobra diadem, was given. This is the crown most associated with images of the Kings of the Old Kingdom, thanks to the Sphinx. Unlike earlier Kings, for some unaccountable reason Redjedef now changed the procedure. He was declared, or declared himself, to be a Son of Re, the first time this had ever happened. Did he then, in usurping the throne, believe himself literally to be a son of god? And if so, then what did this make of his father Cheops? Or is this the reason for his burial near Heliopolis, home of Re – that he was rejecting his father Cheops even as a father? Forever afterwards, future Kings followed his example. The old ways of Cheops were already changing.

Once finally crowned, then in some final, unrecorded act of greatest ritual or magic, King Redjedef was elevated beyond the ranks of man to the ranks of semi-god. The celebration, his 'appearance' in public, was an acceptance of his status before the whole land. From that time onwards, he was secure from attack. Or was he?

We know from inscriptions that Redjedef was King. But how did this all come about? Who backed him and pushed forward his claim against the will of his father?

The conspiracy

On many occasions in ancient Egypt, the order of succession was changed so that the expected heir did not finally come to the throne. In every case, it was for exactly the same reason. A plot was hatched within the harem. The root of this was always the desire for the mother of the future King to gain precedence where she may have had none before. The highest position any women could hold in Egypt was to be the mother of a King: he might have any number of wives but only one woman was his mother. The honour and respect held for a mother was and remains extraordinarily high. The reburial of Hetepheres by her son Cheops only serves to indicate the very special position held by a mother.

In this instance, although we do not know her name, it is more than likely that this conspiracy was hatched jointly between Redjedef and his mother. His mother's name is lost to us, a curious circumstance. She was a nonentity during the life of her husband Cheops, and her son had no hope whatever of any power. In other words, the two of them, mother and son, had everything to gain in fighting for what was not theirs, than they ever had to lose. If they lost, then they remained the same as they had always been, but if, by a miracle, they won, the supreme power belonged to them both.

The reasons, then, are not hard to see. From her birth, Meritetes held the highest position within the family as the eldest daughter of Snofru and Hetepheres. Her younger sisters never had a chance, even though their birth was equally as noble as hers. By the same token, Kawab, as eldest son of Meritetes, was always destined to rule. Within most societies there was always a place for the others; but in the family of the Fourth Dynasty Kings of Egypt, younger siblings lost everything – there was not even a minor position of power that did not owe everything to the King. Redjedef, as Cheops' son, was intelligent enough to understand that new blood and new ideas needed to enter the family from time to time. Perhaps he disliked the treatment of his mother and resented Meritetes. It seems likely that his resentment spilled over on to his father, and he thought he could do a better job of things than Cheops. At all events, he decided to do this not by moving into new, uncharted territory, but by turning the clock back to the 'good old days' of his grandparents.

With his half-brother Chephren, the son of Henutsen and now, since he was married to the daughter of Hetepheres II, his nephew also, there was both alliance and animosity. Both men had turned to Re for support, both men claimed to be 'Son of Re'. Chephren, although the son of a senior Queen to Redjedef's mother, was also passed over during his life. His marriage to Meresankh III changed all of this. He must have simmered with rage as the prize was snatched from him at the last moment.

Redjedef as King

We know now that Redjedef ordered the face of the Sphinx to be carved in his own image. There is no indication that before his time it was anything other than a large outcrop of rock. The half-man, half-lion was the stone embodiment of both the King and Re. The sun, in Egypt, was never considered an entity, a single character from dawn to dusk, but went through a number of changes. At dawn, before it rose above the horizon, he was Khepri. As he sat on the bowl of the horizon, he became Horemakhet, the Horus of the horizon, hovering with rays like great wings waiting to soar. As he rose to the zenith, he became Aten; as he set towards the west, he was Horakhte – the Horus of the second horizon, now hovering again and waiting to dip into the waters of chaos, of Atum at the limits of the physical world. The Sphinx thus became Re-Khepri as he peered eastwards towards the dawn, and Re-Horemakhet as he greeted the first rays of light. He offered shelter under the scorching rays of Aten, and behind his head, like a scarlet halo of light, he waited as Re-Horakhte sank away from sight.

This linking of the Sphinx with the sun remained in the popular memory long after the end of the Fourth and even the Fifth Dynasties. After the end of the Fifth Dynasty, the principal cult of the sun started to fade. As a religious cult it was unsuccessful because it could be seen by everyone. In this respect, it lost the exclusivity of the enshrined secret statue of a god that could only be visited by an elite body of men. By the Middle Kingdom, Amun of Karnak rose to prominence along with Kings who came from his area. Yet the priests of Heliopolis retained their wisdom, passing it down from one generation to another. For them, the Sphinx was the epitome of their god.

Perhaps it was they who told the stories of the old ways to the Crown Princes of the New Kingdom. We know that these young men went to Heliopolis to learn the secrets of governance, of controlling the cosmos. It must have been here that they were taught the secrets of the Sphinx and what it represented. The culmination of all of this, in the late reign of Amenhotep II, meant that his son, Tuthmosis, dreamed that the old god visited him. It was not surprising that the experience almost blew his mind, and that he then created a new cult for the old Sphinx.

Nor, perhaps, that his grandson, Amenhotep, listening at his father's feet, should have believed that this, after all, must be the true religion, so that he changed his name to Akhenaten and tried to bring religious practice back to the way it was during the times of his ancestors. Just as Redjedef had done, 2000 years earlier.

The downfall

Dates from the reign of Redjedef only go as high as the 'fourth occasion'. His rule is believed to have lasted for eight years, a figure agreed by the Turin Canon. But eight years seems excessively high for this King who left so little mark on the land. However, we know from Abu Roash that he and Hetepheres II had two sons and a daughter, so eight years does seem possible. In all probability, his reign was forgotten later.

We have no idea where Redjedef was buried by his half-brother Chephren when he died. It would have been logical to bury him in the middle pyramid at Giza, but workmen's graffiti and ownership of the *mastaba* tombs indicate that this was Chephren's place. Abu Roash was never completed. There is no indication of him having been buried at Dahshur or Meidum. The thought of a King left unburied, with the last rites not said for him, when a pyramid still stood empty at Dahshur and another at Meidum, sums up the viciousness of the feelings involved.

In fact, after his death, both his tomb and images and inscriptions of him at Abu Roash were smashed with great violence. His pyramid was abandoned unfinished, and what was left was deliberately flattened. The ferocity of the destruction was marked. The throne was taken by Henutsen's son Chephren. We do not have to look far for the reason for this venom.

It has been suggested that Chephren's jealousy and anger at his half-brother boiled over so much that he finally killed him. This would have been startling, as a King was believed to be inviolable. Yet we know that he was only a man, no matter what the ancient Egyptians believed. And we can also trace the long resentment between the two of them. After he usurped the throne, Chephren considered himself the true heir and successor of his father Cheops, and was eventually buried at Giza alongside him. It seems that he also usurped the Sphinx at the same time and called it his own, even though the image of the face of Redjedef denied his claims and stood as a permanent reminder. It also seems likely that he also destroyed the tomb of Kawab and Hetepheres II, whose marriage to Redjedef had raised the whole problem in the first instance.

The line of Redjedef was blackened and rejected. His daughter Neferhetepes, however, seems in time to have given birth to a son she called Userkaf. As for Chephren, he had several children by Meresankh III, but they either all died young or were disinherited. In any event, by his sister-wife Khamerernebty he had a daughter who married a cousin, Mycerinus.

When Mycerinus died, the lines of Cheops' heirs virtually died with him. There is no evidence of any child of Mycerinus' except for a daughter. Of all the many children of Cheops, none seems to have survived more than a single generation. This strongly suggests some genetic trait that was causing medical problems.

The ultimate irony is that the throne, after his death, passed into the hands of Userkaf, the grandson of the hated Redjedef. It was, then, Userkaf who ushered in the next dynasty of Kings; and it was the bloodline of Redjedef which continued through that line. Perhaps, after all, there is reason or destiny in everything.

The fearful arguments which split the palace of Cheops must have been dreadful, as brother turned against brother and not even a shared religious belief could help. The Westcar Papyrus relates that Cheops was told, 'after you, your son, and then his son, and then the eldest of the triplets who are in the belly of Ruddjedet, the wife of the priest of Re of Sakhbu'. History tells us a slightly different story. Perhaps it should have gone more like this:

> After you your lesser son; and he shall be murdered by another son; then after him his son; and then, the grandson of the murdered one shall found a new line in your place.

There were lessons to be learned from the whole period.

PART FOUR

BURYING PHARAOH

The End in Sight

—

So far as we can tell, Cheops ruled Egypt for 23 years. This figure is proposed by the Turin Canon. During his reign, a count was made every second year of all he owned throughout Egypt. We have record of the 12th count, which would thus agree with the Turin Canon.

Although Cheops is a shadowy character in history, few other rulers of any civilization have left behind such an impressive monument. As we have seen, using clues from a variety of sources, we can construct some evidence for his life. Scanty though it may be, there is some basis for believing that the several generations of direct inbreeding of which Cheops was the result may have resulted in genetic problems within his family. We cannot be certain if his reclusiveness may in fact have been due in part to some genetic weakness within himself. We know that although he fathered many sons, the line started to dwindle in his grandsons and then left few claimants to the throne.

During his reign, and perhaps from the very start of it, we see the rise of the cult of Re, and with it the increasing importance of the priests of the temple of Heliopolis, ancient Iunu. There is little archaeological or inscriptional evidence of a cult there before this time. The people who worked within the temple here were, unusually, called seers – 'the ones who see'.

We know that the Egyptians were, as Herodotus put it, 'religious to extreme, beyond any other nation'. This fervour was better characterized by Joyce Tyldesley, who stated that religion, to the ancient Egyptian individual, was more a matter of magic laced with superstition. Every event in the life of a King, as an individual or in the state, was hidebound by practices and ceremonies which depended on the observation of nature – timings fixed according to the stars or the solar cycle. We know that in later generations, these observations, together with the wisdom they imparted, were exclusive to Heliopolis. This, then, is why they were called 'the seers'.

Understanding this, then, although we have no direct evidence (the site of the temple of Re in Heliopolis now lies beneath a modern university, called Ain Shams, 'the Sun'), there is good reason to suggest that the cult of Heliopolis was originally formed to interpret the movements of the stars and the constellations through what we might call astrology. At the start of the Old Kingdom, the awareness of how important the role of the passage of the sun was resulted in a major change in thinking. The cult at the heart of Heliopolis was redirected towards Re. It seems probable that all this happened at the same time, at the start of the reign of Cheops.

Many books on ancient Egypt concentrate on the religious revolution at the time of Akhenaten, so-called heretic King of the 18th Dynasty. As I have previously shown, there is no evidence whatever during that period to show that anything new happened. Akhenaten wanted to isolate himself in a new community dedicated to one aspect of the sun, the Aten. In so doing, in religious, social and architectural terms, he was reverting to the solar cult of the Old Kingdom. In his 'revolution' there was nothing which was not an integral part of the older cult of Re.

However, before the Fourth Dynasty, Kings did not reflect either in their names or in their philosophy any inclination towards the sun. This changed during the time of Cheops.

This, then, must have been a true revolution. The darkened temples with their secret cult images within sanctuaries far from man's sight changed overnight to open courts dominated by slender pyramids, which they called *benben* stones and which later became obelisks. The enclosed family status of the Kings opened up to allow in the influence of Re. The priests of Re must have been greatly influential in these changes, and thus we have clear evidence of outsiders infiltrating the thinking of the royal family. That this happened in two of the minor lines of Cheops' sons is probably no accident.

Yet since the very names of Redjedef and Chephren reflect this new allegiance, it has to be to their mothers that we turn. The evidence strongly suggests that several of Cheops' wives were drawn into this revolutionary new faith, going so far as to name their children after the new god. There is no evidence that Cheops himself was of the new faith. So is this another indication of the schism which tore the family apart?

Cheops, if he was aware of the problems, seems to have ridden over them. His death marked the end of an era for Egypt. After him, the rows became more public.

In this section, we shall examine the evidence for his death and the aftermath.

CHAPTER TEN

The Ships

—

The dispute between Cheops' children must have been bitter. The temporary success of Redjedef in holding on to the throne meant that he would oversee the final moments of his father's reign. According to ancient Egyptian custom, a King still ruled after his death, until the time came for him to be buried. After conducting the final rites and overseeing the burial itself, the sealing of the tomb was the moment when the country found itself without a head.

Despite the lack of inscriptions from during his reign, Cheops' power had been that of an autocratic, semi-divine King. So far as his subjects understood, he had steered the ship of state successfully through troubled waters for 23 years. But for all that, he died a very old man and his sons were also elderly.

We know that the funeral, therefore, would have been followed very soon by a coronation at which the new King, Redjedef, was declared to be a Son of the Sun. He was the first King to be crowned under the auspices of the new god whose powerbase was on the other side of the river in Heliopolis. He was confirmed into his position, but only after being given several crowns and titles. It seems that after this, however, another act was carried out at Giza, this time in the name of the new King, Redjedef. At least two huge ships were dragged through the valley temple and outside, into the cemetery of *mastaba* tombs belonging to the new King's relatives, where they were systematically dismantled and buried.

What had they been used for? Why were they buried?

A discovery in 1954

Four and a half thousand years later, on the sands of Giza, a man was checking out the exact layout of the perimeter walls which had once surrounded the Great Pyramid. Inside the massive outer enclosure wall, a smaller wall had once been built close to the pyramid, separating it from the tombs around it. It physically represented Cheops' status in life. The great hub of the city of his family, he remained forever cut off from them at the same time, by reason of his position. This distance had been maintained even in death. In truth, he must have been a very lonely man.

It was two years after the Egyptian revolution had finally removed the last King from the throne. The King who had been ousted had been Turkish, not Egyptian, and he and his family were generally detested. He had ruled as an autocratic Pharaoh and was replaced by a democratically elected president. Despite the new ideas and new processes, however, the Egyptian mentality had been formed and had run for 5000 years, and they understood a system which ran with a single head of state. Thus the new president, whose role had to be worked out just as the first King's had almost 5000 years before, found it easy to slip into a role similar to the old King's.

But for the first time in 3000 years, Egypt now ruled itself. Foreign domination of businesses and offices were all changed at the same time. The Egyptian Antiquities Service, founded in 1857 by a French archaeologist, Auguste Mariette, and controlled thereafter under English or French inspectors, reverted into the hands of the Egyptians themselves.

In 1954, the new inspectors were still finding their feet, coming to terms with the massive responsibility of the ancient civilization they had inherited and which they must, at all costs, preserve for humankind. The new inspectors for all of this were frequently rivals for power. It would be some time before procedures were in place to ensure that all decisions were taken democratically, by councils.

The pyramids and Giza were one of the main focal points for tourism. It seemed reasonable that the area around the pyramids should be tidied up. Two inspectors worked at the site. Zacharia Goneim had excited world interest already when in 1952, the year of the revolution, he had entered into the passages and burial chamber of an unfinished pyramid. This, the pyramid complex of Sekhemkhet at Saqqara, had been known about for over 100 years when the French archaeologist, Jacques De Morgan, had observed a clear series of rectangular enclosures lying in the sand behind and to the west of the Step Pyramid enclosure at Saqqara. Although it had been ascertained that each of these enclosures had been designed to form the burial site of different Kings of the Third Dynasty, none had previously been explored. Goneim decided not even to attempt to start to clear the whole compound of one of these enclosures, but instead to focus on the large mound, clearly the base of an incomplete pyramid. Following known rules for the site, he found an entrance passage that led into a burial chamber cut beneath the bedrock. In the passage, he found rare early jewellery and inscriptions naming the hitherto little-known King Sekhemkhet. In the unfinished chamber he found a rectangular alabaster sarcophagus, similar in design to the one found in the burial of Queen Hetepheres by George Reisner. Just like hers, the sarcophagus of the buried pyramid was empty, never used.

Yet the discovery had excited world interest and focused attention on this new, small group of Egyptians who were starting to cope with the massive inherited burden of controlling excavation and illegal exports of antiquities.

The second inspector at the site was the rising star Kamal El Mallakh. There was intense rivalry between the two men. Goneim's experience on Egyptian sites was remarkable. He had been trained at Cairo University under a series of great Egyptologists, and had worked on sites under Selim Hassan, a man whose careful methodology he emulated. He was made Keeper of the Theban Necropolis in 1943, and was responsible for clearing some fine tombs in the area. In 1951, he was finally made Keeper of the Saqqara Necropolis.

Now, in 1954 at Giza, the routine work of measuring, mapping the wall and tidying the area seemed inauspicious, one of those routine tasks undertaken by us all which typify scientific archaeology. History records that all the work was undertaken by Kamal Ed Mallakh; however, records of the period suggest that it was Zacharia Goneim, instead, who was working the area. There was little expectation of finding anything significant. However, measurements showed for the first time that in two areas to the south of the pyramid, the wall's foundations deviated from the expected straight line.

Having recorded all that there was to see on the surface, the foundations of the wall were tidied up. Underneath, for the first time, the outlines of a series of huge stone beams were seen clearly covering a pit in the rock. The same was found under the second area of deviation of the wall. The stone beams were huge, and in the cracks between each of them had been poured plaster. Into the plaster were impressed the cartouches, the royal names, of Redjedef, the heir of Cheops.

The beams and the pit were instantly recognized as a boat pit. Boat pits were a common feature of many ancient Egyptian royal burial sites. Most of them were boat-shaped, though all except one had previously proved to be empty. The one found intact at Dahshur contained a boat hewn from a solid wooden log. It was relatively small, crudely finished and yet exciting, since it was unique. These pits, it could be seen from the plaster and the beams, were both rectangular. This was unusual. They were also extremely large. It seemed reasonable to believe that they contained a major find.

A few months later, before an invited audience, holes were carefully knocked into the plaster between the blocks and assistants anxiously shone torches into the gaps. The first thing that everyone observed was a rush of air emerging from the pit, filled with the heavy scent of pinewood.

Below, in the light of the torch, planks and beams could be seen, with the clear outlines of a prow at one end and oars laid across the mass of timber. They had found a boat which had lain intact since the time of Cheops' death – but now it was in pieces.

The reconstruction

One thousand two hundred and twenty-four pieces of wood, plus sundry ropes, lay in 11 layers inside the huge pit. The limestone beams which covered the pit had to be lifted first and moved out of the way. This required the use of heavy lifting gear and winches operated by an electric generator which had to be dragged on to the site. Each of the beams weighed in excess of 60 tons. The plaster between them had to be broken away. The lifting job alone took many weeks, during which time the wood was at first exposed to the elements, although slowly bits of it could be lifted.

It was found to be in excellent condition, despite its great age. The pit had been totally sealed, they now realized. With a great deal of excitement, they concluded that the rush of air which had left the pit as they broke through the plaster was literally the breath of the Fourth Dynasty itself, sealed in the pit for 4500 years. The second deviation was a matching pit, also sealed with limestone beams and plaster. It seemed reasonable to expect that a second boat lay in there. However, the wood in the first pit, which had managed to retain both its weight and its patina, slowly began to deteriorate in the modern air and with movement around it.

Ancient ships are extremely rare, and most of those which have survived have been found preserved in deep water, in anaerobic, wet conditions. Experiments showed that they could be conserved indefinitely, first by removing any impurities within the structure of the wood in fresh, clean water. It was especially vital to remove salt from timbers preserved in the sea, and to remove embedded impurities from freshwater beds. The process could be achieved, as with the *Mary Rose*, the flagship of Henry VIII, rescued in 1982, by spraying it for many months. In other cases, such as timbers from Scandinavian ships, they could be laid to soak in water which was continually recycled and renewed. Once the impurities, even to the heart of the timbers, could be expected to have been removed, they could be sprayed for an equally long time with a solution of polyethylene glycol, or PEG. This, a form of antifreeze commonly used in car engines, is diluted in freshwater. The PEG slowly builds up a waxy substance from the middle of the wood, giving it strength and permanent stability.

But this method could not be used on dry-preserved timbers. Any dampness at all on the surface of this very ancient wood would cause it to crumble into dust. Conservators were called in. It was a great concern. The dismantled ship was a masterpiece, its very survival a miracle. Few other areas of archaeology could ever hope to yield ancient timbers such as this. It was vital that every care should be taken with it.

On the other hand, no immediate method of conservation could be used other than to keep it as warm and dry as possible. The priority, it was decided, was to rebuild the ship in order to discover how these sectioned Egyptian boats had been made. It was an unprecedented opportunity. If by chance the timbers did not survive, then experiments could be carried out on the wood to find effective methods to conserve it, knowing that the second boat was still sealed intact in the other pit. It was an easy decision to leave this second pit untouched until the technology to preserve it was right. It was an insurance policy. In the meantime, funding was sought and granted to build a specially designed museum on the pyramid site to house the completed ship.

The woods used for the boat are still a matter of discussion. In *Ancient Egyptian Materials and Technologies*, Russell Meiggs and Paul Lipke have both positively identified the principal wood used as cedar. By the same token, every type of Egyptian wood so far identified except for box, carob and tamarisk were used for boat-building. It makes sense that hull planks, deck planks, oars, rudders and masts needed different types of wood to bring out their strengths. In this book, Ian Shaw discusses the problems over identification of wood from coniferous trees in general, and cedar specifically.

> It seems therefore not only possible, but probable, that the word 'cedar' has always been used in a loose manner and that, even when there is no longer any difference of opinion about the ancient Egyptian name for true cedar, there will still remain a doubt as to whether a particular wood so designated was indeed cedar. Many of the objects loosely described as 'cedar' in museum catalogues most certainly are not.

Cedar is a heavily resinated, decorative wood generally imported from the Lebanon through Byblos. There is a general misconception that wood was scarce if not unobtainable in ancient Egypt, and thus almost all wood had to be imported. This is far from the truth. Certainly in the Old Kingdom, artefacts, inscriptions and images prove that Egypt was heavily wooded by the riverside with all variety of trees, from the willowy, pollarded woods such as acacia and persea, to the hard woods such as oak, ash, elm and lime, and coniferous trees, not to mention the palms. Degradation of the tree resource undoubtedly started as settlement increased, with wood used for basic building material, for fuel and for food for browsing animals. Processing of mineral ores increased the use of wood as charcoal was made in vast quantities to fuel the furnaces to raise the temperatures needed. While wood became a scarcer commodity in the New Kingdom, in the Old Kingdom there were few problems in finding native woods needed.

A closer analysis of the various types of wood used in the boat pit is still needed to identify the usage of variant timbers in some of the smaller sections. For the most part, the hull planks were primarily made of some variety of pine – perhaps juniper; perhaps, although this is unlikely, Lebanese cedar, as there were many native Egyptian varieties of cedar available.

It became immediately obvious that the method of constructing Cheops' boat was unusual. There were a number of ribs, each carved from a single piece of wood with crude adzing marks still visible. It appeared that the ribs were made first and that the hull, made of edge-to-edge fitting planks, curled around them. It also became apparent, since there was no handbook for its reconstruction and since the ribs only fitted in one place, that this process was going to be a matter of trial and error until the correct order was established.

The hull planks were all of different lengths. None of them stretched the full length of the boat. Each plank was drilled through from the inside at an angle of 45 degrees, to appear in the middle of the edge. The planks were then 'stitched' together with strong ropes. At every joint between the planks, a thin strip of wood was placed on the inside face against the joint, held in place by the ropes. These, it appeared, were caulking strips. Many boat-builders making wooden ships caulked, or waterproofed, them from the outside, often using tarred cord rammed into the gaps. This method, to caulk from the inside, was unusual but would have been most effective. As the ropes got wet and shrank, they would tighten over the caulking strips and thus totally seal the joints.

The ship's construction and timbers

Having established the order of the ribs, X-shaped timbers, one end at right angles to the other, were placed into the ribs. The upper part supported one long timber which ran from bow to stern and formed the main support of the decking. Along each side of the hull, right-angled sections of wood were attached and these formed the edges on which the deck planks stood.

The ship was of a very shallow draught and, it became quickly clear, was curved in a very steep angle from bow to stern. Amidships, the boat sat very low in the water indeed. To the bow and stern fitted prows, each fitted with mortice and tenon, which formed the traditional 'divine barque' shape: These two posts were not part of the structure of the ship but could be added or removed at will. Amidships and slightly to the stern stood a cabin, its walls formed with panels of timber, its barrel-vaulted roof supported by internal columns, and slender 'tent pole' columns set against each outer side of the cabin walls. This cabin appears today to slope forwards. However, this is purely because of the modern mountings in the museum. When the ship floated, the rear would have sat lower in the water, making the cabin roof completely flat.

There was no keel. The ship, with its two ends jutting out of the water, would have been a moody craft to sail, barely skimming over the surface of the water, so low amidships that even a slight turbulence would cause a wash over the deck, and so light that in a wind of any strength it would become hard to steer.

At the bow of the ship, a pilot's cabin stood open to the air, clearly once covered with a canopy or awning. From here, a pilot could take soundings of the riverbed. The Nile is notorious for its shifting sand shoals, and even today seldom does any cruise boat make even the shortest of journeys without striking one on the way. Out to one side there jutted a platform, the purpose of which was unclear, but could have served for men to throw ropes ashore to moor, and to push off.

Steering was achieved by two huge rudder oars at the rear of the ship. These were too large in diameter to be handled easily. They would have been lashed to the sides of the boat and had then to be turned. Forward of the main cabin, five pairs of leaf-shaped oars soared above the deck so high that they cross in the centre. Like the rudder oars, they were far too large to be used as ordinary oars and the blades were too narrow to be of any real use. Like the rudder oars, it seems likely that they too were lashed into place and 'decorated' with handsome youths and pretty girls. It is clear that the main purpose of the ship was to be decorative, a royal state barge and not a working ship.

Analysis of the hull showed trace elements of pigment within the wood. The ship had clearly once been gaily caparisoned, with painted sides, coloured awnings over the main and pilot's cabins, and probably coloured sails too, if painted images of Egyptian ships are to be believed. The shape and draught of the hull confirmed beyond doubt that this was intended as a riverine craft. The Egyptians, happy on their river, felt ill at ease if ever they put to sea. By and large they seem to have travelled abroad by hugging the coast and putting into port every night. There was certainly no space below decks on Cheops' boat to stow anything, and certainly no space for sailors to sleep easily.

It took several attempts to rebuild the ship, to ensure that each piece was in the correct place and nothing was left over at the end. As expected, the wood proved to be strong enough even after the long passage of time to bear its own weight in the final display. Only one section, a blade of one of the 10 leaf-shaped oars, was too badly damaged to be used and had to be replaced.

The completed ship was placed on supports in the specially designed museum below the Great Pyramid at Giza in 1972, on top of the pit where it was originally found. It is without doubt one of the masterpieces of ancient Egypt. Yet tourists who come to visit Giza frequently do not even bother to go and look at it. They often seem not to appreciate its miraculous survival. In some ways, its very perfection creates this impression. Somehow, a wreck which has parts missing and looks its age will inspire wonder. The Cheops boat is so complete and perfect, it is almost impossible to comprehend that this is the actual wood, without replacement, which Cheops' sons placed here so very, very long ago. To look at the cabin and truly understand that the builder of the Great Pyramid once sat on these very boards make the intervening years suddenly seem to mean absolutely nothing. Thousands of years drop away in an instant.

As the saying goes: 'All things fear Time; but Time itself fears the pyramids.' In this case, it includes Cheops' ship also.

The use of the ship

The completed ship was 142 feet long, although in the years since its eventual display in the purpose-built museum, it has already shrunk. It is a wooden copy of an earlier reed craft. The Egyptians, despite Thor Heyerdahl's magnificent efforts in building and sailing *Ra* and *Ra II*, never used reed ships in the historical period except for small, one-man skiffs for hunting in the marshes. However, the boat's shape, with its characteristic stern post which bends back over the deck, could only be achieved originally with reeds. Bundles of them would have been lashed together, tapering towards each end, with prows raised high. Then the bow and stern would have to be joined together, tied the full length of the ship with a hogging truss – a rope which was tightened with a stick twisted in the centre. This ensured that the craft would not twist in opposite directions between the bow and stern, but would stay stable along its length. Such a hogging truss produces the distinctive stern post, but would be of no use whatever on a wooden craft. Clearly, by the time the Egyptians became a united nation, they had reverted to the use of wood.

Ever since the ship was first publicized it has been popularly called the 'solar barque'. This term applies to a spiritual ship believed to sail across the sky during the day, and across the sky of the afterlife by night. According to the religion of Re, the King's soul would accompany the sun on such a boat on its daily journey. So it was assumed that the ship would be for this purpose.

This seems most unlikely for many reasons. First, the caulking strips have clear delineations of shrunken ropes on them – in other words, the ship was wet at some point. Secondly, any culture which could build a pyramid accurately out of solid stone 481 feet high could undoubtedly cut a trench for a ship which would be the right size without having to dismantle it first. After all, if religious beliefs stated that the King's soul would join this barque, then was the soul also supposed to emerge with the correct tools to reconstruct it first? It makes no sense. Thirdly, and most importantly, as we have seen, the religious beliefs at the time of the building of the Great Pyramid were associated with the stars, not the sun, going by the alignment of the ventilation shafts. More significantly, these boat pits have been found with every single early royal burial back to the First Dynasty at Abydos and Saqqara – and they most certainly did not have any leanings towards the cult of Re.

The evidence points clearly to the ship having been used during the King's life. The uselessness of the oars suggests it would have had to be towed either by another ship or by a team pulling on land, or that it was going very short distances, such as from the east bank to the west. The use of paint on the hull and the provision for awnings suggest it was intended for use in the full heat of the sun and on public display. And there's the proof that it was wet at an early date.

All forms of archaeology are too keen to attribute 'religious, cultic or mystic significance' to all sorts of artefacts, from tiny ones to hulking ones like this. Often these objects have more practical worth. In this instance there can be no doubt that the ship was used, probably as a state barge, by Cheops himself. Its presence at the site suggests that it was used after the time of the King's burial. In other words, not only may it have carried the King while he was alive – it may indeed have brought his body to the plateau from the palace.

The second pit

The first ship was placed on public display with little attempt to conserve it in any major way. Visitors to the museum are still exhorted to wear crude canvas shoes within the museum to stop sand and dust from the outside being introduced into the display area. To be frank, however, dry dust would do little damage. More harm is caused by the evaporation of body fluids through perspiration or sweat from visitors. This invisible moisture is always present in the air. Even the movement of air caused by people walking around the ancient timbers is destructive in its way. The only way to prevent any future decay would be to seal it anaerobically within a case, where the temperature and humidity could be strictly controlled. With a smaller item, this might be feasible, but with a great ship, even if the technology existed to create a case which could be vacuum-sealed and yet still could be seen through, the cost would be prohibitive. So the ship stands open and moves inexorably to its final collapse and destruction. It simply cannot and will not last forever. In the years since it was opened to the public, the original patina of the wood was the first thing to vanish, leaving the surface matt and darkened. The hull planks which at the time of display formed a smooth exterior, have now shrunk individually and have moved away from each other. The length of the ship has reduced, some say, by as much as a yard overall.

The only optimistic element in all of this was the knowledge that the second pit was still safely sealed. Once the seals had been broken on the first pit, and air had entered in, then there was simply no choice but to remove the wood and to rebuild it while it still existed. Its display was also inevitable, to allow the world also to gaze in awe at the pyramid builder's own ship while it still existed.

Once the urgency over the rebuilding and display was at an end, scientists could sit and reflect on the success of the venture, and start to analyse the whole procedure to learn lessons from what had happened. Attention turned, time after time, to the rush of sweet air from the pit when the first seal was broken. The thought occurred constantly and to many – to see a 4500-year-old object of any kind is overwhelming, but when do we ever have the chance to breathe the actual air that they breathed? Researchers became increasingly disturbed that an element of the first pit had been allowed simply to drift away unexamined. The loss was frustrating.

In the early 1980s it became apparent that the technology which allowed for the gathering of rock and soil samples into lunar landing crafts might be usable on the second pit on the plateau. It seemed reasonable that if the seal on the second pit could be broken under controlled conditions, a fibre-optic probe could be inserted. This could at one time pass light into the pit to illuminate the contents, allow the contents to be filmed to check exactly what was there and what condition it was in and also to sample the air from the pit and test its contents. The seal could then be reapplied without any modern contaminants entering. We could, in effect, answer our questions while leaving the second ship safe in its sealed pit. The notion was so exciting that *National Geographic* agreed to sponsor the tests.

In 1985, equipment originating from NASA was taken to

Giza. The event aroused world media interest. For some months before, the press had become increasingly excited over the possibilities of what might be discovered. The air within the pit, they reported, was going to be tested minutely. We would then be able to compare it with today's air to find out if the structure of the mix had actually changed. We could also compare radioactivity in the two samples, and, more importantly for modern Cairo, test the air quality and measure pollution levels, ancient and modern. Lessons could be learned. The experiment was a serious one, but very quickly, in the glare of publicity, the focus began to shift. Newspaper articles appeared with headlines such as 'Detecting Pharaoh's cooking smells'. Would it be possible, reporters and editors mused, to discern the smoke from ancient cooking fires? Visions swam before the imagination of ancient barbecues on the building site, the smell of roasting meat and fresh bread being captured forever in the pit. In *El Ahram*, the Egyptian national daily paper, one article went even further. One assiduous reporter, noting carved and painted images of an ancient metal-smelting furnace into which workers blew air through tubes, or *tuyères*, to raise the temperature, totally misread the information and got the idea that these were *shishas* or hubble-bubble pipes. They produced an article entitled 'Did the pyramid builders smoke?' Now the popular imagination really ran riot. Did the pyramid builders have breaks for a burger and chips, a quick beer and a quick smoke during their break? The possibilities seemed endless – and hilarious.

The tests were carried out in an atmosphere of scientific caution laced with immense excitement. The use of modern technology that allowed non-intrusive examinations of any ancient material was intriguing as well as ground-breaking. Perhaps the same methods could be used elsewhere – to insert into an unopened tomb, for instance, without having to open it up and thus indicate its existence to tomb robbers. Everyone present knew that archaeological history was about to be made.

In what other form of archaeology could you test the air that our ancestors breathed?

The break having been made in the surrounding plaster infill, probes were carefully inserted, making certain that no modern air was allowed any entry. The lights were switched on and illuminated the pit while filming the contents. To no one's real surprise, the pit, like the first, was filled with layers of wood from a second dismantled ship. To everyone's utter dismay, however, one of the first things to be observed by the screen-watchers was a beetle scurrying across the surface of the wood. The wood, meanwhile, seemed strangely matt, totally lacking in lustre. If the pit had indeed been anaerobically sealed, no life form could exist within it. Their worst fears were confirmed when the air was finally tested. It was estimated as being around 48 hours old!

It was only later that the dreadful truth finally came to light. In 1954, when the first pit was opened and lifting equipment was brought on to the plateau, much of the heavy machinery, plus the electric generators, had been placed on top of the second pit, as it was a smooth, flat surface. The regular throbbing of the generators and the vibrations of the machinery had broken the plaster seal. For thirty years, we had been confident that the second pit was safe forever. Now it seemed that for all that time, air and moisture had been entering the second pit.

Tests later confirmed the awful truth. The wood in the second pit had slowly started to decay from the early 1950s as modern air and rainwater had seeped in. The wood, it seemed, would be brittle and friable. If touched, it would probably simply crumble into dust. It was utterly beyond repair.

The survival of any wood as old as the ship was a miracle. To be able to restore and view a ship in which Cheops had once sailed was a breathtaking opportunity.

It seems that when Cheops had died, his body would have been carried out of the palace and down to the local jetty. From here, although only a matter of a few yards, the boat was drawn by workers to the *re-esh* and the entrance to the pyramid compound. This would probably have happened very soon after he died, as in the stifling heat of Egypt, decay starts rapidly after death. If only the wood of the ship could bear testimony to that day, perhaps it could release for us the keening cries of women, mourning and shrieking as their dead King was carried away from them.

Once arrived at the Valley temple, as we call it, while the body of the King was taken for evisceration and mummification, the boat was probably dismantled then and there and either piled up in a pit to be sealed later, or simply stacked up until the pit was ready. We know beyond doubt that the boats, in their twin pits, would only have been sealed finally after the burial of the old King, since King Redjedef's seals were impressed into the soft plaster which sealed them.

It is a matter of intrigue and deep concern that our chance to test the air of the time of Cheops was thwarted by a preventable mistake. It remains a constant source of theorizing. Would the air have had the same balance in it then as today? Have our years of exploding nuclear weapons had any marked effect on the air around us? And though we can assure everyone that the Egyptians did *not* smoke – still there remains that lingering wistfulness – perhaps, just perhaps, we may have gained a wisp of some ancient smoke lost from a cooking fire and trapped inadvertently in the pit.

It is a sobering thought. Perhaps one day we may be lucky again and find more intact pits. For the moment, we are left with a remarkable archaeological object and a deep sense of regret.

CHAPTER ELEVEN

The End of an Era

—

The reign of Cheops was probably the most extreme example of autocratic power in the whole of ancient Egyptian history. The status of the monarchy was established by Imhotep for his King, Netcherikhe, builder of the Step Pyramid. In building for him the first massive funerary monument at Saqqara, Imhotep created an illusion of separateness and supremacy that continued until the end of the Fourth Dynasty. The building of this first pyramid is more than a problem-solving exercise in technology and organization; it marked the start of the cult of the monarch himself.

It is easy, in retrospect, to understand the elementary mistakes that were made in this way. Imhotep was attempting, it seems, to finally bring some peace to a country which had been torn apart by internal strife for probably three centuries. The unifier of the land had gained little more than time. Although the country had taken shape geographically, politically and economically, it lacked focus. Imhotep's solution, the creation of a single power, seemed to be a good idea based on logical reasoning. But it had one single point of weakness. Who should hold that single power? The allure of absolute power was too great to resist, so little wonder that every head of every family wanted it for himself.

In the creation of an administrative infrastructure brought

together to build a pyramid, a single act designed to unite the people politically, Imhotep tried to give the country a message of hope. The original theory of a single King was good, but for around three centuries no one had seen any benefit from it. Instead they had had to suffer years of jealousy, greed and continual war. People needed to realize the benefits of having one single overlord. They now worked and produced their crops for a King who was effectively their owner, and in return he kept them alive.

Next, using the power of charisma and 'spin', a public illusion was created around the King that he alone was able to communicate with the powers of the universe, and that by maintaining daily order the functioning of Nature itself could be controlled. By making the King responsible for the passage of the sun and the rising of the Nile, a role was created for him beyond the understanding of ordinary men, that was at the same time so vital to the country that everyone was pleased to give him total responsibility for it all. This was a function that in theory none but he could fulfil. It required knowledge that leaders of other families did not have. In a stroke of brilliance, the Egyptian King was lifted beyond petty local squabbles to a new plane, where none except his direct heir could reach him.

Since the fruits of the land were created first by the powers of Nature, these fruits belonged to the King: he created them. But how could they be distributed so that everyone would benefit? He might have the right to bring everything under the roofs of state granaries and treasuries, but how then were they to be distributed? By giving the state, and thus the King, the right of largesse, the sole right to hand out all foods and all benefits in kind, the system made the King the benevolent Father of the Nation. The idea of getting all men to join in some way, to give them a common purpose for the benefit of the man whom they thought gave them life itself was, again, quite brilliant. It took their minds off fighting, brought them together in a single purpose, and allowed the state to create the first pay structure.

The basis of this was food. If you were fed, you were paid. If you were fed by the state, you worked for the state. The King was responsible for the land, so the food was his, and to be paid, you would have to work for him.

It is equally clear in hindsight that Imhotep's plan went somewhat awry. It needed a strong man at the helm other than the King, whose responsibilities were now seen to be elsewhere. The organization lay in the hands of Imhotep, and when he died, although people may have understood a little of how he achieved it, no one was capable of stepping into his shoes. The organization and stability which he created collapsed at his death.

Snofru seems to have resolved the problem. He is remembered as a kindly and benevolent man, but reading from the patterns of history, we know he was a man of brilliance. We know nothing of his ancestors of the Third Dynasty, but we do know that he married his own sister. Was he the first to do so? Once again, the reasoning seemed sound in an age when the shortcomings of incestuous relationships could not be understood. He set a pattern which further isolated himself and his family from the rest of the state. The removal of 7000 Nubians, recorded by the Palermo Stone, leaves us in a quandary. Why precisely did he do this? We know from inscriptions that the Egyptians traded with the south, and it seems reasonable to suggest that he was merely defending his routes from attack. The immigration of thousands of Nubian families into Egypt gave him the controllable manpower resource needed to fire up the pyramid-building industry. It is, therefore, equally feasible that the weakness of Imhotep's master plan was that the Egyptian population was not large enough to spare enough men permanently actually to do the building work.

Cheops' parents were brother and sister, and we know that not only he but also all of his brothers married their full-blood sisters. Snofru and Hetepheres seem to have had a very fruitful relationship. While Cheops' brothers each married only one

317

sister, Cheops himself married at least three of his. We know that at least one of these marriages, with Meritetes, happened long before he became King, but we cannot be so certain about the other marriages. Cheops eventually ruled for 23 years. His children by Henutsen lived long enough to see one of them, Rekhaf or Chephren, inherit the throne. So it may well be that this lesser marriage came only after he became King. Perhaps this accounts for the resentment felt by the children of the lesser wives, that they had been born as sons of a King, whereas the children of Meritetes had been born only to a Crown Prince.

At any rate, it was during the reign of Cheops that the weaknesses in the plan of Imhotep were finally realized. In the case of Old Kingdom Egypt, the wielding of absolute power corrupted absolutely. The practice of internal family marriage, designed to keep others out, missed one vital point: it was based on the false premise that all families would be loyal and stick together and not fight among themselves. This was the undoing of Cheops. There was nothing for his children to do. It was one thing to accept an heir by birth, such as Kawab, but when he died, the various sons had nothing to lose and everything to gain by fighting for their chance to steal the power. It turned son against son, brother against brother; and all of it happened in private, away from the eyes of the public, who could never start to guess what was really going on.

The Westcar Papyrus gives us an insider's glimpse of this tormented family. Cheops is shown to be distrustful, determined to gain for himself the wisdom that, he believed, might solve his problems. When he is told that his family will die out after only two generations, and that the gods were playing games with his fate, there is nothing he can do. His power is stripped away. Although the public may believe that the sun rose and set at his command, in private he was a mere man, incapable of changing a single thing. In one scene Cheops, wanting to test the abilities of the magician brought to him by his son Baufre, orders the magician to take a prisoner, cut off his head and rejoin it to the body. The magician gently refuses. 'Not one of god's cattle,' he replies. This is, in the end, what Cheops is reduced to, a creature at the whim of fate. He may seem to have everything, but once the powers of god are brought into play, there is nothing he can do. No matter how successful he may appear to be, at the end of the day his family will die out, as we know from retrospect, and he will be powerless. The illusion created by Imhotep is shattered. He was only another man.

The battles between Redjedef and Chephren were resolved by the death or murder of Redjedef, leaving the heirs of the deposed Kings in the cold. Chephren maintained the public illusion of control, yet his marriages, although apparently fruitful, resulted in lines which petered out. His son, Mycerinus, passed the bloodline into his daughter who seems, from the family tree, to have no one left to marry except for the grandson of the deposed Redjedef.

The collapse of the family tree may owe something to genetic inbreeding, although we cannot now trace it. The systematic robbery of human remains from the pyramid chambers means no testable material has survived. The prolific families of Cheops and, to an extent, Chephren, which simply vanish away, show us that there was some major health problem. It may simply have been an outbreak of plague, typhoid, cholera – one of those many diseases which spread like wildfire among any population before control existed.

The reign of Cheops was a watershed in the exercise of power. The rapid decline of his family after his death indicated that changes needed to be made. They were slow in coming. But by the end of the Old Kingdom, revolt started to spread against this system which did not work. Naguib Kanawati pointed out, in his *Governmental Reforms in Old Kingdom Egypt*, that at the start of the Fifth Dynasty, Neferirkare issued a 'standard system of ranking titles in place of the informal, rather haphazard system which prevailed before'. In other words, the Fourth Dynasty system of handing out offices at the King's gift to those related to him, regardless or not of whether they were capable of doing anything, had to end. By the start of the Fifth Dynasty, the administrative system was close to collapse and had to be restructured to cope. This could have been because the line of royal men died out. It could equally have been because of incompetence brought about by their genetic make-up. But whatever the cause, the outcome was that the process of revolt started by Redjedef started to creep through society like ripples in a great pond. Once Redjedef started to look beyond his own family for advice and friendship, things had to change.

Cheops' rule may have seemed to be one of glittering, golden sunlight. But every sun had to set, and for Cheops and his family it was only a matter of time.

The death and burial

Soon after Cheops was crowned King, the first cracks of disorder were felt in Egyptian society. At distant Dahshur, the burial of Cheops' beloved mother was broken into by robbers, a most sacrilegious act. During the robbery, many of her belongings were damaged or removed, including, most importantly of all, her body. Who would have dared to enter into the tomb of the King's mother, King's daughter Hetepheres? It would have taken great daring and courage, linked with an increasing sense of frustration and an awareness that this King was, after all, nothing but a man. It seems that the scales were falling from the eyes of the Egyptian workers.

One of Cheops' sons would have had to bring the news of the violation to his father, since all posts of authority, such as they were, were held by them. George Reisner postulates that they did not have the nerve to tell him of the destruction of his mother's body. Arrangements were made for a reburial close to his own chosen place, the completed Northern Pyramid of

Giza. A shaft was quickly hewn into the soft bedrock, with a crude chamber at its foot about 100 feet down. Here were piled her tent and the camping equipment she had used while accompanying her royal husband, Cheops' father, out into the field of battle, such as it was. Her possessions were laid reverentially into the chamber as they were carried over from Dahshur, in reverse order to the original burial. As Cheops watched the lowering of the sarcophagus into the shaft, he would never know that the sarcophagus was empty. As the shaft was filled, he placed three legs of beef and an ox's head, carefully wrapped in linen, with jars of wine, into a niche for her food on her journey into the afterlife among the stars.

Inside the palace at Giza, at the foot of the three pyramids whose platforms, at various stages of completion, were visible over the stone wall which divided their realm from that of the living, a wail of despair would have filled the air. Crown Prince Kawab was dead. While his widow Hetepheres II wept, her half-brother Redjedef, filled with ambition, cast aside or removed his present wife and, some say, forced himself on the unwilling Queen. Hetepheres II, like all Egyptian women of the time, was by tradition a creature of contradiction. Against men she had no real power, no ability to question or to resist. Yet at the same time, whoever controlled her took the crown. It seems that she herself thought that her time was drawing to a close, since she married her blond daughter, Meresankh III, to one of Henutsen's sons, Chephren. It seemed so simple until Redjedef changed the game entirely.

Redjedef, since birth and childhood, was loyal to new ideas. A revolution was underway, starting within the royal family and spreading out into all Egypt. He had powerful supporters outside the palace based on the temple of Heliopolis. Many people in the country showed, through their names and the names they were giving their children, that Re was about to be victorious over the old ways of Cheops. His mother, above all, watched the supremacy of her sisters with jealousy. She began to whisper about how things might have been different. Once the seeds were sown, events moved inexorably towards their conclusion. Her leanings towards the new religion alienated her from her brother-husband, who was too deeply entrenched in the old ways to consider change.

Once Cheops was dead, there was nothing to stand in the way of the powerful new movement. Redjedef controlled enough influence at court, as well as the heiress Hetepheres, to hold Chephren's claim at bay. Unlike his father Cheops, who had kept himself to himself, Redjedef allowed others to influence, perhaps even to control, him.

His ideas were radical, shocking even. At Giza, at right angles to the northern palace wall, he ordered an image to be built from a knoll of rock left from the quarry nearby. This creature, with the body of a lion and the head of a man carved in his own image, represented the sun god to whom he owed his total allegiance. In front of it, he ordered a temple to be built. The front wall, undoubtedly, was high enough to secrete the face of the great statue, since the body had been carved from the bedrock and only the head jutted out above the surface. Anyone who was allowed within the walls of the temple would follow a processional route towards the back where, by tradition, a small sanctuary would have housed the gilded image of a god. Here, it was, like his father's and grandfather's monuments, on a gargantuan scale. Doors flung open brought you out into daylight. It would not do for the image of Re to be kept in darkness! The great, painted face leered down at you, terrifying and awe-inspiring, Redjedef's idea of the very image of god.

Giza now belonged to Re, not to man. Redjedef wanted his own resting place to be built in sight of Heliopolis, home of Re. He turned his back on more than his father's beliefs. He ordered the pyramid to be built on a rectangular base, like the first one ordered by Imhotep, with the walls steep and inclined like that built at Meidum.

Down in Giza, in the palace, plans for his father's funeral had to be made.

The mummification

The journey from the front entrance of the palace to the entrance of the necropolis which had been created for him was only a short one, less than half a mile by modern measurements. The palace building was contained within a great wall with a door facing the necropolis site, through which flooded daily the food and essential supports for the staff working on the building site. It was in effect the tradesmen's entrance, certainly not the door through which a dead King's body could pass. The body was removed from the palace to a jetty where it was carried on to a ship. A second ship, tied behind it, carried equipment needed for the funeral and burial. The state barges – wooden copies of traditional reed ships – were painted gaudily along the sides. The bow-posts were secured with ropes and then towed by gangs along the west bank northwards, while the court wailed, 'Head on knee.'

The ships were dragged into the *re-esh*, the harbour created at the start of the building work at the foot of the plateau. The waters of the harbour, shallow and quiet, reflected the images of four temples. The northernmost of these, standing alongside the workers' village, stood ready to accept the body of the King.

The preparation of the King's body was a matter of sacred ritual. His internal organs would have been removed, as were his mother's before him, and placed in a canopic chest. His body was cleansed. We do not know, at this stage, that it would have been dried at all. Rather, we know that the body would be carefully wrapped, limb by limb, and resins brushed on, constantly and liberally at every stage. Once the wrapping was completed, the last resin hardened, then the face of Cheops would have been shown accurately, as the wet bandages had

followed the lines of his eyes, his nose, his lips. On the hardened case, the face was coloured, the black wig, the eyes,
eyebrows and moustache marked in black, the lips slightly
reddened. At every stage, readings were spoken over the amu-
lets, the wrappings and the body to ensure it was done safely
and correctly.

The body, prepared within the Valley temple and hard as
stone, could now be carried, shoulder high, going by later
images, out of the back of the temple. Here it was quiet and
dark. Once there had been a causeway here. Now it was a
tunnel, walls carved and lightly painted with scenes from his
august life, idealized and propagandized as his public life had
been. Oil lamps burned against the walls to light their way in
the unaccustomed darkness. Outside the corridor walls, where
the tombs stood for his family, some occupied, others standing
empty, perhaps sand had already started to accumulate. Perhaps it already covered the passage. It was of no interest.
Once within the passage, it was like walking through an
underground corridor, and the light of the sun would never be
witnessed again by the remains of the King that they carried.

At the top of a long slope, the height of the ceiling was raised
as they entered into a columned hall with walls of red polished
granite, cold despite the heat outside, in the physical world of
the desert. The final acts had to be carried out by Redjedef, who
touched an adze made from a meteor, iron which they called
'the bones of the gods', to his father's eyes, nose, lips, ears,
throat, hands, genitals and feet, believing, as they all did, that
this would restore the senses of the now vacant shell of a great
man.

The corridors beyond the hall of the Opening of the Mouth
turned slightly to the right as they walked around the
perimeter of the pyramid, its shining, white-cased walls
rising at their left. On the west face, ramps or a staircase had
to rise from the desert floor to give them access to the
pyramid. Redjedef would undoubtedly have accompanied the

procession. Whether Chephren, his rival, was allowed to be there is unknown. Or perhaps all of the children of Cheops were there to witness as he was laid to rest; we cannot tell. There is little doubt that the body was first carried into the central chamber, today misnamed the Queen's chamber, where once again, ceremonies would be carried out, perhaps to free his *ba* to rejoin the constellations through the 'ventilation shaft'. Today the room is bare, but Stadelmann noted its similarity to the *serdab*, or enclosed 'cellar' placed on the face of the Step Pyramid where a statue, the realistic image of Netcherikhe, stood behind closed walls. Here, offerings could be given for the soul of the King. If Stadelmann is correct, the placing of the statue within the pyramid, which was to be sealed, is curious. The *serdab* statue of Netcherikhe was the focal point of offerings made three times a day, every day, so long as the cult survived. The pyramid was about to be sealed, so this statue would receive its offerings once and once only.

Once the ceremony was over, and Cheops' body was safe within its stone womb, the passages were resealed and the pyramid became his eternal mother from which his spirit would be reborn daily to whatever belief he supported. Outside, great pits were cut and lined and the state barges, used to carry him to his final home, were unstitched of their securing ropes, reduced to planks and laid in a grave of their own.

Was there treasure?

The placing of treasure within the pyramid was never the object of the exercise. It is probable that if precious grave goods ever existed at all, they were placed in one of the outer chambers in the halls and corridors below. The layout of the funerary area was later copied exactly in the tombs of the Valley of the Kings. Here, the long, dark, decorated corridor led to a right-angled corner and thence to chambers beyond. In the early tombs of the Valley of the Kings, the same long corridors, in the early days with identical right-angled corners, led also to a series of chambers. In the royal tombs in the Valley of the Kings, the first chambers approached contained a wealth of precious treasures, while the burial chamber was empty save for the canopies or 'shrines' over the sarcophagus. Perhaps it was the same here; perhaps the outer chambers, actually at the foot of the pyramid, would have contained the precious objects.

The similarities in design between the two complexes is startling, once the pyramid areas are examined as they were at the time of burial, not as we see them today. Whereas the tombs in the royal Valley in Luxor were simply passages cut into the bedrock, with the presiding natural pyramid of rock, Meretseger ('She who loves Peace and Quiet') standing at the top of the valley, at Giza both the mound and the covering for the passages were all man-made. Here, once again, is more evidence for the overwhelming traditional need for the King's body to lie beneath a stone mound; and for the architects working on the problem to analyse the previous methods and try to streamline them. In the case of the Valley of the Kings, they saved themselves the need to build a pyramid at all, but simply cut out the passages and chambers.

There is a tendency to see the burials of Egyptian Kings as changing dramatically once the Valley of the Kings was started. In fact, there is instead clear evidence for a long continuity. Once the roofed causeway was entered and the outside world could no longer be seen, the effect would have been identical to the rock-cut subterranean passages of the later Kings.

The aftermath

Redjedef's marriage to Hetepheres II, whether forced upon her or not, was a success in that she bore him several children. Redjedef, meanwhile, imposed his religious views on the land with the creation of the monstrous Sphinx, cocking a snook at his dead father, a matter of yards behind the lion of Re. After some years, as Chephren must have watched his right to the throne slipping away with the births of children who may inherit instead of him, it seems likely that he leaped into action. The disappearance of Redjedef is doubly problematic, as there seems nowhere that he was buried, as his pyramid was not only unfinished but was then systematically smashed apart. What happened at Redjedef's funeral? Did he, in fact, have a funeral at all?

Chephren's seizure of the throne made his mother, Henutsen, into official 'King's Mother' and thus first lady in the land. Perhaps one day her burial will also be found close to his pyramid, as Cheops had placed his mother Hetepheres. He restored the status of his father and returned once more to Giza. His name reflects loyalty to Re, but his actions suggest that family loyalty meant more to him than loyalty to Heliopolis.

The end of Cheops' line may have come about as a result of genetic weakness, or perhaps by chance acts of fate. There is, nevertheless, a curious irony that it was the heirs of the rejected Redjedef who survived into the next generation.

The way it really was

To his family, Cheops was a shadowy creature, removed by virtue of his nature and his office from their company. Few could approach him. He instilled terror into almost everyone. Everyone, perhaps, except his wives who saw him daily, and his sons and daughters whom he controlled in their every action. To the country he was the epitome of terror. No man might ever look into his face and expect to live to tell the tale. To the world, he was the faceless builder of the Great Pyramid, his tomb, which still baffles mankind so long after his death.

As we have seen, how a pyramid was built and why is not so difficult to discover, as long as the evidence is used. The real question remaining to us is the nature of the man behind the public mask. It seems likely that he may have been incapacitated, but the system which existed meant that this was little handicap. He could never have had friends, for the role which had been created for him made of him a man apart.

After his death, things were never the same again. The cult created about him was slowly and steadily knocked down. As others were allowed increasing power and influence, so the status of the King suffered.

No matter which way you look at it, Cheops was a lonely man in life as in death. The Great Pyramid, at the end of it all, stands as a monument to the illusions created by man in order to permit absolute power. Alone in death, alone in life, this is a man who inspires not wonder but pity.

Index

Photographic Credits

Page 42 (below) Ashmolean Museum, Oxford; 98 Drawing by Philip Winton from *The Complete Pyramids* by Mark Lehner, published by Thames and Hudson Ltd, London.

Colour Section: page 1 (above) Egyptian Museum, Cairo, (below) David Couling; 2 Paul Bradbury; 3 Christine El Mahdy; 4 (above) Christine El Mahdy, (below) Paul Bradbury; 5 (above) Paul Bradbury, (centre) Christine El Mahdy, (below) Paul Bradbury; 6 (above) Paul Bradbury, (below) B.V. Bothmer; 7 (above) Christine El Mahdy, (below) Metropolitan Museum of Art, New York/photo W.C. Hayes; 8 (above) Valerie Baker, (below) Christine El Mahdy.